The De-Radicalization of

This book is the first detailed study of the causes of de-radicalization in armed Islamist movements. It is based on frontline research that includes interviews with Jihadist leaders, mid-ranking commanders and young sympathizers, as well as former security and intelligence officers and state officials.

Additionally, it is also the first book to analyze the particular conditions under which successful de-radicalization can take place. The current literature on Islamist movements attempts to explain two principal issues: their support of violence (radicalization) and their changing attitudes towards democracy and democratization (moderation). However, the reasons behind renouncing (behavioral de-radicalization) and de-legitimizing (ideological de-radicalization) violence have not been evaluated to date. The author provides an in-depth analysis of the de-radicalization processes of the Egyptian Muslim Brothers (1951–1973), former allies of al-Qa'ida, such as al-Gama'a al-Islammiyya (Islamic Group of Egypt, 1997–2002) and al-Jihad Organization (2007–present), as well as of Algerian Islamist groups (1997–2000). The book also analyzes cases of de-radicalization failure.

The two questions that the book highlights and attempts to answer are Why? and How? For example, why do radical Islamist militants revise their ideologies, strategies and objectives and initiate a de-radicalization process; and what are the necessary conditions behind successful de-radicalization? De-radicalization of Jihadists shows how a combination of charismatic leadership, state repression, social interactions and selective inducements can ultimately lead Jihadists to abandon "Jihad" and de-legitimize violence.

This book will be of great interest to students of radical Islamist movements and Islamic Studies, terrorism and political violence, security studies, and Middle Eastern politics.

Omar Ashour is a Lecturer in Politics in the Institute of Arab and Islamic Studies, University of Exeter. He has a PhD in International Relations from McGill University in Canada.

Series: Contemporary terrorism studies

Understanding Terrorist Innovation
Technology, tactics and global trends
Adam Dolnik

The Strategy of Terrorism
How it works, why it fails
Peter Neumann and M.L.R. Smith

Female Terrorism and Militancy
Agency, utility and organization
Edited by Cindy D. Ness

Women and Terrorism
Female activity in domestic and international terror groups
Margaret Gonzalez-Perez

The Psychology of Strategic Terrorism
Public and government responses to attack
Ben Sheppard

The De-Radicalization of Jihadists
Transforming armed Islamist movements
Omar Ashour

The De-Radicalization of Jihadists

Transforming armed Islamist movements

Omar Ashour

Routledge
Taylor & Francis Group

LONDON AND NEW YORK

Transferred to digital printing 2010

First published 2009
by Routledge
2 Park Square, Milton Park, Abingdon, Oxon OX14 4RN

Simultaneously published in the USA and Canada
by Routledge
270 Madison Ave, New York, NY 10016

Routledge is an imprint of the Taylor & Francis Group, an informa business

© 2009 Omar Ashour

Typeset in Times by Wearset Ltd, Boldon, Tyne and Wear

British Library Cataloguing in Publication Data
A catalogue record for this book is available from the British Library

Library of Congress Cataloging in Publication Data
A catalog record for this book has been requested

ISBN10: 0-415-48545-2 (hbk)
ISBN10: 0-415-58834-0 (pbk)
ISBN10: 0-203-87709-8 (ebk)

ISBN13: 978-0-415-48545-6 (hbk)
ISBN13: 978-0-415-58834-8 (pbk)
ISBN13: 978-0-203-87709-8 (ebk)

Contents

Illustrations

Figures

Tables

Foreword

Nothing is more gratifying for an old teacher than to see one of his former students upholding the scholarly torch and going beyond his own footsteps to new, untrodden research territory. This is the story of Omar Ashour's book on the deradicalization of Islamist groups in the early twenty-first century.

When I researched Egypt's Muslim militants in the late 1970s, hardly any scholars since Richard Mitchell, in his book on the Society of the Muslim Brotherhood, had visited the subject in two decades. I published my early work in IJMES in December 1980. The following two decades witnessed an avalanche of writings and publications on what were invariably labeled as "Islamic awakening" or "Islamic Fundamentalism", "resurgence", "revival," and "radicalization." This trend was understandably reinforced by major events on the ground: breaking out of the Iranian Islamic Revolution in 1979; and two years later by the assassination of Egypt's President Anwar Sadat by Muslim Jihadists. Another upward turn came with the horrific events of the 9/11 bombing of New York's World Trade Center and the Pentagon Headquarter in Langley, Virginia, allegedly by another more lethal Jihadist organization: the Afghanistan-based al-Qa'ida. The latter has displayed not only an unprecedented organizational capacity, but also a worldwide striking capability and multinational attraction for recruits. Its lethal exploits occurred in such far apart locations as the Bali resort island of Indonesia, the main commercial city of Casablanca in Morocco, a Madrid railway station in Spain, and the London Underground.

The names of the al-Qa'ida leaders, the Saudi-born Osama bin Laden and his deputy, Egyptian-born Ayman Zawahiri, soon would become household names. Bloody events in Algeria, ascendance of Hezbollah in Lebanon and Hamas in Palestine in the last two decades, have compounded both interest and fears in many quarters.

Coinciding with the demise of the Soviet Bloc and the end of the Cold War (1945–1990), many pundits shifted their fame, research interest and media appeals to the emerging industry of the new enemy, " Islamic Menace." Western media, academia, and policy "Think Tanks" have furiously raced to appropriate a share in this new industry. Hundreds of conferences, seminars, and workshops have been devoted to debating, understanding, containing, and combating Islamic terrorism, "Clash of Civilization," and Muslim Exceptionalism. Modes of international and domestic travel would undergo stringent regulations to reduce risks and maximize passenger safety. Racial profiling and difficulties in obtaining entry visas for citizens from Muslim-majority countries became commonplace.

The overwhelming media buzz, scholarly interest, and safety industry seem to have overlooked a growing counter-trend. Below the radar there was another process unfolding – the de-radicalization of some of the oldest and toughest Muslim militant groups. Having been a student of the original subject myself, I stumbled on the new counter-trend by sheer accident: I was arrested, detained, tried, convicted, and imprisoned for my own political activism, which had nothing to do with Islamic radicalism.

My incarceration, between 2000 and 2003, took me back to the same prisons in which various Muslim militants were serving their sentences. I had frequented these same penal facilities twice before. The first was in the 1970s in my capacity as a field researcher, to which I have already referred above. The second time was in the 1980s in my capacity as a Human Rights Defender – as I was the Secretary General of the Arab Human Rights Organization (AHRO) investigating alleged complaints of human-rights violations filed by or on behalf of imprisoned Muslim militants. The third time was as a fellow prison inmate in June 2000.

Although in solitary confinement in Cell Block No. 6 of Torah Farm Prison (TFP), I was surprised when I found one day a written message tucked in my returned laundry, from one of the militants I had interviewed more than 20 years earlier, welcoming me to the TFP, and offering sympathy, support and "help" on behalf of himself and fellow "Brothers." Initially, I was not sure what to make of, or how to answer, the message, until I received a second message wondering why I had not answered, with instructions of how and when to respond. Following the instructions proved to be the beginning of one of the most fascinating dialogues and research ventures of my career as a Social Scientist. The dialogue not only endured throughout my three years spent in TFP, but would also continue with other fellow Islamists outside prison after my acquittal on appeal by the High Court in 2003.

It is in the course of this dialogue that it became increasingly clear that three different Islamic groups had been going through an evolutionary process toward being integrated into the societal mainstream. This is what Omar Ashour is calling "de-radicalization" in this book. The first to do so was Egypt's Muslim Brothers (MB), the mother of all modern Islamic movements. It was likely that its de-radicalization would become an "Ideal Type" in the Weberian sense. As Omar notes, the MB, established by a charismatic young school teacher in 1928, remained a peaceful, faith-based, character-building movement in its first two decades (1928–1948), turned gradually militant in the following two (1948–1968); and gradually de-radicalized in the last four (1968–2008).

Such evolution in the case of the MB was a function of several factors, among which were the ferocious reaction of the Egyptian state to its attempted use of violence, the loss of popular sympathy especially in the presence of a charismatic leadership such as that of Gamal Abdel Nasser (1954–1970), sober revision and self-criticism by the MB leaders of their own beliefs and practices. No less important in this process has been the margins of regime tolerance under President Anwar el-Sadat (1970–1981) and his successor Hosny Mubarak (1981–2009). Although still treated as illegal, the MB members have been able to run as "independents" or under the banner of other legal parties in local and national elections. The fact that they have been active providers of social services to the needy, especially in urban areas, seems to have helped significantly in increasing their share of the popular vote from 2.0 percent in 1984 to 20 percent in 2005. This has been the same general pattern for Islamists who opted to participate in electoral politics in Turkey and Morocco.

The other militant Muslim groups that appeared in Egypt since the mid-1970s were invariably splinters from the MB, ostensibly in disapproval of their elders' moderation, which was interpreted as a "sell out" or as simply "historical fatigue." Under a variety of names – such as Jihad, Repentance and Holy Flight, Mohamed's Youth, The Islamic Group – these groups started mostly on university campuses, and later engaged Egyptian security forces in protracted urban-style guerilla warfare. They also targeted banks, tourist sites, ranking Egyptian officials, members and institutions of Egypt's Christian Copts, and outspoken secular intellectuals. The climax of these confrontations was the Luxor massacre of some 60 foreign tourists in November 1997. That horrific event turned the Egyptian public en masse against armed Islamists, giving the security forces a political carte blanche to eliminate all militants on the slightest suspicion of being armed. This was indeed a turning point. The MB continued to distance itself from any militant activity, disclaiming and condemning such violent action conducted in the name of Islam. Many formerly militant groups followed suit. New splits emerged between leaders and the rank-and-file. A clear fault line appeared between leaders abroad (in exile) and those at home. Another fault line appeared between Islamists in prison and those who were at large.

During my dialogue with the Islamist leaders in prison, one of the vexing questions was why had the world made so much fuss about my case (known in Egypt at the time as Ibn Khaldun Center, IKC) and yet had hardly raised a finger about their plight, which was far worse as it included coerced disappearance, torture, years of detention without trials, keeping many of them in prison long after completing their sentences? I had no definitive answers to these question to give them in prison, as I was a helpless inmate like them, with no access to the outside world to inquire about this "stark differential treatment" of similar "cases of conscience." They were clearly disappointed in my lack of answers. They came back with a request to speculate about why this might have been the case. Among other things, I mentioned "tribalism, since I was one of the old Human Rights Defenders"; so those like-minded rose up in arms to defend one of them. I mentioned that their image of intolerance and violence did not encourage the Human Rights Community to give them priority in light of so many other, apparently more deserving cases.

The question of what was wrong with their image would appropriate nearly a year of the three-year dialogue in TFR. They argued that they had changed significantly; that they now shared many of the common core values that the Human Rights Community held dear. I retorted that even if they have indeed changed in that direction, the world outside did not know; and even if so told, it may not believe that the change was genuine. Ultimately it is both sustainable words and deeds that will get some of the outside world to believe that former Islamist militants have been, in fact, reformed. They asserted that they could start with "words" while still in prison, while deeds would have to wait until they were released. I commended them for this provisional response. In the following two years their leaders issued three volumes of "Muraja'at" (Revisions). When 9/11 happened, they were shaken up by it, as they thought partly morally responsible. This was in contrast to some of the initial denial –or worse, the gloating – that others in prison and outside had expressed at seeing the mighty U.S. being humiliated. The Islamist leaders' reason for concern was that the 19 youngsters who committed that atrocious act may have been emulating elders like the ones in dialogue with me. At that point, I became quite impressed, and suggested they write a fourth volume expressing this candid assessment, which they did.

I was acquitted on appeal in the spring of 2003. I immediately traveled abroad for medical treatment of the nervous disorder caused by the harsh treatment during my incarceration. It took four surgeries in the Johns Hopkins Hospital before I was able to get out of my wheelchair. In 2004, I was honored by McGill University Law School for my supposed defense of freedom and democracy in Egypt and the Arab World. It is on this occasion that I ran into my old student Omar Ashour in Montreal. As I was also asked to serve on the Canadian Board of Rights and Democracy, I would see Omar regularly – at least three times a year. Naturally, we talked at length about my prison experience, prospects of democratization in the Middle East and his other research plans. I was pleasantly surprised when he expressed his interest in writing a book on the topic of de-radicalization of Islamist Movements. I warned him, however, about the numerous "land mines" in the course of researching the topic in general, and if he were to do fieldwork in particular. But he considered it a challenge, and forcefully moved forward.

What he has produced is truly a pioneering work in an area of growing socio-political and geopolitical significance. It is obvious that non-state actors have become among the movers and shakers of international politics. And at the heart of such groups are the faith-based movements. A glance at the media headlines any morning or evening in late 2008/2009 will invariably find the name of one or more of these movements. The latest case in point at the writing of this foreword was the war in Gaza between Islamic Hamas and Israel.

While most are still radical, and hence problematic, to the post-Westphalia "State System" and/or "politics as usual," Omar Ashour's work points to promising directions of how to expedite the de-radicalization of some, if not all, of these movements. The ones he documented and analyzed in Egypt, Algeria, and other areas were involved in terrorism and conflicts that claimed the lives of as many as 100,000 people. Yet now they are integral parts of the accepted sociopolitical landscape in their respective countries. Knowledge is always the first step on the road to change. This book is a giant step on that road, and may very well be one of the turning points of ushering the end of the "Radical Age of Islamic Movements," at least for a generation or more.

Saad Eddine Ibrahim
Professor, American University in Cairo and
Harvard University Founder, Ibn Khaldun Center
for Development Studies and Arab Organization
for Human Rights

Acknowledgments

Writing this book was a long and often arduous process. To all those who helped me to reach the end, I owe my deepest and most heartfelt gratitude.

First, I would like to thank Rex Brynen, to whom I am very grateful for his help and kind support. I also wish to thank Saad Eddine Ibrahim, for years of mentoring and for always being a source of inspiration during both pleasant and unpleasant times.

Thanks are due to Khalid Medani, Mark Brawley, Jean-Louis Tiernan and Robert Stewart for their insightful comments and editorial help. I would of course like to emphasize that any errors in this book are my responsibility alone.

My deepest gratitude extends to my family. To my parents, whose support was the main reason that I have been able to complete this book. To my sister and brother, for their love and encouragement. To my grandmother, whose weekly phone calls from Cairo were always a source of inspiration. To the spirit of my grandfather, who nurtured in me the strong desire to understand and to whom I never had a chance to say a final goodbye. And finally, to my uncles and aunts, whose wisdom and advice are always guiding me.

This book is about ending violence. So these acknowledgments would not be complete without referring to the people who lived through the violence and have suffered under the repression of dictatorships and the terror of non-state actors. Though I do not mention them by name, I am very grateful to all those who shared and trusted me with their experiences, their pains and their hopes – some under conditions of almost unimaginable hardships.

To all of those, I am eternally indebted . . .

Abbreviations

AIS	Armée Islamique du Salut (Islamic Salvation Army) – Algeria
AKP	Adalet ve Kalkınma Partisi (Justice and Development Party) – Turkey
ANP	Armée Nationale Populaire (People's National Army) – Algeria
FIDA	Front Islamique du Djihad Armé (Islamic Front for Armed Jihad) – Algeria
FIG	Fighting Islamic Group (al-Jama'a al-Islammiyya al-Muqatila) – Libya
FIS	Front Islamique du Salut (Islamic Salvation Front) – Algeria
FV	Fighting Vanguards (Al-Tali'a al-Muqatila) – Syria
GIA	Groupe Islamique Armé (Armed Islamic Group) – Algeria
GSPC	Groupe Salafite pour la Prédication et la Combat (Salafi Group for Preaching and Combat) – Algeria
ICV	Initiative for Ceasing Violence (Mubadarit Waqf al-'Unf) – Egypt
IG	Islamic Group (al-Gama'a al-Islammiyya) – Egypt
IMU	Islamic Movement of Uzbekistan (Harakati Islammii Uzbekistan) – Uzbekistan
IRP	Islamic Renaissance Party (Hizbi Nahzati Islammii) – Tajikistan
LIDD	League Islamique pour Da'wa et Djihad (Islamic League for Da'wa and Jihad) – Algeria
MB	Muslim Brothers (al-Ikhwan al-Muslimun) – Egypt
MEI	Mouvement pour l'Etat Islamique (Movement for the Islamic State) – Algeria
MGH	Milli Görüş Harekatı (National Outlook Movement) – Turkey
MIA	Mouvement Islamique Armé (Armed Islamic Movement) – Algeria
OVPV	Ordering Virtue and Preventing Vice
PJD	Parti de la Justice et du Développement (Justice and Development Party) – Morocco
QICM	al-Qa'ida in the Islamic Countries of al-Magreb (al-Qa'ida fi Bilad al-Maghreb al-Islami) – Algeria
RB	al-Rahman Brigade (Katibat al-Rahman) – Algeria

RG	Religious Group (al-Jama'a al-Diniya) – Egypt
RP	Refah Partisi (Welfare Party) – Turkey
SCIRI	Supreme Council for Islamic Revolution (al-Majlis al- 'a'laa lil-Thawra al-Islamiyya) – Iraq
SO	Special Organization (al-Tanzim al-Sirri) – Egypt
SP	Saadet Partisi (Felicity Party) – Turkey
SR	Special Apparatus (al-Nizam al-Khass) – Egypt
SSI	State Security Investigations (Mabahith Amn al-Dawla) – Egypt
UD	Units Department (Qism al-Wahadat) – Egypt
UTO	United Tajikistani Opposition (Itihadi Mu'arazati Tajikistan) – Tajikistan
VT	Vanguards of Triumph (Tala'i' al-Fattih) – Egypt
WP	Wasat Party (Hizb al-Wasat) – Egypt

1 A theory of de-radicalization

Armed wings have dragged Islamist movements into undesired confrontations
with America and the West ... those wings should be banned permanently.
(Nagih Ibrhaim, Ideologue of al-Gama'a al-Islamiyya, Egypt, 2007)

Introduction

In late 1951, Hassan al-Hudaybi, the new General Guide of *Jam'iyyat al-Ikhwan
al-Muslimin* (Society of the Muslim Brothers – MB) in Egypt decided to dismantle the main armed wing of the Society that was known at the time as *al-
Nizam al-Khass* (Special Apparatus – SA). The leadership of al-Hudaybi was
already being challenged, and the decision was extremely controversial. It thus
led to further factionalization and even internal violence within the Society.
Ultimately, it took approximately two decades for the leadership to dismantle the
SA completely. Since the early 1970s, the MB has abandoned violence against
national regimes, and has de-legitimized and prohibited that type of violence by
ideological and theological arguments. Additionally, the leadership of the MB in
Egypt has also dismantled all of its armed units. These conditions indicate a successful, comprehensive de-radicalization process that took place on the behavioral, ideological and organizational levels.

In a very similar but shorter process, *al-Gama'a al-Islamiyya* (Islamic Group
– IG) – the largest armed Islamist movement in Egypt during the 1980s and
1990s – declared a unilateral ceasefire in July 1997 that surprised observers, officials and even many IG members and commanders. The ceasefire declaration
contradicted the militant literature of the group, the previous vows of its leaders
to continue the armed struggle until it had toppled the Mubarak regime and the
increasingly violent tactics used by the IG affiliates since the late 1970s. In 2002,
the leadership of the IG not only dismantled its armed wings, but also renounced
its radical literature, published new books and replaced its curricula with those
of the relatively moderate Muslim Brothers (Zinah 2003, 16). Members of the
shura (consultative) council of the IG issued several books explaining its new
non-violent ideology. As with the Muslim Brothers, this seemed to indicate a de-
radicalization process that had taken place not only on the behavioral (strategic/

tactical) level but also on the ideological level. By 2007, the IG's de-radicalization process looked to have been consolidated: no armed operations since 1999, no significant splits within the movement and around 25 volumes authored by the IG leaders to support their new ideology with both theological and rational arguments. Two of the volumes were critiques of al-Qa'ida's behavior (Zuhdi *et al.* 2002; 2003) and a third was a critique of the "clash of civilizations" hypothesis, arguing instead for cultural dialogue (Ibrahim *et al.* 2005, 225–247). The drafting of these volumes by the same movement that co-assassinated President Anwar al-Sadat for signing the Egyptian–Israeli Peace Treaty was a significant development. This process of de-radicalization removed more than 15,000 IG militants from the Salafi-Jihadi[1] camp currently led by al-Qa'ida.

In 2007, al-Jihad Organization, the second largest armed organization in Egypt, with strong ties to al-Qa'ida, also initiated a de-radicalization process. The process is being led by the former emir (commander) of al-Jihad (1987–1993) and al-Qa'ida's ideologue, Dr. Sayyid Imam al-Sharif (alias 'Abd al-Qadir Ibn 'Abd al-'Aziz as well as Dr. Fadl). To recant his old views, al-Sharif authored a new book entitled *Document for Guiding Jihad in Egypt and the World*. In addition, al-Sharif and other al-Jihad commanders toured Egyptian prisons between February and April 2007 to meet with their followers and discuss the de-radicalization process. That process has been only partially successful however, as three factions within al-Jihad still refuse to uphold it. These factions also refuse to leave the Organization and one of them is in alliance with al-Qa'ida. The process is thus still ongoing at the present time.[2]

In Algeria, similar de-radicalizing transformations occurred in 1997. Like the IG of Egypt, the self-declared armed wing of the Islamic Salvation Front (FIS),[3] known as the Islamic Salvation Army (AIS), declared a unilateral ceasefire. The ceasefire led to disarmament and demilitarization processes that aimed for the reintegration of the AIS members as well as other armed Islamist factions into Algeria's civil ranks. The demilitarization process included subgroups from the notorious Armed Islamic Group (GIA) and the Salafi Group for Preaching and Combat (GSPC).[4] These groups and factions issued several communiqués to explain and legitimize their decisions to dismantle their armed wings. Unlike the Egyptian groups, however, the Algerian groups did not produce any ideological literature to reconstruct a new ideology.

The phenomenon of "de-radicalization" is not only confined to the previously mentioned countries. In the 2000s, it took place in several other Muslim-majority countries, albeit on a smaller scale than in Egypt and Algeria. These de-radicalization cases include Libyan, Saudi, Yemeni, Jordanian, Tajik, Malaysian and Indonesian armed Islamist groups, factions and individuals. Additionally, the Egyptian de-radicalization processes had international repercussions. For example, the transformations of the IG have influenced several leaders from the British Islamic Liberation Party and caused them to abandon the Party's radical ideology (Nawaz 2007, 6). In Libya, factions from the Fighting Islamic Group (FIG) modeled their de-radicalization process after that of the Egyptian IG and recently published several books in which they ideologically and theologically de-legitimized violence against national regimes (al-Tawil 2006, 7; Libya al-Youm 2008, 4). In Saudi Arabia, government-sponsored *al-Munasaha* (Advising) Programs, as well as interventions from independent Islamic scholars, succeed in de-radicalizing mainly individuals and small groups who allegedly supported or were loosely linked to al-Qaʻida Network (Howaidy 2007, 6). In Tajikistan, the Islamic Renaissance Party (IRP) that led the United Tajikistani Opposition (UTO) in the civil war of 1992–1997, again led the UTO into a fragile peace agreement with the Tajik regime. Similar to the IG in Egypt and the AIS and other armed groups in Algeria, the IRP called for "Jihad" in 1992 and then for a ceasefire, a compromise and a peaceful resolution of the conflict in 1997.

Despite the fact that the aforementioned armed Islamist movements, which used to engage in terrorist acts, have shown remarkable behavioral and ideological transformations towards non-violence and despite that the "de-radicalization" processes of these movements had removed tens of thousands of former militants from the ranks of al-Qaʻida's supporters and acted as disincentives for would-be militants, there is not one single detailed book on the causes of de-radicalization processes. Nor there is a comprehensive study about the conditions under which de-radicalization can be successful. This is the case in spite of the great interest in explaining Islamism and the huge volume of literature produced after the 9/11 attacks.

Generally, the literature on Islamist movements attempts to explain two issues: their support of violence (radicalization) and their changing attitudes towards democracy and democratization (moderation). The literature addressed and debated the causes of radicalization since the late 1970s. As for moderation, a smaller number of works have addressed the causes of that process as it is a relatively recent development.[5] More importantly, the reasons behind renouncing (behavioral de-radicalization) and de-legitimizing (ideological de-radicalization) violence were not analyzed before in the literature. None have developed a theoretical account of the causes of the de-radicalization process within armed Islamist movements. As such, this book will address crucial lacunae in the literature on Islamism, security and counterterrorism studies as the first detailed study of the causes of de-radicalization of specific armed Islamist movements, based on frontline research that includes personal, media and archival interviews with Islamist leaders, mid-ranking commanders, grassroots, young sympathizers, Islamist movements' specialists, former security and intelligence officers and state officials. Additionally, it will also be the first detailed study that analyzes the particular conditions under which successful de-radicalization can take place.

To explain these changes within movements that have long glorified violent struggle and upheld continuity, the main question that this book attempts to answer is: why do radical Islamist militants revise their ideologies, strategies and objectives and initiate a de-radicalization process?[6] In other words, can militant Islamist radicals turn into relatively peaceful groups that accept the "other" and, if yes, under what conditions?

In order to answers these research questions, this chapter will begin by providing definitions of key terms and concepts as well as a typology of Islamists and their ideologies in the following section. Thereafter, a theoretical framework will be developed in an attempt to explain the causes of de-radicalization processes. Following this, several case studies will be undertaken. The first case is that of the Muslim Brothers in Egypt between 1951 and 1973. The second and the third cases are those of the Islamic Group, and the related al-Jihad Organization. The fourth case is that of the AIS and the affiliated militias in Algeria.[7] Also, Algeria provides two cases where de-radicalization was attempted but was ultimately unsuccessful. These cases are those of the GIA and the GSPC and they are analyzed in the sixth chapter as well. Finally, in the conclusion, the book will provide a comprehensive theoretical framework that explains the causes of de-radicalization of armed Islamist movements as well as some policy implications.

Definitions and typology

General definitions

In this section, the terms that are used throughout the book are defined. Also, a typology of Islamist groups and ideologies is provided.

Islamist groups that the book discusses are sociopolitical movements that base and justify their political principles, ideologies, behaviors and objectives on their understanding of Islam[8] or on their understanding of a certain past interpretation of Islam.[9] Islamist groups can be distinguished under the broad categories of *moderate* and *radical*.

By a *moderate* Islamist group, I mean an Islamist movement that ideologically accepts, at minimum, electoral democracy[10] as well as political and ideological pluralism, and that aims for gradual social, political and economic changes. Behaviorally (tactically and strategically), moderate groups accept the principle of working within the established state institutions, regardless of their perceived legitimacy, and shun violent methods to achieve their goals. Moderate Islamists could also be called reformists, pluralists or modernists.

By contrast, *radical* Islamist groups are those movements that ideologically reject democracy as well as the legitimacy of political and ideological pluralism. They also aim for revolutionary social, political and economic changes and refuse to work within the established state institutions. Radical Islamist movements can use violent and/or non-violent methods to achieve their goals. Radical Islamists could also be called revolutionaries, extremists or exclusivists.

To highlight and explain nuanced ideological and behavioral changes within relatively moderate groups like the MB in Egypt, I shall divide moderate Islamists into electoral and liberal sub-grouping. Electoral Islamists are the ones who accept the Schumpeterian definition of democracy,[11] tend to emphasize majoritarianism,[12] and are reluctant to accept minority rights in general[13] and those they consider to be "illegitimate" minorities in particular.[14] Electoral Islamists tend to be the majority within Islamist movements and the most popular Islamist movements fit into this sub-group. [15] On the other hand, liberal Islamists accept liberal democracy with its elements of constitutional liberalism and provisions for protecting minority rights. Within the larger Islamist movement, liberal Islamists are a very rare breed, and indeed could even be perceived as a theoretical extreme with little or no concrete instantiations.[16] However, interviews done with the Turkish Justice and Development Party (AKP) and the Egyptian WP leaders suggest that they follow a relatively liberal trend.[17]

Regarding the radicals, three main distinctions should be made to highlight nuanced ideological and behavioral differences and changes. The first distinction is between violent and non-violent radicals.[18] This book is mainly focused on violent radicals, as the concept of de-radicalization[19] is primarily concerned with changing the attitudes of once-armed Islamist movements towards violence.

The second is between the groups that perceive violent combat as means to an end and those groups who perceive it as a "sacred" end in and of itself. I refer to the former as pragmatic militants[20] and to the latter as extremist militants. Examples of the former are the AIS in Algeria and the IRP in Tajikistan.[21] Examples of the latter are the Egyptian al-Jihad, the IG before their ideological transformations, the Algerian GIA and the global al-Qaʻida.[22]

The third distinction is between the radicals who ideologically legitimize and practice violence against civilians and unarmed persons (terrorism) and the ones who ideologically prohibit, and practically refrain from, that behavior. To the extent of my knowledge, all extremist militants ideologically legitimize and practice violence against civilians, whereas pragmatic militants tend to shun that path.[23]

Processes of change within Islamist movements

Radicalization, de-radicalization and *moderation* are processes of relative change within Islamist movements that can occur on the ideological and/or the behavioral levels, evenly or unevenly across issue areas. The three processes are centered on the changes in the stated positions and views of Islamist leaders and groups on violence and democracy relative to their positions in the past.

Radicalization

Radicalization is a process of relative change in which a group undergoes ideological and/or behavioral transformations that lead to the rejection of democratic principles (including the peaceful alternation of power and the legitimacy of ideological and political pluralism) and possibly to the utilization of violence, or to an increase in the levels of violence,[24] to achieve political goals.

De-radicalization

De-radicalization is another process of relative change within Islamist movements, one in which a radical group reverses its ideology and de-legitimizes the use of violent methods to achieve political goals, while also moving towards an acceptance of gradual social, political and economic changes within a pluralist context. A group undergoing a de-radicalization process does not have to ideologically abide by democratic principles, whether electoral or liberal, and does not have to participate in an electoral process.[25] De-radicalization is primarily concerned with changing the attitudes of armed Islamist movements toward violence, rather than toward democracy. Many de-radicalized groups still uphold misogynist, homophobic, xenophobic and anti-democratic views.[26]

As distinct from the ideological level, de-radicalization can occur on the behavioral level only. On that level, de-radicalization means practically abandoning the use of violence to achieve political goals without a concurrent process of ideological de-legitimization of violence. De-radicalization can occur in only one of the two levels.

Finally, there is also a third level of de-radicalization. Following the declaration of ideological and/or behavioral de-radicalization by the leadership of an armed group(s), there is usually the challenge of *organizational de-radicalization*: the dismantlement of the armed units of the organization, which includes discharging/demobilizing their members without splits, mutiny or internal violence.

Several types of de-radicalization correspond to the previously mentioned levels: *comprehensive de-radicalization* refers to a successful de-radicalization process on the three levels (ideological, behavioral and organizational). The Egyptian cases represent comprehensive de-radicalization well as two large Egyptian organizations underwent that process successfully: the armed wings of the MB (1969–1973) and the IG (1997–2002).[27]

Substantive de-radicalization entails a successful process of de-radicalization on both the ideological and behavioral levels, but not on the organizational level (usually a failure on that level is followed by splits, factionalization and internal organizational conflict, and/or the marginalization of the de-radicalized leadership). An example of substantive de-radicalization is the case of the Egyptian al-Jihad which is discussed in the fifth chapter.[28]

A third type of de-radicalization is *pragmatic de-radicalization* which refers to a successful behavioral and organizational de-radicalization process, but without an ideological de-legitimization of violence. The Algerian AIS,[29] discussed in the sixth chapter, is an example of an organization that underwent this type of de-radicalization.

Moderation

Finally, *moderation* is a process of relative change within Islamist movements that is mainly concerned with the attitudes of these movements towards democracy. Moderation can take place on two levels: on the ideological level, the key transformation is the acceptance of democratic principles, most importantly the legitimacy of pluralism and the peaceful alternation of power. On the behavioral level, the key transformation is participation in electoral politics (if allowed).

Different levels of moderation can occur within both non-violent radical and moderate[30] Islamist movements unevenly and across issue areas.

A typology of Islamists

There is a popular misconception that Islamist movements subscribe to the same ideology or to a similar set of ideologies. This section briefly describes the major, and often conflicting, ideological trends in Islamism. These major trends are: Ikhwanism, Salafism, Jihadism, Takfirism and al-Jaz'ara. In the following chapters, the book will analyze the de-radicalization processes of Islamist movements that subscribe to one or more[31] of these ideological trends.

Ikhwanism: the enduring legacy of the Muslim Brothers

The term *Ikhwani* (literally Brother-y) is usually used to describe an MB-affiliated group or individual. However, the term and the ideological trend of *Ikhwanism* transcends the organizational ties with the MB in Egypt or any of its autonomous branches in Jordan, Syria, Libya, Iraq, Palestine, Lebanon, Algeria, Sudan, Kuwait and other countries. The term refers to a set of ideological and behavioral characteristics that were established between the early 1970s and the late 1980s.[32] These characteristics include non-violence against national regimes,[33] acceptance of electoral democracy, relative pragmatism and, since the 1990s, high levels of popularity within several Muslim-majority countries. Groups that belong to this trend[34] include Reform (*Islah*) Party (Yemen), Movement for Peaceful Society[35] (MSP) (Algeria), Islamic Party (Iraq), Islamic Group (Lebanon), Islamic Action Front (Jordan), Muslim Brothers (Kuwait), Muslim Brothers (Indonesia), Islamic Group (Pakistan), Muhammadiyah Movement (Indonesia), National Outlook Movement and its parties[36] (Turkey) and Islamic Society (Afghanistan).

Salafism: the Saudi Arabian impact

A derivative of the word *salaf* (predecessors or ancestors), Salafism is a school of thought in Sunni Islam that attributes its beliefs to the first three generations of Muslims: the *sahaba* (companions of Muhammad) and the two succeeding generations (seventh and eighth century). Literally, the term Salafi means a follower of the *salaf* and Salafism believes that pure Islam was practiced by these first three generations. "Innovations" in religious matters are unacceptable to Salafis. Vaguely and broadly defined, those "innovations" could range from modern ideas like democracy to different understandings of Islam like mystical Islam (Sufism) or Shi'ite Islam.

Aside from the problems arising from attempts to understand religious texts in the twenty/twenty-first centuries via the minds of individuals who lived in the seventh/eighth centuries,[37] contemporary Salafism has several other characteristics including literal interpretation of Sunni Islamic texts. Regarding violence,

Salafis can be both violent and non-violent. Violent Salafis combine elements from Salafism and Jihadism and therefore are called "Salafi-Jihadists." Non-violent Salafism can be political or apolitical. Political Salafis participate in electoral politics after getting fatwas (religious/theological rulings) from leading Salafi sheikhs.[38] Political Salafis can also be a part of state institutions, like in the case of the Saudi religious establishment, an official form of Salafism.[39] The main stream of apolitical Salafism is the so-called "scientific or scholarly Salafism" (*salafiyya-'ilmiyya*) which is concerned with studying and analyzing the texts and the teachings of the *salaf* and their followers, then preaching and issuing (apolitical) fatwas based on that.

About democracy, Salafism gives mixed negative messages. The stances of Salafi groups range from total rejection of democracy (Salafi-Jihadists) to participating in electoral processes as a lesser-but-necessary evil compared to secular dictatorships (regarding that position see for example Belhaj 1992; Qutb 1983). In all cases, Salafism has a strongly critical stance on democracy and does not favour electoral politics, unless the alternative is "worse."

Finally, the origins of contemporary Salafism go back to the eighteenth century teachings of Sheikh Muhammad Ibn Abdul Wahab (1703–1792) of the Najd region in today's Saudi Arabia. Abdul Wahab's Salafism is still upheld and promoted by the official religious establishment in Saudi Arabia. His version of Salafism and Hasan al-Banna's Ikhwanism are considered to be the two most influential ideologies in contemporary Islamism, at least in the Middle East.

Jihadism: between Egypt and Afghanistan

Jihadism is a radical ideology within Islamism that stresses the use of violence as *a* legitimate, and in some versions *the* legitimate, method of political and social change. Jihadists mostly use selective and literal Salafi interpretations of Islamic sources, hence the term "Salafi-Jihadist." Jihadism is also characterized by the rejection of democracy, whether electoral or liberal, as well as by intolerance and the frequent use of violence against political rivals. In many cases, these rivals are Islamists and in some cases mere Jihadists. Some researchers classify Jihadists into global (internationalists), internal (mainly concerned with toppling nationalist regimes) or irredentists/secessionists (ICG 2005, 2–5). However, the activities of Jihadist movements in general can usually fit into more than one of these categories.

The origins of Jihadism go back to Egypt in the late 1960s and 1970s.[40] The ideology was partially built on an interpretation of the writings of Sayyid Qutb, a prominent Islamist intellectual. The ideology and the behavior was also a reaction to Nasser's repressive policies as well as to the failure of the Muslim Brothers in dealing with these policies. A major resource-boost to the Jihadist movement was the Soviet–Afghan conflict, where the ideology was internationalized and the movements adhering to it acquired necessary guerrilla training, logistics, contacts and other valuable resources. Afghanistan, and to a lesser extent other conflict zones like Bosnia, Chechnya, Palestine, Lebanon and Somalia, also acted as training grounds as well as causes to mobilize and recruit potential supporters. Islamist movements that subscribe to Jihadism include the Islamic Group of Egypt (pre-1997), al-Jihad Organization of Egypt (pre-2007), Fighting Islamic Group of Libya (pre-2008), Algerian GIA (pre-1995), Army of the Pure (*Lashkar-e-Tayyiba* – Kashmir), Islamic Party (Afghanistan), Islamic Movement (Uzbekistan), Islamic Group (Indonesia), as well as al-Qa'ida and all of its self-declared branches and affiliates.

Takfirism: another extreme

In the literature on Islamism, there is usually quite a bit of confusion between Takfirism, Jihadism and Salafism. Takfirism is quite different from all of the aforementioned, however. Takfir (excommunication) is the act of accusing a Muslim of abandoning Islam and becoming an infidel or an apostate (*murrtadd*). Based on that concept, Takfirism is an ideology whose basic assumption labels a whole Muslim community (a village, a city, a country or the global Muslim community) as infidels/apostates, unless proven otherwise. This is the core difference between Takfirism and the rest of Islamist ideologies. The rest assume that in predominantly Muslim societies, individuals are Muslims unless declared or proven otherwise.

As opposed to Jihadists, Takfirists can be violent and non-violent. If they are non-violent, they are usually content to live their chosen way of life in isolated societies in deserted areas like the case of *al-Takfir wa al-Hijra*[41] (Excommunication and Migration) in Egypt in the early 1970s. If violent, then their violence is directed against a wide selection of targets from all segments of the society, sometimes including women and children like the case of the Algerian GIA (post-1995). The reason for the wide selection of targets is that the mere apostasy of that community (*riddah*) is believed to be a legitimate reason for a death punishment. Takfirists reject the idea of democracy and use participation in elections and voting as a "proof" of someone being an infidel and of apostasy.

The origins of Takfirism also go back to Egyptian political prisons and interpretations of Sayyid Qutb's writings. After a second wave of violent repression against the members of the MB in the 1960s, some of the younger members started developing a more radical understanding of Qutb's writings, particularly after his execution in 1966. The leadership of the MB had opposed Takfirist interpretations of Qutb's works and was even able to "reconvert" some of the Takfirists and their leaders (Mahfuz 1988, 90).[42] The MB leadership, however, was not entirely successful. By the early 1970s, Takfirists had their first independent organization in the twentieth century: The Muslim Group (known in media as al-Takfir wa al-Hijra or Excommunication and Migration).[43] It was initially non-violent (Mahfuz 1988, 94–96) and then in reaction to repressive state policies, it turned to violence in the mid-1970s.[44]

Indeed, to a large degree Takfirism and Jihadism are products of repressive authoritarianism in Egypt and the consecutive failures of the Egyptian regimes to accommodate political opposition in a non-violent manner since 1952. These ideologies were exported at a later stage to the rest of the Arab world, and ultimately to the rest of the (free and not free) world. Other variables (aside from repression) discussed in the radicalization literature explain the persistence of these ideologies and the behaviors of their adherents.[45] Finally, it is worth mentioning that Jihadism, Takfirism and Salafism are the three "violence-prone" ideologies in Islamism.

Al-Jaz'ara: Algerian nationalist-Islamism

All of the previously discussed Islamist trends have global characteristics. To varying degrees, they are all critical of the nation-state and they are not limited by state boundaries. Al-Jaz'ara is different in this latter regard, since it is an Islamist trend that is limited to Algeria. It literally means "Algerianizing" or "Algerianization." The title al-Jaz'ara was given to that trend by their Islamist rivals,[46] but it was upheld by the adherents at a later stage.

The ideology of al-Jaz'ara is inspired by the thoughts of Malek Bennabi, a French-educated Algerian intellectual who was the director of higher education during the rule of President Boumedienne. Bennabi's writings focused on the reasons behind the relative decline of Muslim-majority countries, as well as the ways to reverse this decline through a focus on the interactions between ideas, cultures and individuals (Shahin 1997, 118; Burgat and Dowell 1996, 317). Bennabi is considered to be the godfather of al-Jaz'ara (Laremont 2000, 186).

The ideology of al-Jaz'ara is characterized by its nationalist-Islamist agenda and its rejection of any forms of non-Algerian Islamist interpretations of Islam and/or influences in Algeria. These rejections include the influences of both the Muslim Brothers, who inspire Algerian Islamist parties like the MSP, al-Nahda (Renaissance) and al-Islah (Reform); those of the Saudi-sponsored international Salafis; and those of Jihadi and Takfiri groups and figures.

Regarding violence and democracy, al-Jaz'ara approach is pragmatic. Like the Ikhwanis,[47] they accept electoral democracy and participate in elections. If the road to democracy is blocked, al-Jaz'ara activists regard armed resistance as a legitimate struggle against dictatorships (Ben Hajar 2000, 8). Al-Jaza'ra current was one of two domineering factions within the FIS[48] and has controlled the Front since the Batna conference of July 1991. It also attempted to influence and/or to control the GIA in mid-1994. That attempt failed and led to the execution of many of al-Jaz'ara leaders and activists by the GIA. It also led to an intra-Islamist war between al-Jaz'ara armed groups and the GIA. Islamist militias that represented al-Jaz'ara during the Algerian civil war included the Islamic League for the Call and the Jihad (LIDD), the Islamic Front for Armed Jihad (FIDA) and al-Rahman Brigade (RB).

The following table summarizes some of the characteristics of the previously discussed trends in Islamism:

Table 1.1 Major trends in Islamism

Islamist trend	Historical origins	Geopolitical scope	Stance on democracy	Stance on violence
Ikhawnism	Egypt	National, international (autonomous)	Acceptance	Rejection (against national regimes)
Salafism	Saudi Arabia (Najd Province)	International	Critical (but mixed)	Mixed
Jihadism	Egypt	International, national, secessionist/ irredentist	Rejection	Upheld and promoted
Takfirism	Egypt	International	Rejection	Mixed
Al-Jaz'ara	Algeria	National	Acceptance	Pragmatic

How does de-radicalization develop?

A theoretical framework

In the following chapters, I empirically show that there has been a change in the ideologies, behaviors and organizational structure of several armed Islamist movements. The process of change that this book seeks to explain is that of de-radicalization. Radicalization and moderation processes have been explained before in the literature, and are therefore only included in the theoretical framework and the empirical arguments when necessary.

Figure 1.1 below summarizes the Islamist typology that was previously outlined as well as the patterns and processes of change within Islamist movements.

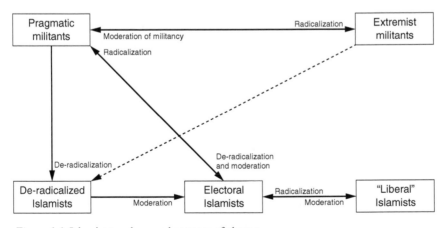

Figure 1.1 Islamist typology and patterns of change.

Bidirectional arrows indicate the possibility of the occurrence of a process and its reversal. Unidirectional arrows indicate a decreased likelihood of a reversal process, at least in the cases under study.

As the figure shows, the following chapters argue that the processes of change within Islamist movements can take three possible paths: the path of moderation, the path of radicalization, or the path of de-radicalization. Needless to say, the processes of change can stagnate or reverse at least in some of those paths.

A complex argument ... simplified

To review, the questions of "why will that de-radicalization process of change start?" and "under what conditions will it succeed?" are the two main questions that the book attempts to answer. To provide an answer, the argument in the book is based on a combination of structural and process-oriented approaches (Kitschelt 1992, 1033). Initially, the argument upholds the primacy of structure over agent. However, once the processes of change occur within the agent(s) as a result of structural conditions and stimuli, those same structural conditions will be responsive to the new agent behavior, which has itself been produced by the processes of change. The importance of agency arises from the assumption that agents could chose to challenge the structural strains and, therefore, give preferences to continuity-under-pressure over change.

In other words, domestic and international structural constraints forces several armed Islamist movements to initiate the aforementioned endogenous processes of change (radicalization, de-radicalization or moderation). Once those processes are running vigorously, structural conditions will respond to them and could

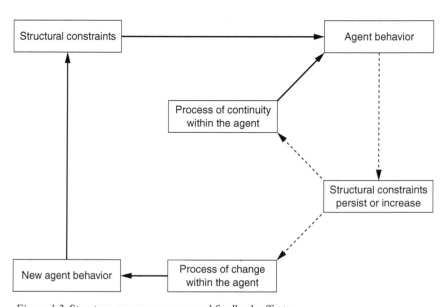

Figure 1.2 Structure, agency, process and feedback effects.

change as well. An Islamist movement could choose to continue challenging the structural strains; in such a situation, there will be no significant changes in its ideology and/or behavior. Figure 1.2 illustrates the pattern of interaction between Islamist movements and their sociopolitical environments. The figure is followed by a justification of the case-selection, discussion of the variables that lead to de-radicalization, as well as by the hypotheses.

Case-selection: why Egypt and Algeria?

The method of investigating the causes of de-radicalization of armed Islamist movements in this book is an inductive, qualitative one. To identify these causes, the units of analysis examined are armed Islamist movements that underwent comprehensive, substantive or pragmatic de-radicalization processes as defined above.

Chapters 4 and 5 argue that the Egyptian MB and the IG represent two pioneering cases of comprehensive de-radicalization: two formerly armed Islamist movements that de-radicalized on the ideological, behavioral and organizational levels. The MB went from pragmatic militancy (1940–1964) all the way to electoral Islamism (1984–present),[49] whereas the IG transformed from extreme militancy (1970s–1997) to de-radicalized Islamism (1997–present). Regarding the IG in particular, several governments and armed Islamist organizations modeled their de-radicalization programs and processes on the example of the IG. These include the cases of the Fighting Islamic Group in Libya as well as factions from the Islamic Group of Indonesia, Salafi-Jihadi factions from Saudi Arabia and even Liberation Party factions from the United Kingdom and Pakistan (Nawaz 2007, 5; Siringoringo 2007).

Egypt also proffers a third case of substantive de-radicalization. In 2007, the leaders of al-Jihad Organization, one of the closest organizations to al-Qaʿida, abandoned violence and ideologically de-legitimized it. Al-Jihad had been struggling with de-radicalization since 1997 and the re-emergence of its former commander, Sayyid Imam al-Sharif (1987–1993), as a leader for the process was crucial to its relative success on the ideological and behavioral levels. On the organizational level, the group still suffers from factionalism, as two of its factions still oppose the ideological component of the de-radicalization process (Jahin 2007, 12) and one faction, in alliance with al-Qaʿida, opposes the whole process (Jahin 2007, 12; al-Zayyat 2007, 5).

Beyond de-radicalization, several sympathizers and former members of the IG and al-Jihad have participated in the 2005 Egyptian parliamentary elections (al-Zayyat 2005, 5). They all lost, but their participation indicates that there is a possibility for relative moderation (from de-radicalization to electoral Islamism).

Because of the richness of the Egyptian case, a richness that is illustrated by the fact that Egyptian groups pioneered both historical (the MB) and contemporary (the IG) processes of comprehensive de-radicalization, as well as that other de-radicalization processes were modeled on the case of the Egyptian IG, Egypt will be the primary case study in this book.

Egypt, however, does not offer cases of pragmatic de-radicalization (behavioral and organizational, but not ideological). Algeria is probably the only country that offers both cases of Islamist pragmatic de-radicalization (AIS) as well as de-radicalization failure (GIA, GSPC and QICM) under the very same structural/contextual conditions. The de-radicalization failure is important because it allows us to test the necessity of the proposed independent variables (will be discussed in detail in the following section). The question then will be: why did the attempted process fail?

Finally, in the last chapter, the book aims to conclude with a generalizable theoretical framework that explains what causes Islamist movements to ideologically, behaviorally and organizationally de-radicalize. That framework would be valuable for both academic research and policy purposes.

Leadership, repression, interaction and inducements: a de-radicalization formula?

The explanatory argument in this book is that a combination of charismatic leadership, state repression, interactions with the "other,"[50] as well as within the organization and selective inducements from the state and other actors, are common causes of de-radicalization. There is a pattern of interaction between these variables leading to de-radicalization. State repression and interaction with the "other" affect the ideas and the behavior of the leadership of a radical organization and probably lead them to initiate three endogenous processes: strategic calculations, political learning, and *Weltanschauung*(s) revision(s). The first process is based on rational-choice calculations and cost–benefit analyses. The second process is a product of socialization and interaction with the "other." The leadership will update its beliefs and reassess its behavior due to the behavior of their interaction partner(s). The third process is mostly based on perceptional and psychological factors. It is a process in which the leadership of an armed Islamist movement modifies its worldviews "as a result of severe crises, frustration and dramatic changes in the environment" (Bermeo 1992, 273). Following these processes, the leadership initiates a de-radicalization process that is bolstered by selective inducements from the state as well as by internal interactions (lectures, discussions, meetings between the leadership, mid-ranking commanders and the grassroots in an effort to convince them about the merits of de-radicalization). Also, de-radicalized groups often interact with violent Islamist groups and, in some cases, the formers influence the latter.

State repression

State repression is defined as "a behavior that is applied by governments in an effort to bring about political quiescence and facilitate the continuity of the regime through some form of restriction or violation of political and civil rights" (Davenport 2000, 6). This behavior incorporates a broad range of actions including "negative sanctions, such as restrictions on free speech, violations of life integrity rights, such as torture and political imprisonment" (Carey 2002, 7), as well as state-sponsored terror in the form of assassinations, civilian slaughters and mass-murders. In short, state repression comprises all confrontational activities, both violent and non-violent, that are directed from the ruling regime towards the population in general and the political opposition in particular. Finally, state repression varies along three main dimensions: intensity (high, medium or low), duration (short, medium or long) and nature (pre-emptive versus reactive; selective versus indiscriminate).

Selective inducements

Selective inducements mean any explicit or implicit sociopolitical/socio-economic incentives proffered by domestic and/or international political actor(s) to an Islamist movement in return for behavioral, ideological and/or organizational changes. Selective inducement varies along the aforementioned dimensions as well: intensity (high, medium or low), duration (short-term, medium-term or long-term) and nature (only pre-emptive versus reactive). Examples of selective inducement proffered by the state could range from ceasing systematic torture in detention centers to offering a power-sharing formula for participation in the government.

Social interaction

Social interaction is a variable with internal and external dimensions. External interaction is a sub-variable featuring a sequence of social actions between a movement and any social actor or entity who/which does not belong to the same ideological camp of that movement or is not recognized by the movement under study as such.[51] Internal interaction is another dimension of the same variable that takes place on the internal level between the leadership, the mid-ranking commanders and the grassroots of the same movement. In the cases under study, social interaction took place mainly in prisons, detention centers or the mountains (where Islamist guerrillas were operating).

Leadership matters

Since change in general, and change towards demilitarization in particular, is often conflated with "betraying the struggle" in many militant Islamist movements, only a leader/leadership that is perceived by the majority of the followers as credible, pious, theologically knowledgeable[52] and, preferably, with a history of "struggle"[53] could cast legitimacy on the de-radicalization processes. In other words, charismatic leadership is based on followers who see their leader(s) as extraordinary due to the aforementioned factors, and are therefore dependent on that leader(s) for guidance and inspiration (Yukl 1998, 337). As a result of this, the leader/leadership exerts control or a high level of influence over the followers' behaviors, thereby eliminating or limiting splits and internal conflict.

Without a leadership having these characteristics, armed Islamist movements tend to fragment under state repression. In most cases, that fragmentation leads to splintering and further radicalization in the form of anti-civilian violence and extreme anti-system ideologies perpetrated and upheld by loosely-structured organizations. Also, fragmentation may engender internal violence within the same organization.

The following chapters demonstrate that the presence of such leadership facilitated the de-radicalization process in the case of the Egyptian IG, whereas the lack thereof in the case of the Algerian GIA led to the fragmentation and the further radicalization of that group in the 1990s. A similar argument could be made regarding the Algerian GSPC which became al-Qa'ida's branch in the al-Maghreb countries (Algeria, Morocco, Tunisia and Mauritania) due to several factors, most notably the lack of a "legitimate" and charismatic leadership.

Hypothesizing on de-radicalization

The arguments above, and throughout the book, can be summarized in two propositions. The first is about the factors driving the initiation and ultimately leading to the success of a de-radicalization process: four variables are necessary for the initiation and the success of a de-radicalization process within armed Islamist movements. These variables are charismatic leadership in control of its followers, state repression directed against the armed movement, selective inducements proffered by state and other actors, and social interaction between the layers of the movement as well as between the movement and the "other." The following hypothesis can be derived from this proposition:

> *Hypothesis 1a: When pressures for de-radicalization build, an Islamist movement lacking charismatic leadership will not de-radicalize successfully. Instead it will fracture, with some elements de-radicalizing while other elements continue with radical goals and violent methods.*

> *Hypothesis 1b: When state repression is high, but selective inducements are low, an armed Islamist movement may be temporarily broken, but it will not de-radicalize. When state repression and selective inducements are both high, an Islamist movement is more likely to de-radicalize.*

> *Hypothesis 1c: When social interaction between the layers of the movement, as well as between the movement and the "other," is low, de-radicalization is unlikely to proceed. When it is high, de-radicalization is more likely to succeed.*

The second proposition is about the pattern of interaction between these variables: state repression and interaction with the "other" affect the ideas and the behavior of the leadership of an armed organization. The leadership initiates a de-radicalization process which is bolstered by selective inducements from the state as well as by internal interactions. A second hypothesis can be engendered from this proposition:

> *Hypothesis 2a: To succeed, de-radicalization must be initiated at the "top" of a movement, usually after a period(s) of repression and external interactions with the "other."*

> *Hypothesis 2b: De-radicalization initiated by the leadership only succeeds when it is bolstered by selective inducements from the state.*

> *Hypothesis 2c: De-radicalization initiated by the leadership only succeeds when it is bolstered by internal interactions between the leadership and the members of the movement itself.*

Finally, it should be mentioned here that the arguments throughout the book are supportive of the claim that *state repression* alone can result in the radicalization, destruction, fragmentation and/or further radicalization of an Islamist movement. However, it will not lead to a de-radicalization process without the other three variables.

Method of investigation

After showing the historical developments and the changes that the aforementioned groups have undergone on the ideological, behavioral and organizational levels, the causes that led to their de-radicalization processes are investigated. The proposed variables are tested empirically in the Egyptian cases first, followed by the Algerian cases.

The framework and the hypotheses are tested through qualitative comparative research (mainly content analysis and interviews). This method highlights both the idiosyncrasies and general explanatory powers of the cases, thus overcoming the problems of a small N case selection. In addition, this method is particularly attractive when researching regions, countries and/or movements that suffer from a lack of reliable aggregate data. Also, the arguments in the book are based on a close examination of many Arabic language sources, both primary (archival interviews, original statements, documents and literature) and secondary.

The following chapters include analyses of personal, media and archival interviews with Islamist movement leaders, mid-ranking commanders, members of the grassroots, Islamist movements' specialists, former security and intelligence officers, and state officials. This analysis helps identify the potential causes of de-radicalization from different perspectives. Also, content analysis is used to examine some of the original ideological literature and statements produced by the Islamist groups under study and their leaders.

The general structure of the book

This book is divided into seven chapters: this chapter and six others. The second chapter is a review of the previous studies on the processes of change within Islamist movements (mainly radicalization and moderation).

The third chapter of the book is a historical overview of the once-armed Islamist movements that the book analyzes. This chapter shows the behavioral, ideological, and structural changes that these movements underwent throughout their history. It also helps highlights the dominant factors that were behind such changes.

The fourth chapter discusses the attempts of the MB's leadership to de-radicalize and dismantle their armed wings since 1951. It analyzes the causes behind the failure of two de-radicalization processes in 1951 and 1964, as well as the causes behind the successful de-radicalization that took place between 1969 and 1973.

The fifth chapter analyzes the two more contemporary and crucial cases of the IG and al-Jihad Organization. Both organizations came from an extremist militant camp similar to that of al-Qaʻida, and ended up arguing for, and promising non-violent political behavior and ideology.

The sixth chapter is on de-radicalization in Algeria. It analyzes both the successful (AIS) and the unsuccessful cases of de-radicalization (GIA, GSPC, QICM) in that country.

Finally, the seventh chapter is the concluding one. It aims to provide a comprehensive theoretical framework that explains the causes of de-radicalization of armed Islamist movements. It also highlights policy implications.

2 The good, the bad and the ugly

Moderation, radicalization and de-radicalization in Islamist movements

The three processes of radicalization, moderation and de-radicalization[1] within Islamist movements are reviewed and analyzed in this chapter. I start by analyzing the studies on radicalization in Islamist movements, since that process has been extensively covered relative to the other two. That is followed by an analysis of the studies on the moderation process in Islamist movements. Given that there are far fewer studies on that process, I will be able to discuss specific case studies of moderation. That will be followed by showing a gap in the literature when it comes to Islamist de-radicalization.

The main focus of this chapter is reviewing the causes of the three aforementioned processes. Radicalization has been discussed extensively since the late 1970s (Ibrahim 1980, 1982; Roy 1994; Esposito 1997; Anderson 1997; Fuller 2002; Hafez 2000, 2004; Wiktorowicz 2004). Moderation is a relatively recent development and, therefore, less work has been done on examining its causes (Wickham 2004; El-Ghobashy 2005; Clark 2006; Schwedler 2006). None of the literature on Islamist movements has distinguished between moderation and de-radicalization. Also, none of it has theorized about the causes of the latter process, as defined in the first chapter, in Islamist movements.

On radicalization

The literature on the causes of radicalization can be divided into two broad approaches: the structural–psychological[2] and the political process approaches. Following Ted Gurr's seminal book *Why Men Rebel* (1970), the classic models of the structural–psychological approach posit "a linear causal relationship in which [socio-structural] strains produce psychological discomfort which, in turn, produces collective action" (Wiktorowicz 2004, 6). Scholars and experts have introduced several types of socio-structural strains and debated their relative importance. The four main types are socioeconomic, identity-based, cultural and political.

Structural–psychological approaches: socioeconomics?

Ibrahim (1980, 1996), Ansari (1984), Zubaida, (1989), Anderson (1991), Ayubi (1991), Tessler (1997) and others have emphasized the importance of socioeconomic factors in explaining the psychological alienation and, therefore, radicalization of Islamist activists. Their arguments mainly recycle relative deprivation models (Gurr 1970) to argue that Islamist movements represent modern reactions to rapid urbanization, overpopulation, unemployment, poverty, marginalization of lower/lower-middle classes, skewed income distribution and corrupt elites. Given these socioeconomic strains, disenfranchized youth seek radical changes through protest and, in some cases, violent struggle (Tessler 1997; Ibrahim 1980; 1996).

As shown by the scholars who uphold this approach, there is some empirical support to socioeconomic explanations of radicalization. The works within this category have shown indicators that membership in Islamist movements are partially correlated with socioeconomic dislocations, including poverty, income inequalities and lack of basic social services (Davis 1984; Dekmejian 1988). Several case studies support this line of argument. These cases include the 1988 riots and the GIA in Algeria (Tessler 1997), and *al-Takfir wa al-Hijra* case in Egypt (Ibrahim 1980).

Despite that, there are several problems with these socioeconomic explanations. First, they fail to answer the question "why Islamism?" These socioeconomically disenfranchized individuals and groups could have chosen ideologies that directly address their grievances, like leftist ones. Instead they chose to rally around Islamist symbols and figures. Given that, socioeconomic explanations do not adequately capture the socio-cultural dimension of radical Islamism.

In addition, when these explanations are tested empirically, there is usually a selective focus on the socioeconomically disenfranchized members and leaders of a specific radical group. Therefore, these explanations do not adequately answer the question of why do members of the upper and upper-middle classes get radicalized.[3] After all, both Usama Bin Laden and Ayman al-Zawahri are members of the Saudi and Egyptian upper classes respectively. In addition, none of the 19 hijackers of 9/11 belonged to the lower classes. Finally, due to that selective focus, socioeconomic explanations fail to provide a general framework to explain the causes of radicalization of Islamist movements.

Structural–psychological approaches: identity?

Other scholars have argued for the relative importance of identity politics in explaining Islamist radicalization (Kramer 1997; Burgat and Dowell 1997, Esposito 1997; Ibrahim 2004). Their arguments attempt to explain radicalization as a reaction to the growing influence of Western and other non-Islamic cultures in predominantly Muslim societies. The primary hypothesis of these arguments is that Islamists will uphold radical religious and religio-national identities in response to what they perceive as "cultural imperialism." That perception is usually bolstered by non-Muslim military presences, like in the Saudi Arabian case, or by long colonial confrontations, like in Algeria and Chechnya (Kramer 1997; Fuller 2002). Following this line of argument, radicalization occurs in a context, or during a process of, "cultural defense."

Another identity-related approach, one that differs from the cultural defense thesis,[4] is the political culture one. The argument of this approach is based on two assumptions. The first, like the cultural defense approach, is that Muslims possess a strong sense of religio-cultural identity that affects their behaviors and worldviews (Sivan 1985; Lewis 1991). Following from that, the second assumption is that Muslim political behavior is influenced by Islamic scriptures and classics (Sivan 1985; Lewis 1991).[5] Given the broadness and, sometimes, vagueness of these textual sources, radical interpretations of them are usually an option. Thus, the political culture approach argues that radicalism can be based on Islamic injunctions and identities. Therefore, as opposed to cultural defense, radicalization can occur without "cultural imperialism."

Despite doing a good job in addressing the salience of cultural norms within Islamist politics and despite being common within some of the literature on Islamist movements, much of the coverage by the media outlets and, sometimes, Western political rhetoric, there are many problems with identity-based approaches. First, as Michael Hudson has argued (Hudson 1995, 29–34), identity-based explanations that invoke culture suffer from definitional and methodological problems: what is culture and how should it be measured in an unbiased manner? In addition, there are several sweeping assumptions at the core of the identity-based approaches. First, there is an assumption that religio-national identities are always strong among Muslims, not only among Muslims who support Islamist movements. Following from that, there is another assumption that political action is a natural derivative of these strong religio-national identities, sentiments as well as religious scriptures. In other words, identity-based approaches assume that there is a linear correlation between identity and political behavior, as well as scriptures and political behavior. More importantly, these approaches fail to account for several empirical cases. For example, if identity determines behavior, why would an Islamist-leaning party like the Turkish AKP relentlessly pursue a European Union membership for Turkey, or why would Iraqi[6] and Afghan[7] Islamist movements cooperate with the US and/or NATO to overthrow nationalists or Islamist regimes in their countries?

Finally, recent empirical works on the relationship between religiosity and political attitudes represent a challenge to identity-based approaches. Based on his surveys and empirical research in four Arab countries, Mark Tessler found that "Islam appears to have less influence on political attitudes than is frequently suggested by students of Arab and Islamic society" (Tessler 2002, 351). For example, his study shows that there is no statistically significant relationship between attitudes towards democracy and personal piety in Morocco and Algeria (Tessler 2002, 350).

More problematic, especially with the political culture approach given its emphasis on primordialism, is the constant failure to explain change within Islamist movements. Case studies and comparative analyses have shown that many Islamist political movements, whether radical or moderate, change their ideologies, identities and behavior over time (Voll 1992; Entelis 1998; Roy 1994; 1999; Wickham 2002; 2004). Then, the problematic question for the political culture approach is: if identities are primordial, classic scriptures do not change and Islamist movements strongly uphold both, why would these groups change their behaviors and ideologies and therefore radicalize, de-radicalize or moderate? Using Olivier Roy's terms (1994), why do "fundamentalists" become "neo-fundamentalists?"

Structural–psychological approaches: politics?

A third approach within the literature on radicalization argues for the relative importance of political stress as a source of psychological discomfort and aliena-tion. Radicalization is perceived here as a reaction to predominant authoritarian-ism, state repression and forced exclusion (Hudson 1995; Anderson 1997, 2000; Ibrahim 2002; Burgat 2002; Nasr 2002; Hafez 2004). Francois Burgat best illus-trates this approach by arguing that any Western political party could be turned into the GIA in weeks if it was subjected to the same level of political repression that Islamists had endured (Burgat 1997, 45).

There is strong empirical support for this particular type of structural–psycho-logical approach, most notably the cases of the MB in Egypt[8] (1954–1969), the MB in Syria (1980s), the FIS in Algeria (1992–1997), the IRP in Tajikistan (1992–1997), among others. In these aforementioned cases, the tendency to work within a democratic framework and/or established state institutions did exist initially, and radicalization has occurred in response to exclusion and political repression. Also, radical Islamist movements and ideologies which are prone to violence were all born in authoritarian states during highly repressive periods. Jihadism and Takfirism were both born in Egyptian political prisons where torture ranged from a systematic daily practice in some periods to a selective-but-widespread practice in others (Ramadan 1993; Ra'if 1993; 2005; Amnesty International 2007). Mainstream Salafism was developed in Saudi Arabia, another country whose ruling regime has an inglorious human rights record. None of those ideologies or movements has come out of a democracy.

However, that is only a part of the whole puzzle. Similar types of political strains have led to the opposite effect: moderation. As opposed to the Algerian scenario of a decade-long and bloody civil war, political pressures[9] on Turkish Islamists in 1997 led to the moderation of their rhetoric and behavior (Yavuz 2006; Ashour and Unlucayakli 2006). Political strains have led to similar effects in the cases of the Moroccan Justice and Development Party (PJD), the Egyptian *Wasat* Party and the Tunisian al-Nahda Party.[10] Thus, while these political strains might be necessary to radicalize a movement, they are by no means suffi-cient to do that on their own.

Relevant arguments about radicalization

Finally, two arguments in the literature on the causes/levels of radicalization should be mentioned here. First, some scholars have attempted to directly correl-ate the shape of Islamist activism as well as the level of radicalism with the intensity of the structural strains within the crisis environment (Dekmejian 1995, 6; Esposito 1992, 12–17). The more severe the socioeconomic, identity and/or political crises are, the higher the levels of violent radicalism.[11]

The second argument is more recent and comes from organizational theorists. The main hypothesis of this argument is that the fundamental cause of radicalization is organizational (Rosa 2006, 3). Based on some of the literature on ethnic conflict and "failed states" (Fukuyama 2004; Mowle 2006; Rosa 2006; Marten 2007), organizational explanations are based on the notion that both state and group factionalization/de-centralization breed radicalization. The state's withdrawal from its classic spheres of influence (Richards and Waterbury 1987), including providing services and having a monopoly over means of violence, allows radical groups to fill that vacuum and challenge the state. This state withdrawal could be due to lack of capacity, will or both. On the other side, factionalization of radical groups is positively correlated with an increase in the levels of violence that these groups perpetrate (Hafez 2004, 23). The empirical examples that are usually cited to support that argument are the cases of al-Qaʻida and other smaller radical groups in Afghanistan, Iraq and Somalia.

Whereas the organizational arguments can partially explain several cases of *further* radicalization, they do not explain the *root causes* of that process. All of the radical Islamist ideologies and movements that this book addresses, as well as many others, were born in strong, centralized states like Egypt and Saudi Arabia. Factionalization and de-centralization have only affected these groups in a secondary stage. "Failed states" acted as facilitating grounds, mainly for mobilization, recruitment, training and resource gathering (like the case of Afghanistan), but not as a cause behind initial radicalization.

Structural–psychological approaches: are they really that useful?

In the literature on social movements, stark criticism is leveled against the structural–psychological models (McAdam 1982). The same critiques are relevant to the study of radical Islamist movements. One of the main critiques is that structural strains, regardless of their versions (socioeconomic, political, identity-based), are ubiquitous to all societies but they do not always lead to violent radicalism. On the contrary, poorer societies coupled with repressive regimes tend to produce fewer rebels – whether Islamists or not. In Leon Trotsky's words, "the mere existence of privations is not enough to cause an insurrection, if it were the masses would be always in revolt" (Trotsky 1961, 249). Regarding Islamists in particular, several scholars have shown that the variations in Islamist violence in the Middle East does not correspond to the variations in structural strains (especially socioeconomic strains). The cases examined include Algeria, Egypt, Jordan, Morocco, Saudi Arabia and Tunisia (Hafez 2004; Fandy 1999).

Another critique to structural–psychological approaches is related to their static nature and the validity of their vision of linear, causal relationships. Islamists do not always turn to violent struggles and radical ideologies whenever there is an intense structural strain. If that was the case, the overwhelming majority of

Islamist movements would be armed and violent.[12] Also, even when the choice is in favour of violent struggle and radicalism, and even when the structural–psychological approaches are successful in explaining that choice in specific cases, the explanation is limited to the nature of the grievances. In other words, the purpose (revolutionary versus pragmatic), the scale (national versus international), the scope (limited versus expansive), the intensity (sustained versus sporadic) and the duration (brief versus protracted) of armed militancy, all associated with the radicalization process, are left unexplained by the structural–psychological approaches (Hafez 2004).

Finally, structural–psychological approaches, at least in their classical versions, imply that structural change is required for a shift towards de-radicalization and moderation. Yet, empirical evidence overwhelms that implication. Among the "anomalies" are the cases of the *Wasat* Party and the Islamic Group in Egypt, the Justice and Development Parties in Turkey and Morocco, and the Islamic Renaissance Party in Tajikistan. Structural–psychological approaches do not adequately explain change under continuous structural strains.

Neither structure nor agent: is it the process?

Despite the aforementioned critiques, most of the literature on Islamist movements in general, and Islamist radicalism in particular, is confined to structural–psychological explanations. Recently, an alternative approach has been advanced to explain the causes of Islamist radicalism as well as the shift towards moderation: the political process approach (Yavuz, 2003; Hafez 2004; Wicktorowicz 2004; Wickham 2002; 2004).

Originally, the political process approach was developed and utilized by social movement theorists (Tilly 1978; DeNardo 1985; Tarrow 1996; McAdam *et al.* 2001). This approach addresses several limitations of the structural–psychological approaches, especially its lack of dynamism and its emphasis on causal linearity. Regarding Islamist movements, the approach premises that "it is neither necessary for Islamists to be contended to become moderate nor sufficient for Islamists to be deprived to become rebellious" (Hafez 2004, 19–20). The approach emphasizes the dynamism of the political environment and asserts the primacy of process over structure. In addition, the political process approach argues for the importance of resource mobilization, whether the resource is material, organizational, ideational or institutional. For the proponents of that approach, "social and political movements do not correspond mechanistically to existing conditions; rather, they continually mobilize resources, apply them in various forms of collective action or 'tactics' and experience the consequences of those strategies in a fully interrelated process that also affects subsequent 'rounds' of mobilization, action and outcome" (Snyder and Kelly 1979, 219). In this sense, Islamist politics is perceived as an intersection of political opportunities, mobilization strategies, as well as ideological frames and symbols that resonate well with Muslim cultures (Tilly 1997, 151–157; McAdam *et al.* 2004).

To sum up, the political process approach attempts to explain Islamist radicalism (and/or moderation) by investigating the political environment in which Islamists operate, the mobilization structures through which they garner resources and the ideological frames through which they legitimize their actions.

The main critique of the political process is that it is a catchall approach – almost the polar opposite of parsimony. The approach fails to provide a manageable set of causal variables that explain Islamist transformations. Terms like "political environment" could include many variables like domestic institutions, regime types, international/regional actors, geopolitics, political cultures and historical peculiarities. Using those broad terms might be useful in studying a single case or a few cases in a relatively homogenous region. However, producing cross-regional generalizable theories will be difficult. Even so, the interplay among the three dimensions of the political process approach (political environment, mobilization structures and ideological frames) can be the key to understanding change within Islamist movements especially under continuity – when some, or most, structural strains remain constant.

Another critique is that, despite the presence of ideological frames as a main dimension in the approach, many scholars assign that dimension a secondary, dependant role. The assumption that Islamists use violent methods only when all other options are exhausted (Shahin 1997; Hafez 2004) represents that demotion of ideology. In several cases, as well as in specific time-frames, ideology became "too sacred" to be violated and thus it determined the strategic choices of a movement, regardless of both the actual capabilities/resources of that movement and the available strategic alternatives. Empirical examples include the case of the Egyptian al-Jihad Organization and its decision, based on its ideology, to militarily confront the powerful, well-established Egyptian regime in the 1970s during a period of relative liberalization.[13] Similar examples supporting that argument can be found in the Algerian case with the Salafi Group of Preach and Combat (1998–2007) and in Saudi Arabia with al-Qaʻida in Peninsula (1995–present).

On moderation

The literature on moderation can be divided under four broad theoretical categories: inclusion–moderation, rule-and-moderate, repression–moderation and political process. Under each of these categories there are empirical cases that can be interpreted as supportive. Therefore, this section discusses some of the literature that focuses on empirical cases of moderation. This is in addition to the theory/hypothesis-focused works.

Despite the fact that most of the empirical literature on moderation is post-2001, the first of these empirical studies was published in 1993 and it discussed Hizbullah's transformation from a revolutionary militia to a political party that participated in the 1992 Lebanese parliamentary election (Hamzeh 1993).[14] Since moderation is associated here with the practical abandonment of violence,[15] groups that have armed wings and use violence like Hamas or Hizbullah will not be discussed, even though they accept electoral democracy and participate in elections. More relevant to the moderation process as it is defined here are the cases of the *Wasat* and the AKP. Those two groups broke away from relatively moderate, larger movements, namely the Egyptian Muslim Brothers and the Turkish National Outlook Movement (*Milli Görüş Harekatı* – MGH). The latter was represented by the Welfare Party (*Rifah Partisi* – RP) between 1983 and 1997 and by the Virtue Party (*Fazilet Partisi* – FP) from 1998 until 2001. The Brothers – *Wasat* and the AKP – FP splits in 1996 and 2001 respectively marked a move by the *Wasat* and the AKP Islamists from the electoral Islamist camp towards a relatively liberal Islamist one.

The inclusion–moderation hypothesis

The inclusion–moderation hypothesis is advanced by Michael Hudson[16] (1995), Gudrun Kramer (1995) and Lisa Anderson (1997; 2000). Generally, their works attempt to hypothesize about the potential causes of moderation. These works are based on modifications/extensions of structural–psychological approaches and they usually follow a linear, conditional "if ... then ..." argument.

More specifically, the inclusion–moderation hypothesis reverses the frustration–aggression models and the political repression–radicalization approach. The main argument is that if Islamists are radicalized due to repression and exclusion, then including them in the political process will have the opposite effect: moderation (Anderson 1997, 24–29). However, as shown before in the previous sections, the relationship between repression and radicalization, although valid in several cases, is not always linear. Repression and exclusion could lead to moderation as the case of the *Wasat* Party and AKP demonstrate (Wichkham 2004; Yavus 2006; Dagi 2006; Ashour and Unlucayakli 2006). In addition, as argued by the proponents of the political process approach, empirical evidence shows that "it is neither necessary for Islamists to be contended to become moderate nor sufficient for Islamists to be deprived to become rebellious" (Hafez 2004, 19–20). Following that line of argument, the inclusion of Islamists can be a necessary but not a sufficient condition for their moderation as argued by the inclusion–moderation hypothesis. Moreover, most of the literature that discussed the inclusion–moderation hypothesis left the space between inclusion and moderation unaccounted for. The mechanism(s) by which Islamists moderate, due to their inclusion, were left largely unspecified (Clark 2006, 342).

Moderation cases ... and critiques

In 1997, Glenn Robinson raised an important question: can Islamists be Democrats? (Robinson 1997, 373). To answer that question, he analyzed the behavior of the Islamic Action Front (IAF), the political wing of the MB in Jordan. He concluded that the IAF/MB "has been consistently in the forefront of democratizing the Jordanian polity since liberalization began in 1989" (Robinson 1997, 374).[17] He attributed that behavior mainly to the inclusive policies of the

Hashemite regime. Therefore, his study confirmed inclusion–moderation in this specific case. His study was followed by several others addressing similar research questions and the same case of the IAF. However, they were more critical of inclusion–moderation. More recent are studies done by Janine Clark (2006) and Jillian Schwedler (2006).[18]

Clark was very critical of inclusion–moderation. She tests the hypothesis by monitoring IAF's "cross-ideological cooperation" as possible evidence of moderation. Clark analyzes the case of the Jordanian Higher Committee for the Coordination of National Opposition Parties (HCCNOP), where the IAF's Islamist and secular parties interact and coordinate policies in several issue-areas. Clark concludes that her investigation sheds doubt on the "inclusion–moderation" hypothesis as well as on the "cooperation-could-lead-to-moderation" argument (Clark 2006, 559–560). This is because her findings show that "the IAF's willingness to cooperate with other HCCNOP parties is limited to issues with no bearing on Shari'a" and therefore, she concludes, the moderation of the IAF is both limited and selective (Clark 2006, 560).

Another empirical study critical of inclusion–moderation is that of Schwedler (2006). As opposed to Clark, however, Schwedler reaches a different conclusion regarding the IAF. When comparing and contrasting the IAF with the Yemeni *Islah* Party, Schwedler concludes that "while the IAF had moved significantly in the direction of accommodating and embracing democratic principles, the *Islah* party, as a whole, had not" (Schwedler 2006, 191). In her perspective, the IAF is a successful case of inclusion–moderation. The *Islah* is not. Therefore, according to Schwedler, including Islamists in the political process could *sometimes* lead to their moderation.

The two authors have reached different conclusions about the same case study for definitional and contextual reasons.[19] First, while Schwedler defines moderation broadly as "the movement from a relatively closed and rigid world view to one more open and tolerant of alternative perspectives" (Schwedler 2006, 3), Clark only mentions the association between moderation and the willingness to participate in a democratic system, without providing a clear definition[20] (Clark 2006, 542). The broad definition in Schwedler's case, coupled with definitional vagueness in Clark's case, has contributed to their reaching different conclusions about the moderation process of the same group.

Also, the comparative contexts and issues-selection were two other factors contributing to the different conclusions. Clark was looking at the IAF's stances on issues like honour crimes, women parliamentary quotas and personal status laws (particularly women's divorce rights) within the HCCNOP context. In other words, she was comparing the IAF's positions on issues of women's rights to those of progressive, leftist and secular parties, which are also members of the HCCNOP. Therefore, her conclusion that the IAF's moderation is limited and selective is not surprising. However, this conclusion was influenced by her selection of issues, context and comparative cases. Schwedler, on the other hand, is comparing the IAF to the *Islah* party, which is relatively new to the democratic process, has historical ties with Saudi Salafis and former Arab-Afghan Jihadists[21] and operates in a more conservative Yemeni context. Compared to the *Islah*, the IAF will consequently tend to look moderate and therefore to confirm inclusion–moderation thesis. Compared to leftist seculars on issues related to women's rights, it will not. Given that, more attention should be paid to definitional, comparative contexts, and issue-selection when studying and attempting to generalize about the moderation process of Islamist movements.

The rule-and-moderate hypothesis

A related hypothesis to inclusion–moderation is the rule-and-moderate one advanced by Saad Eddine Ibrahim (Ibrahim 2006, 2007a, 2007b). Based on his field trips in the Palestinian territories, Lebanon and Israel as well as his interactions with the Egyptian MB, Ibrahim initially hypothesizes that the closer Islamists are to political power in a democratic process, the more they will moderate their behavior (Ibrahim 2007, 13). To support the hypothesis empirically, Ibrahim cites rhetorical and behavioral changes towards moderation within groups like Palestinian Hamas, Lebanese Hizbullah and the MB during the electoral process and after electoral victories (Ibrahim 2006, 13; Ibrahim 2007, 13).

Like inclusion–moderation, the rule-and-moderate hypothesis has some validity. Borrowing from Givonai Sartori's work on European political parties (Sartori 1966), one can argue that most Islamist movements have the status of "permanent opposition." Given the lack of accountability and governmental responsibilities, these movements tend to make wild promises to their supporters and use vague symbolic slogans that resonate well culturally, like "Islam is the solution." However, once close to, or in, office, these movements will need to moderate their behavior and act responsibly if they want to avoid political/economic disasters and keep their base of support.

Despite the argument advanced above, a main problem with the rule-and-moderate hypothesis, in addition to the critiques directed at inclusion–moderation, is that at the core of the argument there is an assumption that the grassroots and supporters prefer moderate policies. Therefore, if the politicians/leaders do not pursue a moderate agenda, these supporters will not vote for them. This is not always true, as the case of Algerian FIS demonstrates, for example (Shahin 1997, 160).[22] In addition, there are several cases that suggest the opposite of the hypothesis: Islamists pursue a more radical rhetoric whenever they are closer to office. In Algeria, one can argue that after the FIS won the municipal elections in 1990, it did not moderate its behavior or rhetoric. For example, Ali Belhaj, deputy leader of the FIS, asserted that he does not believe in democracy (Belhaj 1992, 34; Ayachi 1993, 170), despite the fact that the FIS was closer to power through a democratic process.

The repression–moderation hypothesis

The repression–moderation hypothesis emerged more recently after witnessing the transformations of the Egyptian *Wasat*, the MB and the AKP towards a more liberal Islamist trend under continuous structural strains. This approach argues that applying pressures on Islamists coupled with limited accommodation in the electoral process will lead to their moderation. The works of Mona El-Ghobashy (2005) on the Egyptian MB and Ihsan Dagi (2006) on the Turkish AKP represent that line of argument. It is important to note here that the works focusing on repression–moderation are only attempting to explain a single case study, while inclusion–moderation is aiming at a more general hypothesis.

One of those works that uses repression–moderation to explain a single case study is that of El-Ghobashy (2005). In her study, she traces the transformation of the Egyptian MB[23] from a "highly secretive, hierarchical, antidemocratic organization led by anointed elders into a modern, multivocal political association steered by educated, savvy professionals not unlike activists of the same age in rival political parties"[24] (El-Ghobashy 2005, 374). She mainly attributes that change to the MB's participation in, and experience with, rugged Egyptian electoral politics. El-Ghobashy argues that within the Egyptian authoritarian context, the MB had to moderate their behavior to be able to fend off state repression and maintain their "influence and relevance with the public and influential international actors" (El-Ghobashy 2006, 394). She calls that "self-preservation."

Ihsan Dagi advances a very similar argument to that of El-Ghobashy when he investigates the causes behind the AKP's departure from mainstream Turkish Islamism as represented by the MGH and its moderation of rhetoric and behavior. In a volume edited by Hakan Yavus (2006) about the AKP,[25] Dagi argues that after the 1997 "soft" coup, the insecurity of the AKP led it to internalize the human rights discourse and the pro-democracy position. In other words, the pressures and threats from the military establishment have led to the internalization of liberal behavior/ideas and, therefore, to the moderation of the AKP (Dagi 2006, 103).

The two aforementioned case studies demonstrate that moderation of both behavior and ideology could develop under repressive conditions. However, the main problem with the repression–moderation approach is that it does not answer the questions of when repression leads to radicalization (Algerian FIS, Tajik IRP) and when it leads to moderation (Turkish AKP, Egyptian Wasat). This is one of the reasons that the repression–moderation approach is limited to a few case studies. Even within these case studies, the explanation provided by that approach is incomprehensive. The 1995–1996 military trials for civilian MB activists in Egypt and the 1997 "soft-coup" against the MGH Islamists in Turkey were not the first incidents of repression. The MB activists had been objects of state repression since the late 1940s and the MGH's since the 1970s. Given this timeline, why did they relatively moderate only in the mid-1990s and 2000s? The state repression variable alone cannot provide an answer for this question.

The political process approach[26]

As I argued above in the radicalization section, structural–psychological approaches can not account for change under constant structural strains. Several empirical studies on moderation have shown that this kind of change *could* occur. Among those studies is the one done by Carrie Wickham (2004) about the Egyptian *Wasat* Islamists. Using a more dynamic political process approach, Wickham provides a framework for analyzing the process of Islamist moderation. According to Wickham, the two variables that have led to the *Wasat* ideological moderation are political learning and strategic calculations, much as the comparative theory would predict. She notes that "the *Wasat* party is interesting precisely because it is a hard case, in which the precipitants of moderation are weak and/or the deterrents to moderation are strong" (Wickham 2004, 223). Wickham concludes that "the *Wasat* Islamists revised their ultimate goals and took a public stand in favor of values associated with democratic civil culture when the regime was not democratic" (Wickham 2004, 224). By that conclusion, she demonstrates the limitations of the structural–psychological approaches, the advantages of the political process approach, as well as a main problem with the inclusion–moderation hypothesis.

Moderation, however, is not the only process that merits explanation, and moreover the *Wasat* Party is not the only Islamist "hard case" that moderated under adverse or discouraging structural conditions, as I argue in the following section. Also, Wickham's independent variables need further explanation. What causes Islamists to initially revise their strategic calculations and political knowledge? The research direction of this book is moving in this way, mainly to address the causes that led groups as different as the IG, al-Jihad, the MB and the AIS to rethink their ideologies and behaviors.

On de-radicalization: a gap in the literature

Between the two ends of the Islamist spectrum, taking up arms (radicalization) on one end and accepting/participating in a democratic process (moderation) on the other, there is a point when an Islamist movement decides to abandon violence behaviorally, de-legitimize it ideologically and act on that by dismantling its armed units organizationally. On that spectrum, this is the point where the de-radicalization process starts.

As shown in the above review, the literature on Islamist movements has attempted to explain the two processes of radicalization and moderation. Islamist de-radicalization, as defined in the first chapter,[27] is neither addressed nor theorized about sufficiently in the literature. Therefore, this book is dedicated to investigating the causes and the dynamics of de-radicalization processes within selected armed Islamist movements. The main two case studies that, I argue, underwent comprehensive de-radicalization (behavioral, ideological and organizational) are those of the Muslim Brothers (MB) and the Islamic Group (IG) in Egypt. The MB leadership was able to dismantle its main armed wing, the Special Apparatus, after two failed attempts (1951–1954 and 1964–1965), between 1969 and 1973. Since then, the MB was moving on the moderation path, after abandoning violence against national regimes, prohibiting it on theological and ideological basis and organizationally dismantling its units. Also, the

IG dismantled its military wing, vowed to shun violence forever, and its leadership produced ideological literature that de-legitimizes violence. The IG still asserts its political nature and seeks sociopolitical change (Zinah 2002, 1). It continues to uphold its ideological stance, according to which democracy is "Islamically illegitimate" – not that different from most Salafi-Jihadi movements.[28] The IG is the first, former Salafi-Jihadi movement which produced ideological literature that de-legitimized violence. Recently, following that path, the Egyptian al-Jihad Organization has started a process of ideological and behavioral de-radicalization as well (al-Khatib 2007b, 1).

Finally, as demonstrated in the following chapters, the cases of the MB, IG, al-Jihad and others represent another challenge for the structural–psychological approaches. For example, the IG's de-radicalization process that started with the 1997 unilateral ceasefire was developed under circumstances of repression and stagnant structural conditions. Moreover, the Mubarak regime initially responded to the transformations with several negative signals including apathy, rejection, hesitation and suspicion (Zuhdi *et al.* 2003, 135). Given that, the approach towards explaining de-radicalization will involve several premises form the political process approach. These premises include that "it is neither necessary for Islamists to be contended to become moderate nor sufficient for Islamists to be deprived to become rebellious" as well as the "primacy of process over structure."

Conclusion: what is new?

In this chapter, the literature that discusses and analyzes the two processes of radicalization and moderation within Islamist movements were reviewed. In the literature on Islamist movements, radicalization is the most explored process of change. This is probably due to the fact that it is associated with several important events that sparked Western and international interest beginning in the 1970s with the Iranian revolution, moving into the 1980s with the assassination of President Sadat and continuing into the 1990s and the new millennium with events all over the world from the Algerian civil war to the terrorist attacks of 9/11. Despite that coverage, radicalization was mostly investigated through the lenses of structural–psychological approaches with all of their aforementioned limitations. Recently, radicalization was explored through the more dynamic political process approach, which promises a better understanding of that phenomenon.

In this book, the causes of radicalization will not be the main focus, given the extensive investigation that this process has already received in the literature. However, radicalization will be discussed in the third chapter (Historical Overviews) as a historical process that several Islamist movements have undergone. It will also be discussed in the sixth chapter (De-radicalization in Algeria) where I demonstrate that the lack of leadership and social interaction, in addition to intensive state repression will either lead to the destruction or the fragmentation and further radicalization of an armed Islamist movement.[29]

Compared to radicalization, fewer works have addressed the process of moderation within Islamist movements. The process itself is relatively new, nonetheless investigating it by reversing structural–psychological approaches as well as through the political process approach offered several important insights, as demonstrated for example by Lisa Anderson's works (1997; 2000) as well as more specifically by Wickham's study of the *Wasat* Party and the MB (Wickham 2004).

Given that de-radicalization processes are the least addressed in the literature, the main focus of this book is on those processes, which several armed Islamist movements have undergone, and some are still undergoing. Empirically, the de-radicalization cases analyzed here were not analyzed before in the literature. The oldest, comprehensive de-radicalization case of the Muslim Brothers in Egypt is analyzed in the fourth chapter. The other comprehensive case of the Islamic Group is discussed in the fourth chapter. In the same chapter, I also analyze the very recent, substantive de-radicalization case of the Egyptian al-Jihad Organization (al-Khatib 2007a). The cases of the MB and al-Jihad are not addressed in the literature and the latter only started in 2007.[30] Additionally, the book discusses the case of the Algerian AIS and the affiliated militias in the sixth chapter. Chapter 6 also includes a discussion of Algerian organizations in which de-radicalization was attempted, but failed. Theoretically, the definition of de-radicalization, the distinction between its types and dimensions, contribute to the literature on Islamist movements and security studies. Also, based on the case studies, the book provides a more general framework for analyzing and explaining the causes behind the de-radicalization of armed Islamist movements. That framework can be valuable for both academic and policy purposes.

3   Historical overviews of de-radicalization cases

The historical overviews of several types of de-radicalization cases are discussed in this chapter. The two cases of comprehensive de-radicalization (ideological, behavioral and organizational) are those of the MB and the IG. The case for a substantive de-radicalization (ideological and behavioral) is that of the Egyptian al-Jihad Organization, which is still undergoing the de-radicalization process. The case of pragmatic de-radicalization (behavioral and organizational) is that of the Algerian AIS and the smaller militias affiliated with it. Finally, the case of de-radicalization failure is that of the GIA and its main splinter group, the GSPC (now *al-Qa'ida fi Bilad al-Maghreb al-Islami* or al-Qa'ida in the Islamic Countries of al-Maghreb – QICM).[1] The chapter starts chronologically with overviews of the MB followed by the IG. Then it proceeds with the background of the third case: al-Jihad Organization. This is followed by the Algerian cases: the AIS, the GIA and the GSPC/QICM. These historical overviews are a precursor to a detailed analysis of the causes of de-radicalization in later chapters.

Historical background of the Muslim Brothers

Writing this section was probably the hardest task encountered in this chapter. The history of the MB is extremely controversial, especially with regard to their armed wings, the Special Apparatus (SA)[2] and the Units Department (UD).[3] The controversies not only emanate from the ideological and partisan backgrounds as well as the political motivations of former officials, historians, politicians and activists,[4] but also from the accounts, interviews and memoirs of the MB, the SA and the UD leaders themselves.[5] The latter contradictions are mainly due to factionalism and internal polarization within the MB. Moreover, some historians significantly change their accounts and interpretations of history over time. For example, the two editions of Tariq al-Bishri's seminal work on political movements in Egypt between 1945 and 1952 have conflicting accounts of, and conclusions about, the MB's role in that period. The first edition (1972) is scathingly critical of the MB's political role and portrays them as an antidemocratic, pro-monarchy reactionary force whose armed wing is purely a terrorist organization (al-Bishri 1972, 50). In the second edition (1983), al-Bishri mentions that his first edition lacked impartiality and his version of history was influenced by his ideological orientation[6] (al-Bishiri 1983, 22).

In addition to the ideological biases, another problem is that of methodology. One clear example is the extensive study of the MB and their SA done by the historian Abdul Azim Ramadan (1993). Ramadan was very critical of Nasser's military show-trials of the MB in 1954 and in 1965. He called these trials "the worst disgrace in Egypt's contemporary history" and went so far as to label Abdul Qadr Audeh, the Secretary General of the MB who was executed by Nasser in 1954, a "martyr of democracy who entered history" (Ramadan 1993, 134, 138, 254). Yet despite this critique of the trials, a large part of Ramadan's study is based on the "confessions" of the MB leaders in front of these military tribunals (see for example Ramadan 1993, 89–325).

Taking these controversies and methodological issues into account, I divide the historical and contemporary developments of the MB into five phases. The first phase (1928–1932) was dominated by missionary activities and calls for religio-social reform, while the second phase (1932–1940) was dominated by the MB's politicization. Two themes dominated the rest of the phases: paramilitarization and partial radicalization were dominant in the third phase (1940–1949), especially after the end of World War II. The fourth phase (1949–1966) was dominated by fragmentation (1949–1954) and, again, partial radicalization (1954–1966). Finally, the last phase (1969–present) has been dominated by de-radicalization (1969–1973) as well as by a still-ongoing moderation process (1974–present).

Foundation, social reform and missionary activities (1928–1932)

The Society of Muslim Brothers was a product of the ideas and the activities of Sheikh Hasan al-Banna, an Arabic language elementary school teacher who was born in the town of al-Mahmudiyya in al-Bihira Governorate northwest of Cairo in 1906 (al-Banna 1966, 8). Al-Banna's father, Ahmad Abdul Rahman, was the local imam of the town and brought up his son in a conservative environment. Religiously, al-Banna was a student of Sheikh Muhammad Abduh,[7] was influenced by the thought of Sheikh Rashid Rida on Salafism and Islamic modernism, and joined the *Hasafiyya* Sufi order at the age of 14 (Mitchell 1969, 1–11; al-Banna 1966, 17; al-Banna 1990, 90, 91). Politically, al-Banna was influenced by the nationalist and independence ideas of the leaders of *al-Hizb al-Watani* (Patriotic Party[8]) like Mustafa Kamel (1874–1908) and Muhammad Farid (1868–1919). Although he criticized that party in his memoirs (al-Banna 1966, 58), al-Banna contemplated merging the MB with it in 1945 (Abdul Khaliq 2004, episode 2).

After graduating Cairo University, al-Banna was hired in September 1927 as an elementary school teacher in al-Isma'iliya City (al-Banna 1966, 70). In a notable break with orthodoxy, he began preaching his version of Islam in cafés and local clubs as opposed to in mosques (al-Banna 1966, 83). As a result, he influenced quite a few students, workers, intellectuals and businessmen, some of whom were members of al-Isma'iliya's middle and upper classes. In March 1928, six of al-Banna's friends and disciples met with him at his house and gave him a *bay'a*[9] to preach and struggle for the sake of Islam. When one of the students asked him "what shall we call ourselves," al-Banna replied "we are brothers in the service of Islam … so let us be the Muslim Brothers" (al-Banna 1966, 87).

From 1928 to 1931, al-Banna and his followers were active mainly in al-Isma'iliya. They focused their activities on preaching and education, as well as fundraising for charity/welfare projects. In 1930, the MB officially registered as an Islamic charitable organization and started building its first mosque in al-Isma'iliya (al-Banna 1966, 108; Lia 1998, 40).[10] Above the mosque, they built a social-sports club, a school for boys and another one for girls[11] (al-Banna 1966 113; Lia 1998, 40). By the end of 1931, the MB was able to establish two other branches in the towns of al-Mahmudiyya and Shubrakhit.

The politicization of the MB (1932–1940)

Although several historians argue that the politicization of the MB started in 1938 as a reaction to the unpopularity of the Anglo-Egyptian Treaty of 1936 and the Arab revolt in Palestine (1936–1939) (al-Bishri 1983, 47; Muhammad 1987, 25; Mubarak 1995, 30), much evidence suggests that the MB was engaged in politics from the time of the establishment of their Cairo branch in October 1932. For example, the MB's weekly newspaper, the *Muslim Brothers Newspaper* (MBN), was launched in May 1933 and it mainly addressed political issues (MBN 1934, 1; Lia 1998, 31, 80–81, 97). Other examples of pre-1938 politicization include the MB's calls on King Fu'ad to retain the lost title of "Caliph" and therefore to re-establish the Caliphate in Egypt in the early 1930s (MBN 1933, 1), their 1937 pro-monarchy demonstrations in favor of a pledge of allegiance to King Farouk (MBN 1938, 1), their anti-imperial stance beginning in the early 1930s (Lia 1998, 81) and their criticism of rival Egyptian political parties and groups (MBN 1936, 12).

The politicization of the MB reached another level after 1936. In that year, al-Banna started writing to the leaders of countries that had Muslim majorities, demanding more support for the Palestinians as well as more commitment to Islamic laws and culture (Muhammad 1987, 21). To help him advance these two causes, Al-Banna built a patronage network with several influential Egyptian politicians, most notably Abdul Rahman Azzam, founder and former Secretary-General of the Arab League (1945–1952) and Ali Maher, former Prime Minister of Egypt (1936; 1939–1940; 1950–1952) (Harris 1964, 182).

The major change in al-Banna's rhetoric, however, came in May 1938, when the MB launched their weekly political magazine *al-Nadhir* (The Harbinger[12]) after the MBN folded.[13] In the first editorial of *al-Nadhir*, al-Banna mentioned that the MB had expanded and entered a new phase. He announced that the MB will turn its call (*da'wa*) for Islam from mere words and speeches to activism and struggle. He called on politicians to respond to the MB's calls for the implementation of Islamic rule, and warned that if those politicians did not move in the direction of reestablishing the rule of Islam, the MB would be at war with them (al-Banna 1938, 1). He excluded King Farouk from those leaders by mentioning at the end of the editorial that the MB still perceived the King favourably and had "faith" in him (al-Banna 1938, 1).

Despite the militant rhetoric, al-Banna had emphasized on many occasions that he did not support revolutionary activities for reasons that were more pragmatic than ideological (al-Banna 1990, 271). Specifically, he argued that revolutions have usually led to negative consequences and therefore are not a viable method for "Islamic" change (al-Banna 1990, 268–271).[14]

Ideological, organizational developments and paramilitarization (1940–1949)

This third phase witnessed several important organizational and ideological developments within the MB. The first was the establishment of the *al-Hay'a al-Ta'sisiya* (the Constituent Board – CB), which served as the main consultative (*shura*) body of the MB from 1941 onwards. The first CB had 100 members handpicked by al-Banna himself (al-Nadwa 2002; Lia 1998, 190). It was subsequently enlarged to 150 members due to the expansion of the MB, with the new members chosen by the initial 100 members rather than being elected from below. (Zaki 1980, 99–108; al-Bishri 1983, 62). Parallel to that consultative body, there was an executive body that oversaw all activities and finances of the MB: the General Assembly of the Guidance Office (GAGO). The GAGO also chooses the members of *Maktab al-Irshad* (Guidance Office – GO), the highest executive body in the MB (Abdul Khaliq 2004, episode 2; Zaki 1980, 105). The GO is headed by *al-Murshid al-'Am* (the General Guide).[15]

The *murshid* has most of the executive powers in his hands, despite the complex internal structure of the MB (Lia 1998, 71). This is mainly for two reasons, one of which is structural and the other ideological. In that period, the general structure of the MB was based on the concept of "selection from above" as opposed to "election from below" (al-Bishri 1983, 62, Zaki 1980, 106).[16] Since the General Guide was at the helm of the organization, he could strongly influence the selection process (Lia 1998, 93). Ideologically, the concept of *al-ta'a* (obedience) to the superiors was inculcated in the minds of all MB members during the indoctrination or the *tarbiyyah* (bringing up) process. On many occasions, al-Banna emphasized the importance of obedience to the leadership to become a "true" Muslim Brother (al-Banna 1966, 141–143). In his "Letter of Teachings," an address by al-Banna to the MB members, he elaborates on the ten pillars of the MB's *bay'a*. Obedience is the sixth pillar and he defines it as "executing orders [given by MB superiors] in both good and bad times, easy and difficult situations" (al-Banna 1990, 15). High-ranking MB members like Salih al-'Ashmawy, former leader of the SA and former editor-in-chief of *al-Nadhir*, said that the *murshid* has the "right" to expect to be obeyed by MB members (al-Gindi 1946, 69).

Between 1939 and 1941, al-Banna drew out the main ideological character-istics of the MB.[17] First, the movement's aim is to change Muslim societies and governments, mainly from below (al-Banna 1990, 268). In al-Banna's words, the aim of the MB is "to 'dye' the *ummah* with a comprehensive Islamic dye in every aspect of its life ... through building a new generation of believers in correct Islamic teachings" (al-Banna 1990, 268). The change should start from the individual, then the family, then the society and then the government and, in end, should culminate in the reestablishment of the Caliphate (al-Banna 1990, 285).

Regarding democracy, since the very beginning the movement's ideology did not perceive electoral processes as Islamically illegitimate. Al-Banna wanted to participate and participated in parliamentary elections in 1942 and 1945 respect-ively. In 1942, al-Banna bowed to the pressures of Mustafa al-Nahas Pasha, the Wafdist Prime Minister of Egypt at the time, and withdrew from the campaign to avoid a crackdown on the MB (Lia 1998, 168–270). In 1945, he lost due to the rigging of the elections (Kamal 1987, 91; Lia 1998, 270). However, al-Banna perceived the Egyptian political parties of his period as "corrupt hypocrites" without programs or curricula (al-Banna 1990, 374). He called for their dissolu-tion and formation of a single ruling party in one of his letters entitled "Our Internal Problems: The Ruling Regime"[18] (al-Banna 1990, 376).

On the issue of violence, the MB's ideology, behavior and rhetoric were full of contradictions and mixed signals during this phase (1940–1949) as well as the next one (1949–1966). In January 1939 during the fifth general conference of the MB, al-Banna declared to his followers that the MB does not believe in, or support, revolutions and revolutionary changes (al-Banna 1990, 268–271). He also declared that the MB could use their power only as a last resort and exclu-sively for defensive purposes (al-Banna 1990, 271). Yet while declaring this position in a general conference, al-Banna was in the process of establishing the SA.[19] In addition, while part of al-Banna's rhetoric and ideological literature condemned radical change and revolutionary behavior, another part of his rhet-oric and literature glorified violent militancy, most notably his articles entitled "al-Jihad Letter" and "Solidierism in Islam" (al-Banna 1990, 33–61; al-Banna 1938, 1). Also, the MB after al-Banna's death has strongly supported and was heavily involved in the 1952 coup against the monarchy (Abdul Khaliq 2004, episode 9, 10; Abdul Ra'uf 1989; Shadi 1981; Kamal 1987; al-Sadat 1977). Later on in 1954, there were several armed confrontations between the SA members and the new military regime, most notably the attempt on Nasser's life in October 1954. Similar confrontations took place in 1964 and 1965. In sum therefore, between 1938 and 1966, the MB's ideological and behavioral stance on the issue of violent activism was vague.

The special apparatus: purpose, ideology and behavior

Like other aspects of the MB's history, the date of the establishment of the SA is controversial. According to Ahmad Adel Kamal, one of the few SA leading operatives who are still alive, the SA was co-founded by al-Banna and Abdul Rahman al-Sindi, who ultimately became the SA's commander (Kamal 1987, 120–121). Mahmud Abd al-Halim, a GO member, and Salah Shadi, the commander of the UD, have different stories in their memoirs, however. They both assert that al-Banna had the idea of establishing a well-trained military wing for the MB. He consulted five GO members, including Abd al-Halim, discussed the issue with them and then took the decision to establish the SA in 1940 (Abd al-Halim 1979, 258; Shadi 1986, 127).

The reason for the establishment of the SA is a source of much less disagreement. Most of the accounts show that it was a reaction to the failures of the MB to gather arms and militarily assist the Arabic uprising in Palestine in 1936 (Kamal 1987, 120; Shadi 1981, 128; Abd al-Halim 1979, 259; Mitchell 1979, 171). In a 14 hour extensive interview on *al-Jazeera* network, Farid Abdul Khaliq, another influential member of the GO and al-Banna's disciple, adds to that account by mentioning that the idea of establishing the SA was developed after a discussion between al-Banna and Sheikh Amin al-Husayni, the former Mufti of Jerusalem. According to Abdul Khaliq, they both agreed that Zionist paramilitary organizations in Palestine should be confronted by similar types of guerrilla organizations. The SA was a product of this idea. In addition to the Palestinian issue, other regional and international factors had an impact on the establishment of the SA, most notably the British presence in Egypt.[20] Also, both Abdul Khaliq (2004, episode 4) and Norwegian researcher Brynjar Lia (1998, 167, 175, 179) refer to the impact of the new militaristic trends in Europe, especially the rise of Nazi-German and Fascist-Italian paramilitary units, on al-Banna's decision to establish the SA. They also refer to the impact of the national experience with armed wings for political parties on al-Banna's decision.[21]

Finally, liberal historian Abdul Azim Ramadan adds another dimension to the question of the purpose of the SA's establishment. In his extensive study of the SA, Ramadan argues that the notion that the SA was initially established with an eye toward the Palestinian issue is only partially correct. To complete the picture, he argues that the SA was established for a national agenda as well: to protect the group from regime crackdowns especially after al-Banna's brief internment in October 1941 (Ramadan 1993, 44, 57, 84). In addition to citing some statements of al-Banna, like the aforementioned ones in *al-Nadhir* editorial, Ramadan also points to the operations of the SA in targeting Egyptian figures like the Judge Ahmad Bek al-Khazindar in March 1948 and the Prime Minister Mahmud F. al-Nuqrashy in December 1948 to prove his point. Despite the fact that this argument is controversial,[22] the SA, in a later stage (post-1944), was used by the MB against state institutions and figures on several occasions (see for example Kamal 1987, 147–152).

Ideologically, al-Banna elaborated on his vision of the militarization of Islamist activism in several works. The SA represented an embodiment of that vision. In one of his letters published in 1936, he argued in a section entitled "solidierism in Islam" that Jihad, defined here as armed struggle, is an Islamic obligation (*fard*) and that it should be carried out to attain "Islamic objectives" (al-Banna 1990, 176). He argued that Islam had made military power "sacred" (al-Banna 1990, 176). He also argued that the main difference between militarization in Mussolini's Fascism, Stalin's Communism and Hitler's Nazism on one hand, and Islam on the other, is that the latter upholds peace above power and militarization. Al-Banna concludes that section by saying that militarization in Islam is a power for law, order and justice, whereas current militaristic trends in Europe are armies of "greed and injustice." In another letter titled "Letter of al-Jihad," he advances his theological evidence mainly to support the argument that Jihad is *fard 'ain*[23] to defend Muslim lands against foreign aggression and *fard kifaya*[24] when Muslim lands are not under threat. He concludes by saying that "ultimate martyrdom" can be attained only through getting killed for the sake of God (al-Banna 1966, 59).

Finally, al-Banna considered Jihad as the fourth pillar of the MB *bay'a*[25] (al-Banna 1966, 7, 14). The main slogan of the MB has five phrases. The fourth one is *al-Jihad Sabiluna* (Jihad is our way) and the fifth translates as "the death in the way/service of God is our most sublime wish" (al-Banna 1967, 14). Whereas these pillars and slogans apply to the MB members in general, the SA represented an institutional embodiment of that military dimension in the MB's ideology. The SA was mainly the institution that was responsible for executing violent tactics.

The SA operatives were trained by Egyptian army officers like Maj. Mahmud Labib, a veteran of guerrilla warfare in Libya against the Italians (Labib 1980; Kamal 1987, 299; Ramadan 1993, 44; Adul Khaliq 2004, episode 4, 5) and Maj. Gamal Abdul Nasser, who ultimately became the Egyptian President (Abdul Khaliq 2004, episode 5; Kamal 1987, 300; Abdul Ra'uf 1989, 136). Starting in 1946, the SA conducted several violent operations against both national and colonial targets. In December 1946, SA operatives attacked bars where British soldiers were celebrating New Year's Eve[26] (Kamal 1987, 149). On 22 March 1948, the SA assassinated Court of Cassation Judge Ahmad al-Khazindar and on the 8 December 1948, the Egyptian Prime Minister Mahmud Fahmy al-Nuqrashi. In November of the same year, the SA attacked several Jewish-owned civilian targets like the Eastern Media Company,[27] as a reaction to the first Arab-Israeli War (Kamal 187, 189). The SA was also involved in the armed resistance against the British army in the Suez Canal area in 1951 (Ramadan 1993, 50, 227; Kamal 1987, 269).

Internationally, the SA played a role in the Arab-Israeli conflict of 1948 with as many as 2000 MB volunteers and SA operatives fighting along the side of the Palestinians (Ramadan 1993, 75; al-Sisi 1986, 178–184). They started their first operation in Gaza around the settlement of Dier al-Balah (Kamal 1987, 187). Once the war started, the SA operatives fought on the side of the Egyptian army under the command of Generals Ahmad A. al-Mawawi and Ahmad F. Sadiq respectively (Kamal 1987, 204, 205).

Fragmentation and partial radicalization (1948–1966)

This phase was marked by a cycle of violence and counter-violence between the Egyptian regimes, both monarchic and republican, and the MB. The fragmentation of the MB in this phase can be seen in the autonomous status of the SA under the leadership of Abdul Rahman al-Sanadi, as well as in the internal factionalism that reached its zenith with the appointment of Hasan al-Hudaybi as a new *murshid* after al-Banna's assassination in 1949.

The phase started with the assassination of Ahmad al-Khazindar, a judge who was perceived as sympathetic to the British presence in Egypt and the 1936 Anglo-British Treaty (al-Sisi 1986, 207; Kamal 1987, 148). Al-Banna did not know about the planning of the assassination (Kamal 1987, 236; Ramadan 1993, 70–79; al-Sabbagh 1998, 83–95; Abdul Khaliq 2004, episode 6), a fact that illustrates the autonomous status that the SA acquired even under al-Banna's leadership. As a result of the operation, al-Banna held an emergency meeting with the commanders of the SA and the MB to investigate who ordered the assassination (Abdul Khaliq 2004, episode 4). According to Abdul Khaliq, who was present at the meeting, al-Banna did not reach any conclusions. Abdul Rahman al-Sanadi, the head of the SA, Mustafa Mashhur, an SA high-ranking commander and a former *murshid* (1996–2003), and all others denied responsibility (Abdul Khaliq 2004, episode 4). Thirty-nine years later, Ahmad A. Kamal, al-Sanadi's aide, mentioned in his memoirs that al-Sanadi was the one who gave the order for the assassination of al-Khazindar, without al-Banna's knowledge or permission (Kamal 1987, 236).[28]

That was not the end of the SA's autonomous behavior. On 28 December 1948, Abdul Majid A. Hasan, an SA operative, assassinated the Egyptian Prime Minister Mahmud F. al-Nuqrashi. The operation was a response to the banning of the MB, the arrest of its volunteers in Palestine and their incarceration in the al-Tur and other detention camps in the Sinai desert (Al-Sisi 1986, 226; Kamal 1987, 223). For the second time in less than a year, the assassination was not ordered by al-Banna. The latter issued his famous communiqué entitled "Not Brothers and Not Muslims" to distance himself and the MB mainstream from the assassin, specifically condemning the assassination, and describing the plotters as not "true" brothers and not Muslims (al-Banna 1948, 1; Abdul Khaliq 2004, episode 4, 5).

The cycle of terror and counter-terror between the Egyptian regime and the MB was now underway. A major crackdown on the MB began and al-Banna himself was assassinated on 12 February 1949. In response, the SA attempted to assassinate the new PM, Ibrahim Abdul Hadi, but the operation was a fiasco (al-Sisi 1986, 235). The SA also widely distributed a communiqué calling for the assassination of King Faruk. It was entitled "The Head of Faruk for the Head of al-Banna" and it escalated the situation with the monarchic regime (al-Sisi 1986, 236).

Leadership crisis

Following the assassination of al-Banna, there was a severe leadership crisis. The GO and the CB could not agree on a candidate to replace al-Banna until 19 October 1951, more than two years after al-Banna's assassination (Abdul Khaliq 2004, episode 7). Four competing factions had emerged by that time. The first was led by Salih al-Ashmawy, the first commander of the SA. The second was led by Sheikh Ahmad Hasan al-Baquri, who was practically leading the MB in the period between 1949 and 1951. The third was represented by the ones who had blood ties to al-Banna like his brother, Abdul Rahman al-Banna and his brother in law, Abdul Hakim Abdin, and their supporters. The fourth faction was a coalition of upper-class MB elites, including Justice Hasan al-Ashmawy, Justice Munir Dallah, Farid Abdul Khaliq and Abdul Qadir Audeh. The first faction had the arms, the second had the theological credentials, the third had the genealogical legitimacy and the fourth had the funds. In the end, the fourth faction gained the upper hand and chose Hasan al-Hudaybi, a judge in the Egyptian Court of Cassation.[29]

Given his career background, upper-class status and personal behavior, al-Hudaybi's leadership style proved to be very different from al-Banna's. His main problems were failing to connect with the MB grassroots and middle-ranks as well as to rise above factionalism[30] (Kamal 1987, 251–254; Abdul Khaliq 2004, episode 6). Moreover, given the assassination of fellow judge al-Khazindar, al-Hudaybi insisted initially on the controversial policy of dismantling the SA. He upheld the slogan that there should be "no secrecy in serving God" (Mitchell 1969, 88; Ramadan 1993, 96). Given the harbingers of an upcoming confrontation with Nasser's regime, al-Hudaybi changed the policy from dismantling the SA to "reforming" it and keeping it under the leadership's control. He appointed Sayyid Fayez to lead the armed wing[31] and assigned to him the job of dismantling it (Kamal 1987, 282–287; Ramadan 1993, 153; Abdul Khaliq 2004, episode 4). Fayez, however, was assassinated by a bomb hidden in a mail parcel that was delivered to his house on 19 November 1953, one day before he was supposed to submit a database of the SA members and units to al-Hudaybi (Mitchell 1979, 242; Ramadan 1993, 121, 155; al-Sabbagh 1998, 130–131; Abdul Khaliq 2004, episode 5). Suspecting their involvement in the assassination, al-Hudaybi fired some of the SA commanders including al-Sanadi, Kamal and others. Abdul Khaliq, Salah Shadi, Ahamd Hasan al-Baquri and other MB leaders, as well as historian Abdul Azim Ramadan, accuse al-Sanadi and Kamal of being behind the assassination (Shadi 1980, 198; al-Baquri 1988, 71; Ramadan 1993, 153; Abdul Khaliq 2004, episode 4). The latter denies any responsibility in his memoirs (Kamal 1987, 116, 331). His denial is supported by Mahmud al-Sabbagh, another deputy of al-Sanadi who was fired by al-Hudaybi in 1953.[32] Official investigations did not lead anywhere. However, such accusations reflect the intensity of the internal rivalry and factionalism within the MB (see for example al-Sabbagh 1998, 222–293).

Relationship with the Free Officers

This period (1948–1966) was marked by varying relationships with the Free Officers movement and the military regime it produced. Those relationships ranged from alliance and coordination in the pre-1952 period, to differences and frustrations between 1952 and 1954, and then to outright hostility in the post-1954 period.

The relationship between the MB and the leaders and members of the Free Officers movement goes back to 1941. Some of the Free Officers members were also MB members, for instance Abdul Mun'im Abdul Ra'uf, one of the seven officers who founded the first Free Officers cell in the Egyptian army (Abdul Ra'uf 1989, 41–61; Ramadan 1993, 158). Others were MB members, and even SA members, at one point. Then they left the MB officially but kept their contacts with the group. The most famous of these is Gamal Abdul Nasser.[33] According to Farid Abdul Khaliq, Nasser at one point had a debate with al-Banna and Mahmud Labib about whether the Free Officers should be an MB unit in the army or whether they should be an independent, more inclusive organization. Ultimately, the latter type of organization was chosen by Nasser and al-Banna agreed (Abdul Khaliq 2004, episode 9).

The cooperation with the Free Officers led to internal polarization within the MB. The two armed wings of the MB were in support of Nasser and the revolutionary path[34] (Shadi 1981, 177–178; Kamal 1987, 303), while Abdul Khaliq and other members of the "elite" faction were not. In the end, al-Hudaybi agreed to support Nasser based on several conditions, including reinstalling civilian leadership, reforming the army and redistributing land (Mitchell 1979, 276; Abdul Khaliq 2004, episode 10). Salah Shadi, the head of the UD, mentioned to al-Hudaybi that Nasser agreed to these conditions. However, in a meeting held on 27 July 1952 – four days after the coup – between Nasser, al-Hudaybi, other Free Officers and MB leaders, the former denied that he had agreed to the re-installation of a civilian leadership (Shadi 1981, 177; Abdul Khaliq 2004, episode 10). That sparked the first differences between the MB and the Officers, as Nasser stated clearly that the MB would have no guardianship over the coup (Nasr 1984, 118; Ramadan 1993, 108, 147; Abdul Khaliq 2004, episode 10). These differences accumulated and led to an anti-Nasser demonstration on 28 February 1954 (Ramadan 1993, 126; Abdul Kaliq 2004, episode 11). The MB was the main organizer of that demonstration, whose demands were a return to a civilian rule and the release of all political prisoners (Ramadan 1993, 124). More than 100,000 demonstrators surrounded Nasser and Naguib in Abdin Palace in Cairo and Nasser asked Abdul Qadir Audeh, the Secretary-General of the MB, to dismiss the demonstration. Abdul Qadir complied.[35] Nasser's supporters organized a counter-demonstration on 29 March 1954, chanting slogans including "down with democracy" and "down with educated people" (Mansur 2004; Ramadan 1993, 117; al-Tilmisani 1985, 70). Following that, a crackdown on the MB and other opposition groups took place. The crackdown led to another reaction by the SA. Although al-Hudaybi called off all violent operations, Hindawy

Duwayr, the SA commander of the Imbaba district in Cairo, planned with some of his followers an attempt on Nasser's life, which took place in October 1954 (Ramadan 1993, 220–225; Abdul Khaliq 2004, episode 13).

Periods of repression

Since the early 1940s, the MB was subjected to various types of state repression, with different levels of intensity. Between the 1940s and the 1970s, three periods stood out as being particularly brutal. The first was between 1948 and 1949 when the Prime Ministers Mahmud F. al-Nuqrashi (December 1946–December 1948) and Ibrahim Abdul Hadi (December 1948–July 1949) were in power. This period featured military rule, torture of some defendants and dissidents in cases of political violence, administrative detention and state-sponsored terrorism (Ramadan, 1993, 80–84; Abdul Khaliq 2004, episode 6).

The second period started in 1954, after the attempt on Nasser's life. Repression was more intense in this period, featuring longer prison sentences and systematic, indiscriminate and often brutal torture (Kamal 1987, 308–348; Ra'if 1989; Ramadan 1993, 249–325; Abdul Khaliq 2004, episodes 13, 14). In June 1957, the infamous Limane Turah massacre took place. This involved the Limane prison guards opening fire on MB prisoners inside their cells, killing 23 of them and wounding 46 (Hammuda 1987, 129–131; Mubarak 1995, 47).

The 1965 organization

The final repressive period under Nasser was between 1964 and 1966. It started with an attempt led by two MB leaders Abdul Fatah Isma'il, who was a former SA operative, and Zaynab al-Ghazali, who was the head of the Muslim Sisters Department and a leading Islamist feminist figure, to reorganize the MB again in the early 1960s (al-Ghazali 1989, 19, Ramadan 1993, 311; Abdul Khaliq 2004, episode 14). Farid Abdul Khaliq (1987; 2004) and Zaynab al-Ghazali (1989) have different accounts about the reorganization attempt. The former insists that the organization had an armed wing, aimed to assassinate Nasser and that the *murshid* Hasan al-Hudaybi did not order any type of reorganization at all. Moreover, Abdul Khaliq mentions that he received a direct order from the *murshid* in mid-1964 to stop any further reorganization-related activities and to dismantle any nucleus of an armed wing. Zaynab al-Ghazali and others have another story. She mentions in her memoirs that the reorganization was mainly aimed for propagating the MB ideology, that there was no planning for a military action, and that the *murshid* gave her a direct order to reorganize (Zaynab 1989, 40–47).

In any case, the early 1960s saw an attempt at reorganization by the MB that involved rearmament. In the beginning, Abdul Aziz Ali, a former minister of municipal affairs in the early days of the coup[36] was at the head of the new organization. Later on, al-Ghazali and Isma'il chose Sayyid Qutb to take up this position for his symbolic status and the popularity of his literature that had been smuggled from prison.[37] However, the reorganization attempt was discovered and the organizers were arrested in 1965. This initiated another major crackdown on the MB including the military decree of "detaining whoever was detained before in 1954." The same 1954 processes and policies of systematic torture, military show-trials, executions and long-term prison sentences were repeated again in 1965, though now these had what would ultimately become national and even international consequences.[38] It was during this specific period of repression that both the Takfiri and the Jihadi ideologies were born. It also saw the birth of the "cult of Sayyid Qutb," featuring his glorification as a "grand-martyr," the wide popularity of his writings among Islamists, and the understanding of his literature as basis of a comprehensive confrontational ideology.[39]

De-radicalization and moderation (1969–present)

Nasser died in September 1970, and a de-Nasserization period ensued with Sadat's "corrective revolution" of 1971. Concurrently, the MB was undergoing a process of de-radicalization and relative moderation. It featured first a decision by the *murshid* Hasan al-Hudaybi to permanently forgo any military or paramilitary activities. As opposed to in the 1950s, al-Hudaybi did not face any organizational opposition this time.[40] As a result, the organizational dimension of the process was not as difficult compared to that earlier period. To support the decision to de-radicalize theologically and ideologically, al-Hudaybi wrote the book *Preachers Not Judges* in 1969 (al-Hudaybi 1985; Voll 1991, 366). The book represented a counterargument to mainly Takfiri ideologies and, to a lesser extent, Jihadi ones.[41] More specifically, it represented a critique to Sayyid Qutb's *Milestones*,[42] especially the concept of *al-Hakimiyya*,[43] a cornerstone in the arguments of both Takfirists and Jihadists.[44]

Behaviorally, al-Hudaybi and his successor 'Umar al-Tilmisani were active in de-radicalizing the MB and distancing themselves from any armed Islamist movement. Both General Guides gave an oath to Sadat not to use violence against the ruling regime (al-Zawhiri 1993, 91; Abdul Khaliq 2004, episode 14).[45] Al-Tilmisani went so far as to call Sadat a "martyr" and his assassins "Kharijites" in a statement by the MB (al-Tilmisani 1981, 1). Since the 1970s, the MB's position on the issue of using violence has become clearer: no armed wings, no secret organizations and no violence against any national or Muslim figures/targets.[46] This position has drawn condemnation from other Islamist movements, most notably the ones who belong to Takfiri and Jihadi trends. Ayman al-Zawhiri, the leader of al-Jihad organization (1993–2000) and the second-in-command in al-Qa'ida dedicated his book *The Bitter Harvest of the Muslim Brothers* (1993) to harshly criticizing the MB's behavior and ideology in general, and the post-1970 changes towards de-radicalization and moderation in particular (al-Zawhiri 1993). By the mid-1980s, however, non-violence had become an important characteristic of the MB's behavior not only in Egypt but also in Algeria, Libya, Jordan, Iraq, Kuwait, Yemen, Indonesia and other places. In some cases, the MB leadership went so far as to support or to offer support to military and dictatorial regimes against rival Islamist movements and secular political groups, most notably in Algeria.

Historical background of the Islamic Group[47]

In the English-language literature on Islamist movements, the historical background of the IG has been discussed very briefly in a few works (Gerges 2000; Hafez 2004; Wiktorowicz 2004). In the Arabic literature, by comparison, fewer works have discussed that history compared to the volumes of literature focusing on the history of the MB (Hammuda 1985a; 1986; Mubarak 1995; al-'Awwa 2006). The main difference is that many of the works on the MB's history were memoirs written by the group's leaders and other non-MB actors who participated in relevant events. In the IG's case, with the exception of only two works,[48] the leaders have not had the chance to write their version of history yet, since their release from prison has been a recent development.

The historical and contemporary development of the IG can be organized into five phases: a decentralized, movement-building phase (1974–1981), an organizational consolidation phase (1981–1984), a rebuilding phase (1984–1989), a confrontation phase (1989–1997) and a maturation, de-radicalization phase (1997–present).

The movement-building, decentralized phase (1974–1981)

The decentralized phase of the IG started in the early 1970s, when President Sadat decided to release the Muslim Brothers from prison and permit them to be active on university campuses. That decision coincided with a growing interest in religion and the initiation of religiously oriented activism amongst students at Egyptian universities. Religious students established *al-Jama'a al-Diniya* (The Religious Group – RG), an inter-university club that aimed to enhance Islamic awareness and promote religio-social as well as religio-political activism on campus (Uthman 1967, 17). Most of the RG activism took place at Cairo, Alexandria and Assyut universities. By the mid-1970s, the clubs had been transformed into a nation-wide organization with a well-defined structure. Each university had a *shura* (consultative) council and an *emir* (leader/commander) (Hashim 2000; Madi 2005). There was also a national '*emir al-umara*' (leader of all leaders).

Despite having such a structure, the RG was a multi-ideological, decentralized organization. The *emirs* and the *shura* councils of each university were operating autonomously. In 1977, the Muslim Brothers were able to recruit the *emirs* of Cairo, Alexandria and al-Minya universities.[49] The MB, however, was not able to recruit the leaders of the RG in Assyut University, Nagih Ibrahim and Karam Zuhdi. Both figures emerged later among the co-founders of the IG. Indeed, Zuhdi currently heads the *Shura* Council of the IG and Ibrahim is the principal ideologue of the Group (Ahmad 2002a, 4).

The interference of the MB in universities and the reaction to such interference in Assyut were among the factors that ignited the idea of the establishment of a new Islamist movement, less compromising and more puritanical than the relatively pragmatic MB. In March 1978, Nagih Ibrahim was elected the *emir* of all Upper Egypt in Omar Makram's Mosque in Assyut (al-Zayat 2005, 27). His election marked the beginning of the transition towards the centralized phase, in which the IG emerged as an Islamist movement with a distinct leadership and ideology, as well as a base in Upper Egypt.

The differences between the MB and the IG in this early period were both ideological and behavioral. Ideologically, the leaders of what would later become the IG considered the MB's political pragmatism Islamically unacceptable. Also, the leaders emphasized the importance of a puritanical Salafi creed[50] to guide Muslim behavior (Habib 2002, 30). The relative toleration of Sufis, Shi'ites and other versions of Islam by the MB was another ideological divide (Habib 2002, 31). Behaviorally, although the IG in the 1970s did not exclusively rely on military means to achieve sociopolitical goals, violence was still accepted as one of the three major means to attain their objectives (Ibrahim *et al.* 1984, 16).[51] By contrast, the MB had excluded violent means to achieve political goals since their release from prison in the early 1970s.

The IG had numerous contacts with other like-minded, small Salafi-Jihadi factions in Cairo and the Delta region. The most notable of those factions was that of Muhammad Abdul Salam Farag. The latter came to be known as the principal organizer behind President Sadat's assassination. On 28 September 1981, Farag and several leading members of the Egyptian Jihadi movement including Ibrahim, Zuhdi, 'Abbud al-Zumur,[52] and Khalid al-Islambulli[53] held a meeting in Cairo to plan the assassination of Sadat (Qasim 1993, 3).

The consolidation phase (1981–1984)

The major crackdown that followed the assassination of Sadat gathered more than 300 Islamist activists and suspects in Egyptian prisons. That prison phase was crucial in transforming the IG into the distinct, Upper Egypt-based Islamist movement that we know today. Two main developments that took place during this prison phase have led to the consolidated form of the IG: Jihadi splits and literature production.

Jihadi splits and distinctions

The first development was the official split between the Islamic Group and other smaller Jihadi factions, most notably al-Jihad Organization, which was then led by 'Abbud al-Zumur and Ayman al-Zawhiri (al-Zayyat 2005, 229–235; Habib 2002, 41). That development occurred between 1982 and 1983 in the Turah prison complex and was mainly due to disagreements on three issues: leadership, ideology and tactics (Habib 2006, 41; Mubarak 1995, 184–189; al-Siba'i 2002, 6; al-Jihad Organization 1984). Regarding leadership, there was a consensus among the IG's leading figures, who were exclusively from Upper Egypt, that a *'alim* (scholar of Islamic theology/jurisprudence) must lead the IG. They felt that this *'alim* should be Dr. Umar Abdul Rahman,[54] a radical scholar from al-Azhar University (al-Zayat 2005, 221; al-Siba'i 2002). Other leading figures in the general Jihadi movement, almost all from Lower Egypt,[55] refused Abdul Rahman due to an eye deficiency that rendered him blind. Those figures included Jihadists from the military like Major 'Abbud al-Zumur and Captain 'Issam al-Qamary, as well as Dr. Ayman al-Zawhiri. Al-Qamary authored a 64-page document in which he argued that the leadership of a blind man in military or paramilitary matters is Islamically unacceptable[56] (al-Jihad Organization 1984; al-Siba'i 2002c, 10).

The second difference was centered on an ideological concept: *al-'uzr bil Jahl* (excuse due to ignorance) (Ibrahim *et al.* 1984; Mubarak 1995, 186; al-Siba'i 2002c, 10). The concept is well established in Sunni theology, and its simplest version argues that if a person has violated Islamic values/laws/rituals due to "ignorance" and/or a misunderstanding, he/she should not be punished. The IG has upheld the concept without modifications, while the leaders of al-Jihad Organization have argued that if the violating person did not exert "enough effort" to know/understand those Islamic values/laws/rituals, then that person should be punished. The practical implication of the argument has to do with fighting Muslim soldiers protecting "secular" regimes. Whereas the IG gave those Muslim soldiers an "excuse" due to their "ignorance" and therefore argued for narrowing the selection of its targets, al-Jihad did not. The Jihad leaders argued that both soldiers and leaders of secular regimes are "apostates" and, therefore, "legitimate targets."[57] Another practical implication concerns the legitimacy of forming alliances with groups that do not uphold the concept (mainly Takfiri groups). Considering *al-'uzr* an integral part of the Sunni creed, the IG refuses any potential alliance with Takfiris. Al-Jihad does not. The disagreement regarding *al-'uzr bil jahl* and its practical implications has allowed the IG leaders to accuse al-Jihad Organization of following non-Sunni "deviations" and forging alliances with "neo-Kharijites" (Takfiri groups).

The third main disagreement between the IG and al-Jihad was regarding tactics. The IG leaders preferred to be publicly active in mosques, universities and on the streets. Indeed, their charter describes two means for changing the society that emphasize publicity: *al-da'wa* (proselytizing) and *al-'amr bil ma'ruf wal nahyi 'an al-munkar* (ordering virtue and preventing vice – OVPV) (Ibrahim *et al.* 1984, 31). On the other hand, al-Jihad Organization by its very nature was a secret society that emphasized covert action. According to Kamal Habib, a former leader and a co-founder of al-Jihad, the tactic strongly advocated by al-Jihad leaders for bringing about sociopolitical change at that time was an Islamist-led military coup (Habib 2002, 33). In other words, al-Jihad exclusively advocated change from above, whereas the IG partially advocated change from below.

Literature production

The second development that marked the consolidation phase was the production of literature that highlighted the IG's ideology. This literature included books like *Islamic Action Charter* (Ibrahim *et al.* 1984), *A Righteous Word*

(Abdul Rahman 1984), *The Desisting Party from a Law of Islamic Laws* (IG Research Unit 1988), *Another God with Allah? Declaration of War on the People's Assembly* [Parliament] (IG Research Unit 1990) and *The Inevitability of Confrontation* (Ibrahim 1990). As some of their titles suggest, the books represented the so-called *Fiqhul 'unf* (jurisprudence of violence) in Islamist literature. This literature and others have provided Islamically based ideological legitimacy for militarizing Islamist activism and violently confronting political rivals. In this particular case, the main political rival was Mubarak's regime in Egypt. The ideological frames and the literature, however, were disseminated around the globe. Other rivals and enemies of different armed Islamist movements, whether on the national or the international level, did fit conveniently into these ideological frames.

It can be concluded here that this phase that led to the consolidation of the IG as a distinct Islamist movement defined by its ideological preferences took place in Egyptian prisons. Characterized by various forms of repression and isolation, the prison environment was likely an important factor contributing to the production of the radical *Fiqhul 'unf* literature. Indeed, this argument was made by several Jihadist leaders, including the IG's main ideologue Nagih Ibrahim and Kamal Habib, a co-founder of al-Jihad Organization (Ibrahim 2005, 106; Habib 2006, 136).

The rebuilding phase (1984–1989)

It can be said that the IG has one history inside the prisons, and a concurrent one outside it. The rebuilding phase is part of outside-the-prison history. That phase featured energetic attempts to rebuild the IG after the devastating strikes and sweeps conducted by the Egyptian military and security forces in the aftermath of the Sadat assassination. The rebuilding process was conducted by the so-called second-in-line leaders[58]. Most notable of these second generation militants were Safwat Abdul Ghani, the leader of the *da'wa* wing,[59] Mamduh Ali Yusuf, the former commander of the military wing and Mustafa Hamza the former head of the *Shura* Council abroad (al-'Awwa 2006, 118; Ahmad 2002a, 11).

The rebuilding strategy of the IG was developed during the prison period between 1981 and 1984. Three main objectives were identified: popular expansion through *da'wa*,[60] broadening the geographical area of support for the Group (with a special focus on Cairo and other urban areas) and building two branches of an armed wing (Yusuf 2005, 118). The first branch would be trained locally with light arms for quick and small-scale operations. The *raison d'être* of that branch was to protect the *da'wa*[61] from the regime's paramilitary forces and state security officers. The second branch was called the military wing and its members were supposed to be the nucleus of an IG "army" (Yusuf 2005, 119; State Security General 2002). In 1988, several mid-ranking IG leaders and activists were sent abroad to Afghanistan to get more sophisticated military training, with the idea that they would constitute the nucleus of the military wing. Most notable among those activists was Muhammad Shawqi al-Islambulli[62] (Yusuf 2005, 120; al-Hakayima 2006).

The "division of labour" to reach such objectives was based on the length of the prison sentence. The ones who were to be released in three years (in 1984), like Safwat Abdul Ghani, were to carry on *da'wa* works. The ones who were to be released in five years (in 1986) would use the new recruits to expand the geographical area of support for the IG in different Egyptian cities, most notably Cairo (Yusuf 2005, 121). Finally, the ones who were to be released in seven years (in 1988) had the task of building the two branches of the armed wing (Yusuf 2005, 117). Hence 1988 was the year in which IG leaders and activists started to travel to Afghanistan to acquire military skills and guerrilla training that could be used later in a confrontation with the Egyptian regime (Yusuf 2005, 117; Habib 2006, 103). In 1989, some of the Afghan-trained IG members returned to participate in the first terrorist operation since the assassination of President Sadat: an assassination attempt targeting the former interior minister, General Zaki Badr. The violent confrontation with the regime began at this point.

The confrontation phase (1989–1997)

The successful expansion of the IG in Cairo's poor suburbs and universities, its radical rhetoric, and its attempt to change traditional practices that were deemed "un-Islamic" through violent means[63] in the period between 1987 and 1989 had alarmed the regime. As a result, the security forces started a crackdown on IG activists. By early 1989, the IG had attempted to stop the crackdown by issuing the so-called "six demands" appeal. These six demands appeared regularly in the IG's communiqués and publications of that period and can be summarized as follows:

1 Releasing all detainees who were not charged
2 Ceasing torture in prisons, detention centers and state security buildings
3 Improving the prison conditions for IG activists who were sentenced by civilian courts[64]
4 Releasing female hostages who were taken to force their male relatives to surrender to state security agents
5 Reopening the IG mosques that were shut down
6 Ceasing the policy of renewing detention indefinitely[65]

The security forces ignored the demands and continued the crackdown. In reaction, the military wing of the IG, which was led by Mamduh Ali Yusuf at that time, decided to assassinate General Zaki Badr (Yusuf 2005, 125). The operation was carried out on 16 December 1989. It was a fiasco, but it did initiate a cycle of assassinations like the one between the regime and the MB in 1948 and 1949. By 2 August 1990, the spokesperson of the IG, Dr. 'Alaa' Muhhyidin, was found shot dead near his apartment in Giza. The IG accused the State Security Investigations (SSI), one of the Egyptian security agencies, of being behind the assassination.

The murder of Muhhyidin marked the shift of the IG's activities from partial militarization to total militarization.[66] Members of the supposedly peaceful *da'wa* wing were participating in violent activities, including the assassination of Dr. Rif'at al-Mahjub, former speaker of the parliament, on 12 October 1990. The vicious cycle of violence had begun and was exacerbated by the notorious Dayrut events[67] that started in June 1992. The cycle only ended with the Luxur massacre in November 1997.[68]

According to official records, the death toll resulting from the confrontation period between 1992 and 1996 was 471 IG members, 401 from the security forces, 306 Egyptian civilians and 97 tourists (Abdul Fattah 1996, 71). The number of detainees during the mid-1990s reached a maximum of 30,000 people (al-'Awwa 2006, 143). This period also featured an insurgency based in Upper Egypt, a rise in the use of terror tactics in Egyptian cities, many assassinations/ assassination-attempts, bombings, extra-judicial killings, mass-murders, systematic torture in prisons,[69] military show-trials, regular curfews in many Upper Egyptian towns and villages and the destruction of hundreds of acres of arable land.[70]

The de-radicalization phase (1997–2002)

The de-radicalization phase can be divided into four stages. The first stage began with the declaration of intent to de-radicalize and the search for consensus amongst the leadership for this policy. The second part was marked by the ideological legitimization of the behavioral transformations, mainly through the production of new literature. The third part was organizational: convincing the middle-ranking leadership, the grassroots and the sympathizers to support the new ideology, as well as addressing their questions, critiques and concerns through conferences, small meetings and lectures. Finally, the fourth part involved addressing the general Egyptian public, the Muslim world and the international community.

On 5 July 1997, during one of the military tribunals for IG activists, Muhammad al-Amin Abdul 'Alim asked the generals presiding over the tribunal for a brief opportunity to address the "court" (Zuhdi *et al.* 2003, 7; al-Zayat 2005, 299; Abdul 'Alim 2007). The generals agreed and, to the surprise of everyone, Abdul 'Alim read a statement signed by six of the IG "historical" leaders declaring a unilateral ceasefire and calling on IG affiliates to call off all military operations at home and abroad. It was this declaration that heralded the beginning of the de-radicalization phase.

It is important to note that there was no consensus about the de-radicalization process across the organization in the beginning. It was an initiative taken by the imprisoned historical leadership, without approval from the leaders outside prison and abroad. Therefore, the declaration initially drew condemnation from several IG leaders abroad,[71] al-Jihad Organization leaders,[72] as well as several local and international radical figures and smaller groups (Hashim 2000, 1). Since there was no proper communication, some of the IG radicals hiding and operating in remote Upper Egyptian areas did not hear about the declaration and carried on with an older order given to them in 1996: the Luxur operation. Whereas Rifa'i Taha, who headed the *Shura* Council abroad at this point took responsibility for the Luxur massacre, the IG's historical leaders and the leaders in Europe strongly condemned it (Rushdi 2005). The massacre was the last violent act perpetrated by IG affiliates. The leadership consensus about the unilateral ceasefire, which was called in the media the "Initiative for Ceasing Violence" (ICV), was reached only on 28 March 1999, when the leaders in Egypt and abroad declared their unconditional support for the initiative.

At that point, the behavioral dimension of the transformation was much more developed than the ideological one. The second stage of the de-radicalization process however featured a comprehensive attempt to ideologically legitimize the transformation, as well as to publicize that ideological component. To do this, the IG issued four books in January 2002 under the general title of *Correcting Conceptions Series*. The first was titled *The Initiative for Ceasing Violence: a Realistic View and a Legitimate Perspective* (Hafiz and Abdul Majid 2002). Authored by two of the *Shura* Council members and revised by six others, the book generally addressed the practical and the ideological reasons behind the initiative.[73] The three other books, published concurrently, addressed what went "wrong" during the "Jihad" (that is, the confrontation with the Egyptian regime), issues of ideological extremism and excommunication of Muslims, and gave advice to those who participate in the OVPV process.[74] These books were followed by 12 others, two of which provided an ideological–theological critique of al-Qa'ida's ideology, strategies and tactics (Zuhdi *et al.* 2003; Zuhdi *et al.* 2002). A third book criticized the "clash of civilizations" hypothesis (Ibrahim *et al.* 2005a, 236).

Finally, the fourth stage of that de-radicalization process was to address the communities that were affected by the IG activities. These communities were mainly the Egyptian public, the Muslim world and the international community. To do so, the IG established an official website, upon which the new literature was published. The IG leaders have also been interviewed on state-sponsored Egyptian television as well as independent satellite networks like al-Jazeera and al-'Arabiya (Zuhdi 2006).

Historical overviews of other armed Islamist movements

In this section, I provide an overview of two de-radicalized groups: the Egyptian Jihad Organization and the Algerian Islamic Salvation Army (AIS). I also briefly discuss the background of the GIA and its splinter groups as cases of de-radicalization failure. As mentioned before, the Egyptian al-Jihad is still an ongoing case of substantive de-radicalization (ideological and behavioral, but not organizational). Several leaders from al-Jihad in Egypt have declared that the organization has ceased violence forever (al-Tawil 2007, 1). Sayyid Imam al-Sharif, the emir of al-Jihad between 1987 and 1993, have recently issued a book entitled *Document for Guiding the Jihad in Egypt and the World* to ideologically and theologically legitimize the new position of the organization (al-Sharif 2007; al-Shaf 'i 2007, 1, 7; Zinah 2007a, 1). However, the organization is still suffering from factionalism, as at least three factions refuse to de-radicalize and dismantle their armed units (al-Shaf 'i 2007, 1, 7). In the Algerian case, the AIS and its affiliated militias are a case of pragmatic (behavioral and organizational) de-radicalization in which these groups have ceased violence and rejoined society as a part of a political deal with the ruling regime. However, these groups have not ideologically de-legitimized violence against the state.[75] Finally, the case of de-radicalization failure is that of the GIA and its main splinter group, the Salafi Group for Preach and Combat (GSPC) (now al-Qa'ida in the Islamic Countries of al-Maghreb – QICM).

The al-Jihad Organization in Egypt

De-centralization and Movement Building (1968–1984)

The Egyptian al-Jihad Organization was the second largest armed Islamist movement in Egypt after the IG. Al-Jihad is older however, as the history of its first cell can be traced to the 1960s. According to Ayman Al-Zawhiri, Hani al-Siba'i, Anwar 'Ukasha and other Jihad commanders, the first nucleus of al-Jihad cell was established in 1968 (al-Zawhiri 1993, 144; al-Siba'i 2002a, 10; 'Ukasha 2002). The execution of Sayyid Qutb in 1966 and the Arab defeat by Israel in 1967 were all factors contributing to the establishment of this cell (al-Siba'i 2002a, 10; al-Zayyat 2005, 135).[76] By the early 1970s, there were several small factions operating under the name of al-Jihad, most notably Ayman al-Zawhiri's, Salem al-Rahhal's and Kamal Habib's, as well as others. What connected these factions were informal contacts through personal relationships, and Salafi-Jihadi ideological links without a clear organizational structure or hierarchy. Also, these factions were all operating in Lower Egypt, mostly in Cairo, Alexandria and al-Sharqiyya. In the late 1970s, Muhammad Abdul Salam Farag was able to establish organizational links between these Jihadi factions (al-Siba'i 2002b, 10; Hammuda 1985b, 115). Farag was also able to connect these Lower Egyptian factions with the IG in Upper Egypt. As a result of these contacts, Farag was able to organize the assassination of President Sadat.

Despite the factionalism, lack of central leadership and organizational structure, the al-Jihad factions had several common features in this early stage that distinguished them from relatively consolidated groups like the MB and the IG. First, they all preferred covert action as opposed to public activism in universities, mosques and on the street (al-Siba'i 2002a, 10; Habib 2006, 26–37). Second, they all focused on infiltrating the army as there was an early realization that a coup is the shortest and most decisive way to the establishment of an Islamist state (al-Siba'i 2002a, 10; 'Ukasha 2002). Finally, all these factions preferred to avoid any indecisive action that would lead to a prolonged confrontation with regime. In that regard, al-Jihad leaders like al-Zawhiri and al-Zumur strongly objected to the assassination of President Sadat. According to them, the assassination was not going to lead to the establishment of an Islamist state and yet would provoke a confrontation with the regime that these factions were unprepared for (al-Zumur 1990, 7, 16; Hafiz 2006, 95; al-Siba'i 2002b, 10).

Between 1981 and 1984, the aforementioned disagreements between the IG and al-Jihad over leadership, ideological and tactical issues led to the separation of the two groups under clearer organizational structures.[77] Post-1984, al-Jihad became known as a distinct radical Islamist organization with a separate leadership from the IG and a small support base in Lower Egypt. It was also known for preferring covert action and avoiding public activism (al-Jihad Organization 1989, 145).

The Afghan years: rebuilding and consolidation (1987–1993)

The period between 1984 and 1986 saw relatively little activism from al-Jihad (al-Siba'i 2002b, 10; Mabruk 1995, 267). In al-Siba'i's words, it was a period of "healing" after the major crackdown following the assassination of President Sadat. By 1987, two of the al-Jihad leaders had reached Afghanistan: Ayman al-Zawhiri[78] and Sayyid Imam al-Sharif.[79] Other middle-ranking leaders and members followed. Al-Zawhiri was able to reorganize the group in that year and there was a consensus on giving the *bay'a* to al-Sharif as an Emir of al-Jihad, given his theological credentials.[80] Most of the organizational and logistical work, however, was accomplished by al-Zawhiri (Diraz 1993, 73; al-Zawhiri 1995, 269; al-Siba'i 2002, 11; al-Zayyat 2005, 246). Other well known names that contributed to the reorganization process of al-Jihad in Afghanistan were Subhy Abu Sitta (alias Abu Hafs al-Masri)[81] and Ali Amin al-Rashidi (alias Abu 'Ubayyda al-Panjsheiri)[82] (al-Siba'i 2002b, 10).

Several reasons were behind the move to Afghanistan. The first was to find new freedoms and opportunities to rebuild the organization away from the eyes of the Egyptian security services and state repression. The second was to implement an idea that 'Issam al-Qamary[83] is credited for. Al-Qamary argued that the reason behind the defeat of the Egyptian Jihadists in 1981 was their lack of military skills. Therefore, he insisted on implementing training programs for al-Jihad members similar to those of regular armies (al-Siba'i 2002c, 10, Mubarak 1995, 269). Following that line of reasoning, al-Zawhiri thought of Afghanistan as a possible training ground (al-Zayyat 2005, 246–247). The recruitment, however, was mostly done in Egypt. Between 1987 and 1992, al-Jihad members would be recruited in Egypt, trained in Afghanistan and then would return to Egypt. Al-Zawhiri's orders to the trained militants were clear: no publicity of a person's Islamist identity, no confrontation with the regime, and no activities until further notice (al-Siba'i 2002c, 10). However, the IG's confrontation with the regime in 1989 and 1990 led to the discovery of the Afghan trail, since the IG's militants were also trained in Afghanistan. Moreover, large-scale security sweeps and contacts between the activists of the IG and al-Jihad in Afghanistan and Egypt allowed the SSI to discover that the Afghan trail was being used by both the IG and al-Jihad. As a result, a major sweep took place on al-Jihad suspects and more than 800 persons were detained (Siba'i 2002c, 10; Mubarak 1995, 410). This became known as the "Tala'i' al-Fatah" (Vanguards of Triumph – VT) case, because the media referred to the detainees with that term.[84]

Factionalism and confrontations (1993–1995)

The VT case sparked an internal crisis within al-Jihad Organization that reached its zenith in 1993. Ahmad Hussein 'Igiza (alias Abdul Hamid), a middle-ranking leader in al-Jihad, led a faction that condemned al-Zawhiri's policy of temporarily avoiding a confrontation. Al-'Igeiza's faction, composed entirely of younger al-Jihad militants, had two grievances (al-Siba 2002c, 11). First, they thought that the leadership's incompetence had led to the arrest of the 800–1,000 persons taken in during the VT case. Also, they protested that the arrests of those Jihadists happened without any form of resistance, at a time where their rival, the IG, was leading an insurgency whose main objective was to release their detainees. "One thousand of our brothers were detained, tortured and sentenced by military tribunals without even firing one shot … what exactly is the purpose of an armed organization if we cannot protect ourselves…" a statement by 'Igeiza read ('Igeiza 1993, 1).

At this time, most of al-Jihad leaders and many members were in Sudan as the Sudanese government was pursuing a policy of accommodation and coordination with Islamists of all ideological brands. Al-Zawhiri was in Sudan, but al-Sharif, the official Emir and the spiritual leader, was in Pakistan (al-Saba'i 2002c, 11). The latter did not want to go to Sudan to reconcile the two factions, and ultimately tendered his resignation as leader of the group calling upon his followers to choose a new emir. After deliberations within two of al-Jihad's top organizational bodies, the Constitutive Council[85] and the Legitimate Committee,[86] the leading members agreed on giving a *bay'a* to Ayman al-Zawhiri (al-Saba'i 2002c, 11).

This was not the end of the internal crises that followed the VT case. Several members who gave *bay'a* to al-Zawahiri still insisted that the organization should avenge the arrest of its members in the VT case through violent operations (al-Shaf'i 2002, 7; al-Siba'i 2002c, 7). This led to the assassination attempts on the former Interior Minister, Hasan al-Alfi, and the former Prime Minister, 'Atif Sidqi. Both operations failed. Moreover, the SSI was able to kill the head of al-Jihad Organization in Egypt, Adel Awad, in 1994. As a result, al-Zawahiri ordered a tactical ban on all violent operations in Egypt in mid-1995 due to an inability to carry out such operations. The order was internal, but it became public knowledge in the late 1990s (al-Siba'i 2002c, 10; al-Shaf'i 2002, 7).

Finally, another severe problem faced al-Jihad's leadership in Sudan and put an end to their presence there. The Sudanese intelligence warned al-Zawahiri that the Egyptian intelligence had succeeded in infiltrating the organization by recruiting two teenagers, one of whom was the son of Muhammad Sharaf (alias Abu al-Faraj al-Yemeni), a member of the Legitimate Committee of al-Jihad (al-Zawhiri 2002). After a process of coordinated investigation with Sudanese intelligence, al-Zawhiri set up a "trial" for the two teenagers and the Legitimate Committee sentenced them to death! (al-Zawhiri 2002b; al-Siba'i 2002). Also, in response to the infiltration, al-Zawhiri ordered another terror act: the blowing up of the Egyptian embassy in Islamabad in 1995 (al-Zawhiri 2002b). At the same time, the Sudanese authorities were concerned with the behavior of al-Jihad Organization on its territories after the murder of the two teenagers and the bombing of the embassy. Therefore, they asked al-Zawahiri and other al-Jihad militants to leave the country (al-Siba'i 2002c, 10). The former and his followers started a second migration to Afghanistan in early 1996.

Afghanistan again: ideological changes, behavioral changes and internationalization (1996–2006)

By 1996, there was an ideological rapprochement between Bin Laden and al-Zawahiri that had started earlier in Sudan and that became more apparent in Afghanistan. The rapprochement resulted in a shift within al-Jihad's ideology, followed by behavioral changes. To elaborate, one of the ideological pillars of al-Jihad[87] was that fighting the nearby enemy[88] is to be given priority over fighting the faraway enemy.[89] Abdullah Azzam, Usama Bin Laden, Abdul Majid Zendani and other leading Afghan-Arabs upheld an opposing ideological concept: fighting the faraway enemy is to be given priority[90] (Azzam 1987). By 1998, it was clear that al-Zawhiri and a faction within al-Jihad Organization had shifted their ideology and were now upholding the latter concept[91] (al-Zawhiri 2001, 10). The act of signing the declaration of the Global Islamic Front for Fighting Jews and Crusaders[92] represented a tangible manifestation of that ideological change within al-Jihad. This action, however, led to splits within the Organization, since several leaders protested the ideological and behavioral shifts and called for a focus on the Egyptian national level of engagement. By 2000, it became clear that al-Zawhiri was only leading a faction within al-Jihad and not the organization as a whole.

De-radicalization (2007–present)

Post-2000, four main groups existed within al-Jihad. The first and largest group of all was comprised those in Egyptian prisons; its number ranged from 2,000 to 3,000 militants (al-Khatib 2007a, 1). This faction was led by the old generation of the al-Jihad leaders who were sentenced in the 1981 trials that followed the Sadat assassination. Most notable among these leaders are Anwar 'Ukasha[93] and Nabil Na'im.[94] The second faction owed allegiance to al-Zawahiri and joined al-Qa'ida. The title *Qa'idat al-Jihad* (The Jihad Base), which is used post-2001 by al-Qa'ida's members, is a reflection of that merge between al-Qa'ida and that faction within al-Jihad Organization. The third faction was the Jihad members and leaders outside of Egypt who did not join al-Zawhiri and opposed his policies of internationalization. A fourth faction, the smallest in number, was the al-Jihad leaders who "disappeared" after 9/11 and reappeared again in Egyptian prisons. Most notable of those is Dr. Sayyid Imam al-Sharif, the former leader of al-Jihad, who is currently leading the de-radicalization and ideological reform process.

Like with the IG, the process of de-radicalization of al-Jihad started in Egyptian prisons. More particularly it began with the former leader of al-Jihad, 'Abbud al-Zumur, supporting the IG's ceasefire in 1997. Back then, al-Zumur only supported the behavioral component of the ICV and wanted in return immediate political gains (al-Khatib 2007, 1; Abu Ruman 2007, 1). Almost none of the other al-Jihad leaders, whether in prison or outside, have supported the IG's ICV in 1997. In 2004 and 2005, there were several attempts led by Nabil Na'im, a co-founder of al-Jihad, to organize a peace initiative. These were not successful however due to internal organizational differences.[95] Then, in 2007, Cairo declared that Sayyid Imam al-Sharif was present in Egypt.[96] In March, *al-Hayat* newspaper announced that al-Sharif and other al-Jihad commanders were leading a de-radicalization process inside the prison. The process featured meetings with the grassroots and middle-ranks along the lines of what happened with the IG (Zinah 2007a, 1; al-Masy al-Youm 2007, 1). A statement from al-Sharif sent from inside the Scorpion Prison in Cairo confirmed the process (Al-Sharif 2007, 1; Al-Shaf'i 2007, 1). In April 2007, several middle-ranking leaders outside of Egypt declared their support for the new transformations (al-Khatib 2007a, 1). In May 2007, al-Sharif, who had previously authored *al-'Umda*, a large book on the "jurisprudence of violence,"[97] issued a statement saying that he was going to publish a reversionary document entitled *Document for Guiding Jihadi Activism in Egypt and the Islamic World* (al-Shaf'i 2007, 7). At the same time, al-Jihad as an organization declared that it was going to publish a book under the title *The Perception* to outline its new ideology (Zinah 2007a, 1). However, the final draft was delayed on several occasions, mainly due to organizational differences on framing the new ideology, as well as about the future behavior of al-Jihad (Zinah 2007a, 1). Finally, al-Sharif's *Document* was published in November 2007. Needless to say that the process of de-radicalization was harshly criticized by al-Zawhiri's faction, who now used the title of *al-Qa'ida fi 'Ard al-Kinana* (al-Qa'ida in the Land of the Quiver[98]) in their statements and documents (al-Tawil 2007b, 6). Also, some of al-Jihad factions still oppose de-radicalization, including those of Magdi Salim[99] in al-Marj Prison and Ahmad S. Mabruk[100] in Abu Za'abal Prison. This is in addition to a few former al-Jihad figures in Europe.[101]

The Algerian armed Islamist movements: the Islamic Salvation Army (AIS) and the armed Islamic group (GIA)

The GIA and the AIS were established in reaction to a series of events at a critical juncture that occurred in Algeria in the early 1990s. In 1997, the AIS was able to lead a successful process of pragmatic de-radicalization. The leadership of the AIS was successful in dismantling the organization as well as several affiliated armed bands. Moreover, at least 22 of the GIA-affiliated militias joined the de-radicalization process led by the AIS (al-Hayat 2000, 1, 6). However, the bulk of the GIA failed to de-radicalize. Instead, part of the GIA was destroyed and another part became the Salafi Group for Preaching and Combat (GSPC). The latter allied itself with al-Qaʻida and recently changed its name to *al-Qaʻida fi Bilad al-Maghreb al-Islami* (al-Qaʻida in the Islamic Countries of al-Maghreb – QICM) (Ghimrasa 2006, 1; Ghimrasa 2007, 1). Chapter 6 will attempt to explain the causes of the success of the de-radicalization process of the AIS and the failure of that process in the GIA's case.

The foundation of the GIA and the AIS (1992–1994)

Immediately following the capture of an overwhelming majority of parliamentary seats by the Islamic Salvation Front (FIS) in the first round of the Algerian parliamentary elections of December 1991, an anti-Islamist military coup took place in that country. A major crackdown and mass arrests of the FIS's suspected supporters followed the coup. The cancellation of the elections and the crackdown drove many Islamists[102] to flee to the mountains, especially the ones who were inclined to take up arms against the coup plotters.

The military coup triggered the re-emergence of several armed Islamist groups as early as March 1992. The first two were the Armed Islamic Movement (MIA) under the leadership of Abdul Qadir Chabouti[103] and the Movement for the Islamic State (MEI) led by Said Makhloufi[104] (Roberts 1995, 239; Sheikhy 2007, 6). Several other smaller groups came to be known later, most notably the two armed bands that were led by Mansour Meliani and Muhammad Allal.[105] These two bands constituted the nucleus of what came to be known as the Armed Islamic Group of Algeria (GIA) (Hussein 1998, 108; al-Tawil 1998, 104–106; Willis 1997, 268–274; Sheikhy 2007, 6; Layada 2007, 6). After the arrest of Meliani in July 1992 and the death of Allal in September 1992, Allal's deputy, Abdul Haqq Layada (alias Abu Adlan), was able to unite the two bands under the title of the Armed Islamic Group in October 1992 (Hattab 1998, 6; Layada 2007, 6, Zitouni 1995, 16).[106]

There were several attempts to unite these small armed bands under one banner. The first of these attempts took place in the Tamasguida[107] meeting of September 1992, with the plan of uniting the armed groups under the leadership of Chabouti. According to Muhammad bin Hussein, an Islamist activist who was in direct contact with the attendees in the meeting, the united organization was to become an armed wing for the FIS (Hussein 1998, 61). The Algerian army, however, was informed about the meeting and launched a surprise attack in which Muhammad Allal was killed (Hussein 1998, 62). When Allal's deputy, Layada, took over, he refused to unite under Chabouti's leadership and refused the idea of being an armed wing for the FIS. An armed wing of the FIS would be fighting for the return of the electoral process (Ben Aicha 2000, 8), and Layada as well as future GIA emirs did not consider that objective as a Jihad or even as legitimate justification for a fight (GIA 1995, Communiqué no. 36). The ultimate objective of the GIA was the establishment of an Islamist state and possibly a Caliphate.[108] While upholding that ideological stance in 1992, Layada refused unity and established the autonomous GIA in October 1992.

In response to the GIA's militancy, radical ideology, autonomous behavior and insistence upon remaining distinct from the FIS, some of the latter's mid-ranking leaders established the Islamic Salvation Army (AIS) to become an armed wing for the FIS. The first few cells of the AIS were established in early 1993 in Western Algeria under the command of Ahmad Ben Aicha, a FIS MP who was elected in December 1991 (Ben Aicha 1996, 8).[109] In July 1994, the AIS issued a communiqué declaring that it is was expanding its operations to the national level under the joint leadership of Ben Aicha (emir of the west) and Medani Mezraq (emir of the east).[110] The latter was declared the national emir of the AIS in March 1995 and played a crucial role in the de-radicalization process of his organization as well as others in 1997.

Ideological nuances and confrontations (1994–1997)

Since its formation, the AIS has been behaviorally and ideologically different from the MIA, the GIA and even the smaller MEI. First, it believed in the "Islamic legitimacy" of electoral democracy[111] and claimed in its communiqués that it fights for the "Algerian people's choice" (Ben Aicha 2000, 6). Also, the AIS and the political faction within the FIS that it aligned itself with[112] have repeatedly justified their support for violence only as a reaction to the violence perpetrated by the regime after the cancellation of the elections (Guomazi 2000, 8; Jeddi 2000, 8; Kabir 1994, 6).[113] In addition, in its first communiqué the AIS declared that Jihad is only *a* mean, as opposed to *the* mean, to establish an Islamic state in Algeria (see AIS Communiqué in al-Tawil 1998, 169–171). Finally, in contrast to the GIA, the AIS accepted diversity and pluralism between Islamist factions.[114]

As a result of these differences between the AIS and the GIA as well as the former's constant criticism of the GIA's indiscriminately violent tactics and rhetoric threatening excommunication, the relationship between the two groups was characterized by rivalry until 1994 and then escalated to threats and outright hostilities in 1995. In that year, Djamel (Jamal) Zitouni (alias Abu Abdul Rahman Amin) became the national emir of the GIA and led his group towards a Takfiri trend. The hostilities between the GIA and the AIS manifested themselves in several ways. One of them was the GIA's *fatwas* to execute several FIS and AIS figures (GIA 1995, Communiqué no. 30, 1). This was followed by Zitouni's orders to execute former leading figures in the FIS who joined the GIA in an attempt to unite the Algerian Jihadists (Boukra 2002, 198; Zitouni 1995, 27). These figures included leaders as high-profile as Muhammad Said and Abdul Razzaq Rajjam, who were the first and third provisional leaders of the FIS respectively[115] (Waly 1995, 125, 131). Finally, on 4 January 1996, the GIA officially declared war on the AIS and any group affiliated with it (GIA 1996, Communiqué no. 41). In the context of this war, Zitouni was ambushed and killed by militants from a smaller militia that belonged ideologically to the al-Jaz'ara camp, and which later on joined the AIS (Hattab 1998, 6; Ben Hajar 2000, 8). At the time, the militia's name was the Islamic League for Preaching and Jihad (LIDD). The assassination of Zitouni was interpreted as an operation to avenge the death of Muhammad Said, al-Jaz'ara's leader (Ben Hajar 2000, 8). Following Zitouni, Antar al-Zouabri (alias Abu Talha) became the seventh emir of the GIA (1996–2002). He issued a *fatwa* in September 1997 declaring the rest of the Algerian population to be apostates and hypocrites because they withheld their support from the GIA (al-Zouabri 1997, 1). This *fatwa*[116] was preceded by a series of massacres against civilian villagers that started in 1996 and reached its zenith in 1997. The GIA claimed responsibility for some of those massacres in a communiqué issued by al-Zouabri in 1998 (al-Zouabri 1998, 1; Hattab 1999, 6).

The de-radicalization of the AIS

In this context of intense, chaotic violence that involved a war between the regime and armed Islamists, another war between various armed Islamist groups and a third war against the civilian population,[117] the AIS declared a unilateral ceasefire on 21 September 1997.[118] Like the Egyptian case of the IG, the ceasefire marked the beginning of a long process of de-radicalization. That process was not limited to the AIS but also included smaller groups like the LIDD, al-Rahman Brigade, the Islamic Front for Armed Jihad (FIDA)[119] and even several GIA's brigades, including the notorious "Calitos Unit" that operated in Algiers and was responsible for several bombings in that city (Ben Hajar 2000, 8; Kertali 2000, 8; Mezraq 2005b, 6; Sheikhy 2007, 6). As will be outlined in the sixth chapter, the process was successful both behaviorally and organizationally.

The 1997 ceasefire that started the process of de-radicalization was a result of negotiations between the commander of the AIS, Medani Mezraq (alias Abul Haytham), and the deputy-head of the military intelligence, General Isma'il Lamari.[120] After the "election" of Abdul Aziz Boutflika in 1999, a general "amnesty" was given to the AIS members through two presidential decrees issued in 1999 and 2000 (Presidential Decree no. 2000, 2000).[121] Around 7,000 AIS militants benefited from that amnesty in 2000 (Hafez 2000, 579). A limited amnesty was also given to other de-radicalized groups.[122] As a result, around 800 GIA militants joined the process to benefit from that amnesty (al-Hayat 2000, 1). The legal framework of the amnesty was known as the "Law for Civil Concord" (LCC). The Mezra–Lamari negotiations followed by the LCC were two important landmarks that led to the de-radicalization of several armed Islamist groups, including the permanent dismantling of the AIS. Another general amnesty, which targeted the rest of the armed Islamists,[123] was declared and approved through a national referendum in September 2005, after the "re-election" of Bouteflika. It was called the "Charter for Peace and National Reconciliation" (CPNR) and its provisions included immunity against prosecution for guerrillas who renounced violence[124] and army personnel, as well as aiming to end legal proceedings against individuals who were no longer fighting, and providing compensation to families of people killed by government forces. The CPNR was implemented in September 2006.

The transformation and the partial destruction of the GIA (1998–present)

The 1995 Clemency Law, the 1997 Mezraq–Lamari negotiations, the 2000 Law for Civil Concord and the 2005 Charter for Peace and National Reconciliation were not sufficient initiatives to put an end to violence in Algeria. The GIA continued its terror campaign until its partial destruction in 2005 after killing its eighth emir, Rashid Quqali (alias Abu Turab) and the arrest of its ninth emir, Noureddine Boudiafi (alias Abu Uthman and Hakim RPG) (Ghimrasa 2005a, 1; Le Quotidien d'Oran 2005, 1; Muqqadim 2007, 1). Moreover, its main splinter group, the GSPC, allied itself with the al-Qa'ida network, changed its name to "al-Qa'ida in the Islamic Countries of al-Maghreb" (QICM) and continued perpetrating violence. Chapter 6 analyzes the causes of the failure of the de-radicalization of the GIA and the GSPC/QICM. In the following section, I provide a brief history of the transformation of a part of the GIA into the GSPC/QICM.

As mentioned before, after the death of Cherif Gouasmi, the fourth emir of the GIA, there was significant change in the Group's behavior and ideological orientation. More specifically, the GIA's behavior and ideology became more similar to that of Takfiri groups after Gouasmi's death. Djamel Zitouni, the fifth emir of the GIA, upheld a policy of wider selection of targets, including Algerian civilians, foreigners and rival Islamists. Internally, Zitouni started purging former FIS leaders who joined the GIA in an attempt to unite armed Islamists. Zitouni and his successor Zawabri legitimized those actions through excommunications and claims of apostasy. These actions and the new ideological orientation not only alienated potential supporters and sympathizers from the GIA but also the militias who signed the unity agreement of May 1994, including al-Rahman Brigade (led by Mustafa Kertali), LIDD (led by Ali Ben Hajar), FIDA (led by Abdul Wahab Lamara) and others (Kertali 2000, 8; Ben Hajar 2000, 8; Layada 2007, 6; Sheikhy 2007, 6). These militias left the GIA by late 1995 and early 1996. Moreover, the LIDD, a 500 men-strong militia operating mainly in al-Medea, was able to ambush Zitouni and kill him in July 1996. In 1998, Hassan Hattab (alias Abu Hamza), the commander of the second zone[125] of the GIA declared that he had officially left the GIA with his followers due to its behavior (massacring civilians) and theological "deviation" (excommunicating Algerians in general as well as rival Islamists) (Hattab 1998, 6). On 14 September 1998, Hattab also declared the foundation of the GSPC with other leading former members of the GIA. According to the official estimates, Hattab had around 1,300–1,500 armed militants under his command (Ghimrasa 2005b, 6). In a series of published correspondences between Hattab and *al-Hayat* newspaper in 1998, the former vowed to continue the "Jihad" that the AIS and others had "abandoned" (Hattab 1998, 6).

Under Hattab, the GSPC declared that it would only target security/military personnel and avoid civilians (Hattab 1998, 6). In 2003, the GSPC claimed that Hattab "resigned"[126] from leading the group, mainly in protest of coordinating with al-Qa'ida (al-Hayat 2007b, 1; Hattab 2007, 8). While Hattab started coordinating with the Algerian regime to join the de-radicalization process (Ghimrasa 2005b, 6), his successor, Nabil Sahrawi (alias Abu Mustafa Ibrahim), declared his allegiance to al-Qa'ida on 11 September 2003, one month after he became the new GSPC emir. After Sahrawi's death in June 2004, Abdul Malik Drukdal (alias Abu Mus'ab Abdul Wadud) took over and after getting an approval from al-Zawhiri in end of 2006, Drukdal changed the GSPC's name to QICM in January 2007 (al-Tawil 2007, 378). In addition to the hit-and-run guerrilla tactics and assassinations, QICM recently started using the simultaneous suicide bombing tactics that al-Qa'ida is known for, most notably in the coordinated attacks on the government HQ, the Eastern District Anti-Terrorism Center and the HQ of the Interpol, all in Algiers, in April 2007.

Conclusion

To recap, Table 3.1 highlights some of the characteristics of the previously discussed armed Islamist movements (characteristics pertaining mainly to their processes of radicalization and de-radicalization).

The main focus of this chapter has been the historical patterns of change within armed Islamist movements, whether towards radicalization, de-radicalization or, to a lesser extent, moderation. The three processes are centered on the stances of these movements on the two issues of violence and democracy. The chapter provided a historical overview of five cases: the armed wing of the MB (the SA), the IG, al-Jihad, the AIS and its affiliates, and the GIA and its main splinters (GSPC and QICM). The first four cases demonstrate several types of de-radicalization. The first two cases (MB and IG) demonstrate comprehensive de-radicalization: ideological, behavioral and organizational. The third case (al-Jihad) demonstrates substantive de-radicalization, lacking only the completion of the organizational dimension. The fourth case (AIS and affiliates) demonstrates a pragmatic de-radicalization process without an ideological dimension. The fifth case (GIA, GSPC, QICM) demonstrates a case of de-radicalization failure. Chapters 4, 5 and 6 investigate the causal variables behind the success and failure of the de-radicalization processes of the aforementioned cases. Chapter 7 concludes by identifying the patterns of change within armed Islamist groups towards radicalization and/or de-radicalization, the dominant causal variables behind those changes, and the relationship between those variables.

Table 3.1 Characteristics of armed Islamist movements

Islamist organization	Place/date of establishment	Scope of violence	Periods of armed action	Type of violence	Declared reasons for violence[1]	De-radicalization period(s)
MB armed wings (SA, UD, SO, 1965 Org)	Egypt, 1940 (SA)	Egypt, Palestine/Israel	1946–1954, 1964–1965	Anti-colonial, anti-regime, terror acts	Colonialism, Palestine, repression	1951–1953; 1964–1965; 1969–1973
IG	Egypt, 1978	Egypt, Afghanistan, Bosnia/Croatia, Chechnya, Ethiopia[2]	1979–1981, 1989–1997	Anti-regime, anti-colonial, secessionist, terror acts	Mainly repression, "defense" of Muslims	1997–2002
al-Jihad	Egypt, 1968	Egypt, Afghanistan, Pakistan	1981, 1993–1995, 1998–2007 (faction coordinating with al-Qa'ida)	Anti-regime, anti-colonial, anti-US, terror acts	Repression, US presence/influence in ME (faction coordinating with al-Qa'ida)	2007–present (excluding the faction coordinating with al-Qa'ida)
AIS	Algeria, 1993	Algeria	1993–1997	Anti-regime, pro-electoral process	Repression, coup against electoral process	1997–2000
GIA	Algeria, 1992	Algeria, France	1992–2005	Anti-regime, anti-France terror acts (including massacring civilians)	Repression, "apostasy" of the regime	2000–2005
GSPC	Algeria, 1998	Algeria, Sub-Saharan Africa	1998–2007	Anti-regime, terror acts	Repression, "apostasy" of the regime	Failed attempts
QICM	Algeria, 2007	Algeria, Mauritania, sub-Saharan Africa	2007–present	Anti-regime, terror acts	Repression, "apostasy" of the regime	No attempts

Notes
1 As they appear in the literature of these groups and statements of their leaders during confrontation periods.
2 IG affiliates and sympathizers were implicated in the 1993 bombing of the World Trade Center in New York City. However, the leadership never took responsibility for terror acts against the US and it stressed in the 1990s that it does not target the United States (see for example Zuhdi et al. 2003, 18). Also, there was an assassination attempt in 1995 against an Egyptian diplomat (or an intelligence agent) in Geneva, Switzerland. The Egyptian regime blamed the IG, but the leadership did not take responsibility.

4   The untold story

The de-radicalization of the armed wings of the Muslim Brothers

> The persons who assassinated the Prime Minister are not Brothers and are not Muslims.
>
> (Hasan al-Banna, Founders of the Muslim Brothers, 1948)

> The Muslim Brothers did not and will not drop their weapons and leave jihad but the behaviour of some young men had tarnished Islamist action.
>
> (Mustafa Mashhur, Fifth General Guide (1996–2002), 1986)

This chapter investigates two questions. The first is what caused the initiation of the de-radicalization process of the MB's armed wings, a question that was overviewed in Chapter 3. That process had three dimensions: the first was behavioral, and involved the decision of the MB's leadership to abandon violence permanently. The second dimension was organizational, and aimed at dismantling the armed wings, seeking consensus among their commanders and convincing their foot soldiers to uphold the transformation towards non-violence. The third dimension was ideological, and had as its objective the legitimization of the de-radicalization process, and thus ultimately ensuring the permanent abandonment of violence along ideational and theological lines.

The second question flows from the historical fact that the leadership of the MB[1] attempted to de-radicalize the group three times: between 1951 and 1953, between 1964 and 1965, and between 1969 and 1973. The first two attempts were complete failures, with both national and international consequences.[2] The third attempt was successful and, at a later stage, led to the promotion of the moderation process that the MB underwent during the leadership of its third *murshid* Umar al-Tilmisani (1972–1986).[3] The second research question that this chapter attempts to answer is: why did that third de-radicalization attempt succeed, when the other two had failed?

The argument proposed to answer the two questions can be summarized as follows: first, the four causal variables[4] behind a successful de-radicalization process were only present in the third attempt. Second, the interaction between those variables, especially the coordination between President Sadat's regime (selective inducements) and the MB's consolidated leadership following a long period of sustained repression, was reinforcing the third de-radicalization attempt, leading ultimately to its success in the early 1970s. In the previous attempts at de-radicalization, some of the necessary causal variables were missing, and the patterns of interaction between the variables were impeding the de-radicalization process. More specifically, state repression was constantly undermining the leadership, which was willing to de-radicalize in 1951 and, less evidently, in 1964. In addition, state repression was impeding the process of internal interaction between the members of the MB's leadership, the middle-ranking commanders and the grassroots, especially in the early 1960s.

The de-radicalization attempts: successes and failures

In this section, the de-radicalization attempts that the leadership of the MB has initiated since 1951 are discussed. But first, it is important to note that al-Banna attempted to "reform" the SA before 1951. (Shadi 1981, 93–100; al-Sabbagh 1998, 31–34; Abdul Khaliq 2004, episode 5). The "reformation" process included purging disobedient SA members, focusing armed operations on colonial targets and limiting the authority of the then-SA commander, Abdul Rahman al-Sanadi, especially after the assassination of Judge al-Khazindar in March 1948 (Kamal 1987, 236; Shadi 1987, 33; Abdul Khaliq 2004, episode 5). Al-Banna's assassination in February 1949, less than a year after al-Khazindar's assassination, put an abrupt stop to the still-incomplete "reform" process. There was no evidence to suggest that al-Banna had taken any practical steps to dismantle the SA, even after it conducted attacks on civilian targets and assassinated politicians.[5] Moreover, al-Banna established another armed wing, the Units Department (UD), to counterbalance the influence of the SA within the MB (Shadi 1981, 32–33; al-Baquri 1988, 69; Abdul Khaliq 2004, episode 5). He assigned the leadership of the UD to Police Major Salah Shadi, who had an intense rivalry with al-Sanadi (Shadi 1981, 33; al-Sabbagh 1998, 73–74; Abdul Khaliq 2004, episode 7).[6]

The first attempt (1951–1953)

Like the following two attempts at de-radicalization, this attempt was mainly led by the second *murshid*, Hasan al-Hudaybi. It started when al-Hudaybi was chosen by several influential members of the GO, on 19 October 1951, thereby ending the two-year leadership crisis that had plagued the MB since the assassination of al-Banna. Al-Hudaybi initially started a process that aimed to completely dismantle the SA. He legitimized that process through the slogan "no secrecy in serving God and no terrorism in Islam" (Mitchell 1969, 88). Facing several obstacles, al-Hudaybi pragmatically changed the objective into the reformation, rather than the dismantling of the SA. Both the obstacles and the reformation process will be discussed in detail in the following sections.

Leadership status: controversy, rivalry and mutiny

Al-Hudaybi became the *murshid* of the MB in October 1951 mainly as a result of a power struggle between four competing factions:

1   The SA and their allies bolstered by their arms and led by their former spiritual leader, Salih al-'Ashmawy (1940–1947)
2   The *Azharis*[7] and their supporters bolstered by their theological credentials and led by Sheikh Ahmad Hasan al-Baquri
3   Al-Banna's relatives and their followers bolstered by blood ties to the founder of the MB and led by his brother Abdul Rahman al-Banna and brother-in-law Abdul Hakim Abdin
4   Finally, the "elite" faction, bolstered by their financial capabilities and upper-class status. The leading figures of this last faction included Justices Munir Dallah[8] and Hasan al-'Ashmawy[9] as well as Farid Abdul Khaliq (al-Baquri 1988, 87–91; Ramadan 1993, 89–93; Mubarak 1995, 40; Abdul Khaliq 2004, episode 7).

Extensive deliberations took place between Salih al-Ashmawy, al-Baquri, Abdin, Abdul Rahman al-Banna and Dallah, in which they failed to choose one of them as a General Guide. In reaction, Dallah recommended al-Hudaybi as a compromise (Ramadan 1993, 89; Mubarak 1995, 40–42; Abdul Khaliq 2004, episode 8). The others agreed to give *al-bay'a* to al-Hudaybi, thinking that he would be a nominal figure without actual powers.

In addition to being a compromise between competing factions, the choice of Judge al-Hudaybi as a *murshid* aimed at refurbishing the image of the MB after it had been tarnished following the assassinations of Judge al-Khazindar and Prime Minister al-Nuqrashi (Mitchell 1979, 184; Abdul Khaliq 2004, episode 8). Several sources also allude to the possibility that al-Hudaybi might have been the "candidate of the Palace." Al-Hudaybi's brother-in-law, Nagib Salim, was the chief of the royal household. Salim was widely regarded as the link between the MB and the Palace, representing the King's wishes (Mitchell 1979, 182–188; Ramadan 1993, 91–94).[10]

Challenged leadership, controversial decisions

Al-Hudaybi was an accomplished judge and a well-known legal figure. During al-Banna's life, he acted mostly as an advisor to the latter on political and legal matters, beginning in 1944 (Mitchell 1979, 185, Abdul Khaliq 2004, episode 8). However, he was not a regular member of the MB – indeed, to most of the MB leaders and members he was an unknown figure[11] (Kamal 1987, 253; Abdul Khaliq 2004, episode 8). Moreover, the fact that he was recommended for leadership and then strongly supported by the "elite" faction made the rest of the factions uncomfortable and suspicious about his intentions. Also, his personality and leadership style added to the already tense situation. As opposed to al-Banna, a "mover of the masses" par excellence, al-Hudaybi was a man of few words, with a personal style that was perceived as arrogant by some of the MB members, as well as by other politicians (Kamal 1987, 253; Mitchell 1979, 185–187; Mansur 2004, episode 8).[12] Given this fact, Mitchell argues that al-Hudaybi's early years in leadership risked transforming the MB into an elite-dominated/elitist movement, as opposed to a mass movement (Mitchell 1979, 187–188; Abdul Khaliq 2004, episode 8).

On the issue of violence, al-Hudaybi was not a supporter of any type of armed action,[13] whether against the ruling regime or against the colonizer (al-Hudaybi 1951, 3; Mitchell 1969, 85; al-Baquri 1988, 92; Ramadan 1993, 94, Abdul Khaliq 2004, episode 8). In an interview with the *al-Jumhur al-Masry* news-paper in 1951, al-Hudaybi declared that the MB was only interested in spiritual power, while material power was the exclusive domain of the government (al-Hudaybi 1951, 3). He also denied the involvement of the MB in fighting the British in the Canal Zone in 1951[14] (al-Hudaybi 1951, 3) and was quoted as saying that armed resistance would not lead to the departure of the British from Egypt (al-Hudaybi 1951, 3). In addition, Ali Ashmawy, a former SA member and a leading figure in the so-called 1965 Organization, mentions in his memoirs that al-Hudaybi initially refused to meet with the SA members after their release from prison in 1951 (Ashmawy 2005, 20). Ashmawy quotes al-Hudaybi as saying that "he [would] not meet with murderers" (Ashmawy 2005, 20). Al-Sabbagh, one of the top commanders of the SA and a deputy of al-Sanadi in 1951, similarly mentions in his memoirs that during the first meeting between al-Hudaybi and the SA leadership, al-Hudaybi told the SA commanders that he had come to "purify the MB from crime" (Al-Sabbagh 1998, 93).[15] Given these pos-itions and statements, al-Hudaybi quickly became the focus of hostility from several SA commanders, including their leader, Abdul Rahman al-Sanadi.

Moreover, al-Hudaybi took a decision that transformed the tensions into a crisis: the dismantling of the SA and the incorporation of its members into the General Apparatus[16] (*al-Nizam al-'Amm*) of the MB (Mitchell 1979, 246). Al-Hudaybi's argument[17] was that there was no reason for the existence of the SA in a group that preaches Islam[18] (Mitchell 1979, 189, 238; al-Baquri 1988, 92; Ramadan 1993, 96; al-Sabbagh 1998, 92; al-Zawahiri 1993, 111). As a result of this decision, in late 1951, he demanded a database of the names of the SA members and commanders, as well as the locations of the arms warehouses, training camps and other logistics. Given the existing level of mistrust however, al-Sanadi refused to give the information, and responded by starting to criticize al-Hudaybi's leadership. Al-Sanadi argued that al-Hudaybi should not be a *murshid* since he was not a regular member of the MB and did not become a *murshid* through the legal organizational methods[19] (Mitchell 1979, 238; Ramadan 1993, 98). Many of the SA commanders took al-Sanadi's side, most famously the fifth and the seventh *murshids* Mustafa Mashhur and Mahdi Akif, as well as high-ranking commanders in the SA like Ahmad Adel Kamal, Mahmud al-Sabbagh, Ahmad Hassanein and Ahmad Zaki (Kamal 1987, 286; Ramadan 1993, 98; al-Sabbagh 1998, 131). Their argument was that the dismantling of the SA would not only violate the concept of Jihad in Islam and render the MB slogan "al-Jihad is our way" hollow, but would also remove the MB's major instrument of defense (Mitchell 1969, 119; Kamal 1987, 260–266; al-Sabbagh 1998, 90). During this crisis, several meetings were held between al-Sanadi and al-Hudaybi to try to reach a compromise. Al-Sabbagh attended some of those meetings and described the tensions in his memoirs by saying that al-Sanadi told al-Hudaybi once that "he (al-Sanadi) cannot protect his Islamic beliefs except by staying away from al-Hudaybi" (al-Sabbagh 1998, 99).

It was obvious to al-Hudaybi at this point that the dismantling of the SA would not be an easy task. Therefore, he appointed a committee of GO members[20] to investigate the possible dismantling or the reformation of the SA as an alternative option (Ramadan 1993, 98; al-Sabbagh 1998, 117). The committee quickly arrived at the conclusion that because the SA was armed, had a charismatic leadership, as well as a strong *esprit de corps* and a sense of mission, was the most well-established MB institution. Therefore, it could not be dismantled at that point in time. Instead, the committee recommended a reorganization process which had three objectives. The first was to narrow the gap between the MB's General and Special Apparatuses by merging the *'usar*[21] of both Apparatuses under one command. The leaders of the *'Usar* Department would receive orders directly from the Guidance Office.[22] The second objective was to gradually remove the cult of secrecy surrounding the Special Apparatus by introducing the largest possible number of MB members into it, regardless of the SA's old standards for membership[23] (Kamal 1987, 282–283; al-Sabbagh 1998, 67–68). The committee thought that the new members would be more loyal to the *murshid* and therefore would limit the authority of the SA leadership within its own ranks (Ramadan 1993, 99; al-Sabbagh 1998, 90). Finally, the third objective was to weaken the influence of al-Sanadi by firing him from his position as the commander of the SA. The committee members did not however address two important issues: the arms and the databases. This was, arguably, because they knew they would not be able to do much about them without the cooperation of al-Sanadi and his supporters, who were still in control of the hearts and minds of many SA members.

The mutiny

The committee's decisions did weaken the SA, but they did not put an end to the conflict between al-Hudaybi and his elite faction on one side and al-Sanadi on the other. First, the decisions of the committee could not be fully implemented without the databases and the cooperation of al-Sanadi. Many of the SA members were simply unknown and therefore their *'usar* could not be merged with the General Apparatus[24] (Mitchell 1969, 119; Ramadan 1993, 97–99). Other SA members were loyal to al-Sanadi and therefore taking their orders directly from him, regardless of the leadership appointed by the *murshid*. Between November 1951 and November 1953, al-Hudaybi appointed two commanders to lead the SA and neutralize al-Sanadi's influence: Helmi Abdul Majid (1951) and

Sayyid Fayez (1951–1953) (Mitchell 1979; al-Sabbagh 1998, 111, 130). The former soon resigned in protest, due to the lack of cooperation from al-Sanadi and his followers. The latter was assassinated by a bomb hidden in parcel that was sent to his house on 19 November 1953 (al-Sabbagh 1998, 130). At this point, the confrontation between al-Hudaybi and al-Sanadi escalated to another level.

Following the assassination of Fayez, al-Hudaybi took a decision to fire four SA commanders who he perceived as being disloyal to the official leadership and who he suspected of having been involved in the assassination. Those commanders were al-Sanadi, al-Sabbagh, Kamal and Ahmad Zaki (Ramadan 1993, 121; al-Sabbagh 1998, 131; Abdul Khaliq 2004, episode 11). In protest, the supporters of al-Sanadi stormed al-Hudaybi's house to force his resignation.[25] When the latter refused and his followers started to gather around the house to protect him, the mutineers left the house, bolstered their numbers with another 100 or so supporters, and stormed the MB's general headquarters to stage a sit-in (Ramadan 1993, 122–123). Two accounts exist regarding the objectives of the sit-in. Kamal, al-Sabbagh and others claim that their objective was to identify the reasons behind their having been fired along with the other commanders (Kamal 1987, 285; Ramadan 1993, 122–124; al-Sabbagh 1998, 131). However, the supporters of al-Hudaybi argue that the objective was to topple al-Hudaybi and replace him with Salih al-Ashmawy, the first commander of the SA, as a General Guide[26] (Shadi 1981, 105–110; Abdul Khaliq 2004, episode 11; Ashmawy 2005, 25).

In the end, the mutiny was a fiasco and the SA's old guard seemed to have underestimated the resilience of al-Hudaybi. Not only was the decision to fire the four SA commanders upheld, but the sympathizers with the mutineers were also fired on 10 December 1953. These included Constituent Board members like Salih al-'Ashmawy, as well as leading figures form the *Azharis* faction like Sheikh Muhammad al-Ghazali[27] and Sheikh Sayyid Sabiq (Ramadan 1993, 125; Kamal 1987, 288).[28]

In addition, al-Hudaybi was able to appoint a new commander for the SA in the same month: Yusuf Tal'at. Because of his record in fighting the British in the Canal Zone, Tal'at was respected by many SA members and commanders[29] (Kamal 1987, 290; Abdul Khaliq 2004, episode 13). Moreover, al-Hudaybi was able to recruit Abdul Mun'im Abdul Ra'uf[30] to his side to help Tal'at in reorganizing the SA (Abdul Ra'uf 1989, 119–120; Ramadan 1993, 158). At this point, there was a complete transformation in the SA, not only in its leadership but also in its organizational structure. A new name was given to the armed wing: *al-Tanzim al-Sirri* (Secret Organization – SO) (al-Tilmisani 1985, 68; Kamal 1987, 290–291; Ashmawy 2005, 284).[31]

A final note on the leadership struggle within the MB and the regime's policy towards it should be mentioned here: while the internal conflict between the MB leaders was going on, President Nasser's secretary for military police affairs, Muhammad Abdul Rahman Nusayr, contacted al-Sanadi and suggested the assassination of al-Hudaybi (Kamal 1987, 288). When al-Sanadi consulted with other SA commanders, they refused to escalate the situation to that level (Kamal 1987, 288).[32] By early 1954, the balance of power in this struggle for leadership of the MB was tilting heavily towards al-Hudaybi and his camp.

State repression: intermittent, intense and reinforcing radicalization (1953–1954)

As mentioned before in Chapter 3, the relationship between Nasser's regime and the MB fluctuated significantly between 1952 and 1954. In 1953, the relationship was characterized by rivalry and mistrust,[33] and by 1954, by outright hostility. The intensity of these fluctuations, leading ultimately to a policy of repression, directly affected the de-radicalization process of the MB. It will be shown here that the main result of state repression between 1953 and 1954 was the radicalization of the MB moderates led by al-Hudaybi.[34]

Al-Hudaybi was not enthusiastic about supporting the 1952 coup, a position that stood in marked contrast to that taken by the SA, the UD and many GO members.[35] Four days after the coup, Nasser told al-Hudaybi that the MB would have no guardianship over the revolution in exchange for their initial support. On 29 December 1952, Nasser made it clear in a private meeting with the MB leaders that he had no intention of holding elections or of withdrawing the army (Abdul Khaliq 2004, episode 10). This situation escalated because of differences regarding the future of the army in politics, the role of parliament, al-Hudaybi's refusal to participate in the government, and the latter's declaration that the coup was not an Islamic one. Moreover, Nasser was successfully manipulating the internal splits within the MB, mainly between al-Hudaybi and al-Sanadi.[36]

On 15 January 1954, the RCC issued a decree banning the MB for the first time since the 1952 coup. A crackdown followed and around 450 MB leaders were arrested, including al-Hudaybi (Abdul Khaliq 2004, episode 10). Another crackdown occurred between late February and early March of that year, this time arresting Abdul Qadir Audeh, Secretary General of the MB, for his leading role in the massive pro-democracy demonstration of 28 February 1954 (Ramadan 1993, 134, 138, 254; al-Shaf'i 1999, episode 6; Abdul Khaliq 2004, episode 12). In addition, MB officers in the army and the police force were either fired or arrested and court-martialled. These included leading MB figures in the army like Colonel Abdul Mun'im Abdul Ra'uf, Colonel Abu al-Makarim Abdul Hayy[37] and Major Ma'ruf al-Haddary[38] (Abdul Ra'uf 1989, 106–108; al-Shaf'i 1999, episode 6).

Following the so-called 25 March crisis,[39] al-Hudaybi and most of the MB leaders were quickly released (Abdul Khaliq 2004, episode 12). Although Nasser visited al-Hudaybi at his house to "congratulate" him on his release, the confrontation was far from over (Abdul Ra'uf 1989, 114; Ramdan 1993, 140; al-Masry 1954, 1). The MB leadership was sure that the crackdown would continue (Abdul Khaliq 2004, episode 12).

Half-hearted radicals?

Given such developments, Abdul Mun'im Abdul Ra'uf – who was himself detained in January 1954 – mentions in his memoirs that he sent a note to al-Hudaybi[40] requesting the latter's approval for his escape from prison. He also requested from Hussein Kamal al-Din, a GO member and a former member of the SA "reform" committee, 500 fully armed and trained SA members to topple Nasser's regime (Abdul Ra'uf 1989, 148–149). He only received al-Hudaybi's approval for the first request however. When he met the latter after his escape in May 1954, he asked about the MB's strategy as regards Nasser, to which al-Hudaybi responded by showing him an open letter to the President requesting the reinstatement of the parliament and the holding of elections (Abdul Ra'uf 1989, 154). Abdul Ra'uf also asked what the alternative strategy was if Nasser re-iterated his refusal and detained them again. At this point, al-Hudaybi said "ask Yusuf Tal'at and Ibrahim al-Tayyib" (Abdul Ra'uf 1989, 155). The former was the head of the SO, handpicked by al-Hudaybi, and the latter was the SO Commander for Cairo.

Despite the fact that this statement seemed to indicate openness to armed confrontation, the MB's leadership was actually still hesitant as regards this course of action. For example, Abdul Ra'uf demanded the organization of an armed demonstration that would go to the RCC, attack it and topple the regime. Al-Hudaybi denied the request, ordering only an unarmed one similar to the 28 February demonstration.[41] That unarmed demonstration was planned for 29 October 1954 (Abdul Khaliq 2004, episode 12). Tal'at also refused another request by Abdul Ra'uf to authorize the organization of a wide-scale insurrection (Mitchell 1979, 277), as well as a similar request from Justice Hasan al-Ashmawy.[42] Al-'Ashmawy mentions in his memoirs that in his last meeting with Tal'at, the latter refused to launch a large-scale armed campaign against the regime despite the availability of arms and trained men. Al-Ashmawy attributes this to the orders of al-Hudaybi, as well as to the fact that Tal'at was fearful of three possibilities: foreign intervention, the execution of MB prisoners held by the regime, and losing control over the SO (al-Ashmawy 1977, 75–76). Al-Ashmawy concludes that Tal'at became obsessed with the three possibilities in 1954, and that as a result the SO was crippled (al-Ashmawy 1977, 76).[43]

In any case, Abdul Ra'uf was able to internally reorganize the SO, as well as coordinate with Tal'at and al-Tayyib to collect and study the databases to estimate the actual capabilities of the Organization. The three leaders were also able to arrange several training camps and workshops in summer 1954 (Abdul Ra'uf 1989, 179–194; Ramadan 1993, 159). However, Abdul Ra'uf expressed his frustration over the leadership's lack of initiative, its constant delays in taking action, and its hesitation at confrontation (Abdul Ra'uf 1989, 175–176, 179–192). At best, the MB leadership was giving conflicting signals to its followers under conditions of state repression. Thus it ordered the reorganization and rearmament of the SA, changed its name to the SO, signalled an alternative, more violent strategy, and continued issuing firebrand communiqués. At the same time, between

1953 and 1954 it denied all requests for armed action (Ramadan 1993, 245; Abdul Ra'uf 1989, 155; Mitchell 1969, 85; al-Ashmawy 1977, 61).

In September 1954, following news about the regime's plan to assassinate him,[44] al-Hudaybi disappeared, fearing for his life (Ramadan 1993, 189; Abdul Khaliq 2004, episode 12; al-'Ashmawy 1977; 59). Yet the MB's statements and pamphlets criticizing Nasser and the 1954 treaty with the British were still signed by the *murshid*. (Abdul Ra'uf 1989, 179; Ramadan 1993, 193; Abdul Khaliq 2004, episode 12). Hasan al-Ashmawy, al-Hudaybi's companion in his hideout, describes the MB at this stage as being organizationally chaotic: there were more than 500 MB detainees, the group had a hidden, isolated and still controversial leadership,[45] there was widespread organizational disorder plaguing both the General Apparatus and the SO, and there was a continuing crackdown by the regime[46] (al-Ashmawy 1977, 59–60). On 26 October 1954, Mahmud Abdul Latif, an SA/SO operative, attempted to assassinate Nasser in al-Manshiyya square in Alexandria.[47] Following the failed attempt, state repression was taken to a whole new level: thousands of MB members and leaders were arrested and court-martialled, a death-sentence was handed out to al-Hudaybi,[48] six MB leaders were executed – including Abdul Qadir Audeh[49] – and many others received jail sentences.[50]

Social interaction: failure to support de-radicalization (1952–1954)

The social interaction variable has affected the MB's attitudes towards violence since the late 1930s. Regarding radicalization, as mentioned in Chapter 3, the new militaristic trends in Europe – especially the rise of Nazi-German and Fascist-Italian paramilitary units – had influenced al-Banna's decision to establish the SA at the outset. The existence of the armed wings of Egyptian political parties like the Blue Shirts of al-Wafd Party and the Green Shirts of the Young Egypt Party[51] similarly encouraged al-Banna in making his decision (Abdul Khaliq 2004, episode 4; Lia 1998, 167, 175, 179).

In the post-coup period, there were quite extensive internal interactions between the leaders of several MB factions, as well as between those leaders and the grassroots.[52] Externally, there were also some interactions between the MB and other political parties/groups, most notably al-Wafd (nationalist liberals), Young Egypt (radical national-socialists) and the communists (Ramadan 1993, 198–203; Mitchell 1979, 247–262). However, most of these parties/groups were not supportive of the de-radicalization process that al-Hudaybi had initiated. This opposition was for three reasons.[53] The first had to do with the afore-mentioned problems of leadership: if the leader is controversial and the leader-ship is factionalized, then the interaction variable will not be as effective in influencing the de-radicalization process.[54] The second reason had to do with the consequences of state repression: the post-coup anarchic context was marked by the lack of political will to support democracy/democratization by most of the coup-plotters,[55] as well as a strong interest in consolidating the new military regime and ousting/liquidating potential rivals. These were all contextual factors that contributed to the radicalization of the opposition, or more accurately, the post-coup political losers.

External interaction

Given these conditions, social interaction – and particularly the external dimension of social interaction – was a contributing factor in the move down the path of armed conflict with the RCC. Abdul Ra'uf mentions in his memoirs that after being arrested with other less-cooperative-with-Nasser army officers, Yusuf M. Siddiq, a communist army colonel,[56] was constantly blaming al-Hudaybi and the MB for Nasser's success in maintaining the military regime and in cracking down on the opposition. He says to Abdul Ra'uf that he requested assistance from al-Hudaybi to coordinate a multi-ideological armed movement against Nasser's regime, to be led by the MB, the communists and other army officers. But al-Hudaybi refused his initiative, in spite of his lack of an alternative strategy (Abdul Ra'uf 1989, 115).

A different type of interaction occurred between civilian communists and the MB. In June 1954, al-Hudaybi said that communism should be not confronted by laws or state violence, and that the MB did not oppose the idea of having an Egyptian communist party (Siddiq 1954, 5). Following that statement – according to Dr. Fu'ad Mursi, president of the Egyptian Communist Party at the time – talks took place between Sayyid Qutb, who was then the editor-in-chief of the *Muslim Brothers Newspaper*, and a delegate from the Communist Party (Mursi 1975, 57). The general objectives discussed were to topple the military regime, to suspend martial law and to reinstate general freedoms. In the view of the Communist Party, the only way to topple the regime was through demonstrations and a wide-scale resistance campaign, a tactic that was refused by al-Hudaybi (Ramadan 1993, 200–201).

Finally, it should be mentioned here that many MB leaders supported General Naguib and the anti-Nasser movement in the army led by the left-leaning army officer, Major Khalid Muhhiy al-Din[57] (Shadi 1981, 117; al-Tilmisani 1985, 110; Abdul Ra'uf 1989, 114). The latter demanded that the army give up political power and reinstate the parliament in March 1954 (an incident known as the March Crisis).

Internal interaction

The interactions between the MB's leadership and the commanders and foot soldiers of its armed wings were frequently tense in the period between 1951 and 1954. These interactions aimed initially to dismantle the SA, and later simply to control it. The interactions did not however meet either objective, mainly due to the aforementioned problems of leadership. More specifically, the perceived elitism and arrogant behavior of al-Hudaybi, the firing of popular dissidents without consolidating his leadership, and his use of statements describing/implying that the SA members were criminals meant that the objectives were not achieved. Kamal mentions one interesting incident that reflects that failure. In December 1953, following several meetings with the SA commanders, the mutiny, and the firing of dissidents, around 40 armed SA members gathered in a house near the headquarters of the MB, where al-Hudaybi and his supporters from the Constituent Board were in the process of firing those who had sympathized with the mutineers. The SA group's plan was to storm the headquarters and liquidate the leadership. According to Kamal, he interrupted their meeting and dismissed them in his role as a senior commander before the start of the attack (Kamal 1987, 288). The incident reflects the failure of internal dialogue in that period, which resulted in even more radicalization and potential internal violence.

Selective inducements: co-optation of some radicals and radicalization of some moderates

In the period between 1952 and 1954, Nasser's regime was able to co-opt many of the MB leaders and SA commanders, most notably Ahmad Hasan al-Baquri, Abdul Rahman al-Sanadi and Abdul Aziz Kamil, as well as several other members of the Guidance Office and about one third of the Constituent Board (Mansur 2004, episode 11; Abdul Khaliq 2004, episode 11). Al-Baquri, who was a de facto leader of the MB between 1949 and 1951, was one of the four candidates for the position of the *murshid* in 1951, had been a close disciple of al-Banna, and was the leader of the *Azharis* faction, became the Egyptian Minister of Religious Endowments between 1952 and 1959 (al-Baquri 1988, 117–119; 247). Abdul Aziz Kamil was an influential member of the GO who had been recommended as al-Banna's successor by al-Banna himself in the late 1940s (Abdul Khaliq 2004, episode 4). He was also one of three members who sat on the committee that oversaw the "reformation process" of the SA, and he became the Deputy Minister and later the Minister of Religious Endowments under Nasser (al-Tilmisani 1988, 134; al-Sabbagh 1998, 358; Ibrahim 2007). Middle-ranking leaders were also co-opted and hired for governmental positions, most notably Ahmad Kamal Abu al-Majd, who became the Cultural Attaché in the Egyptian Consulate in New York[58] (Ibrahim 2007). Finally, and most importantly, Nasser was able to co-opt the former commander of the SA, Abdul Rahman al-Sanadi, as well as many of his followers. According to the third *murshid*, Umar al-Tilmisani and al-Sanadi's deputy, Mahmud al-Sabbagh,[59] al-Sanadi was given a financially lucrative position in an oil company until his death in 1962 (al-Tilmisani 1985, 67; 135–136; al-Sabbagh 1998, 358–360). He was also given some real estate and a villa in al-Isma'illiya governorate (al-Tilmisani 1985, 67; 135–136). Ali Ashmawy mentions in his memoirs that al-Sanadi asked Nasser to "secure" his followers (Ashmawy 2005, 166). He elaborates on one example that he witnessed personally: Mohammed Fisha, an SA foot soldier from a small village who was loyal to al-Sanadi was hired as a mechanic in the government's agricultural unit in the town of Meet Ghamr by presidential decree! (al-'Ashmawy 2005, 167) That was in 1954, following the crackdown on the mainstream MB. Nasser was successfully using selective inducements to co-opt the SA radicals who did not oppose him.

However, the objective of Nasser's regime was neither de-radicalization nor democratization, but rather the consolidation of the new military regime and the creation of a cult of personality around Nasser. The selective inducements were employed in that context and were guided by those objectives. The result was the co-optation of some of the SA radicals and other MB leaders who saw Nasser as being one of them, and who argued that his revolutionary/confrontational rhetoric was consistent with the MB ideology (al-Sabbagh 1998, 360; Ashmawy 2005, 166–167).[60] Al-Hudaybi and the members of his faction, however, were neither interested in Nasser's SA history nor in his revolutionary ideas and programs.[61] They were more interested in sharing power, reinstating political parties and holding elections. Their political stance regarding electoral democracy made them the focus of Nasser's wrath, and the following 1952–1954 crackdowns pushed many of them along the path of radicalization. The leaders of this MB faction were, however, only half-hearted radicals. They failed (or chose not) to call for a wide-scale insurrection or to coordinate with other political groups for an armed opposition movement. By 1955, most of the leaders of this faction were either executed, like Audeh, or sentenced to long terms in prison, like al-Hudaybi, Abdul Khaliq, Dallah, and others. Whereas selective inducements were employed successfully to co-opt some of the radicals, state repression contributed to the radicalization of the relative moderates.

The second attempt (1964–1965)[62]

The second attempt to de-radicalize the MB occurred in the period between 1964 and 1965. It followed a time of intense repression (1954–1964) and a concurrent radicalization process (1958–1964). The latter process led to the establishment of the fourth armed organization in the MB's history,[63] known in the literature as the 1965 Organization (Ra'if 1986, 233 Ramadan 1993, 316; Allam 1996, 121). In the period from 1954 to 1964, the leadership was weakened organizationally mainly due to state repression that caused the MB to go underground and to become more decentralized. The affiliated factions had different objectives that ranged from collecting funds for the families of the MB detainees to finding jobs for the released members to re-establishing of an armed wing to take revenge on Nasser (Abdul Khaliq 2004, episode 14; Issa 2004a, 8; Ashmawy 2005, 125, 142). This period also witnessed the development of the Takfiri and Jihadi ideologies within the MB, as a result of the very influential writings of Sayyid Qutb, which were produced in prison between 1957 and 1964.

The focus of this section is the 1965 Organization (*Tanzim* 1965) and the attempt to dismantle it. That attempt was mainly led by Farid Abdul Khaliq and Munir Dallah, two leading members in the pro-Hudaybi "elite" faction. The attempt was upheld at a later stage by al-Hudaybi (Ramadan 1993, 318; Abdul Khaliq 2004, episode 14; Issa 2004a, 8).

The analysis in the following sections is mainly based on the memoirs of, and interviews with, MB leaders opposed to the 1965 Organization such as Farid Abdul Khaliq and Umar al-Tilmisani, as well as on the memoirs of the 1965 Organization founders and leaders such as Zaynab al-Ghazali, Sayyid Qutb and Ahmad Abd al-Majid, on the memoir of Ali Ashmawy's,[64] and finally, on the memoirs of security officers such as Generals Fu'ad 'Allam, deputy head of the SSI (1981–1985) and Salah Nasr, head of the Egyptian General Intelligence (1957–1967).

Leadership status: fragmentation

Al-Hudaybi was released from prison due to old age and health problems in 1957. He was followed by a few other MB leaders, including Farid Abdul Khaliq, who became the MB leader of Cairo. Given the regime-imposed restrictions on political activities and the ban on the MB, none of their public organizational bodies such the GO or the CB were functioning. In that context, Abdul Khaliq became the main link between al-Hudaybi and other MB affiliated groups in 1958 (Abdul Khaliq 2004, episode 14; Issa 2004a, 8; al-'Ashmawy 2005, 161). With the approval of al-Hudaybi, the activities of Abdul Khaliq were focused on collecting funds for the families of the MB detainees as well as in finding jobs for the released members, particularly because Nasser enforced the law of "political dismissal," which allowed the regime to dismiss employees affiliated with political opposition from their jobs (Abdul Khaliq 2004, episode 13).

As mentioned in Chapter 3, Zaynab al-Ghazali, former head of the Muslim Sisters Society in the 1950s, and Abdul Fattah Isma'il, an SA member in the 1950s, initiated an attempt to unify several MB affiliated groups. The largest of these was a group of former SA grassroots members who had not been arrested in 1954, and who were led by Ali Ashmawy. The result of the unification efforts was the nation-wide 1965 Organization. The memoirs of the commanders differ as regards what the Organization's objectives were. There is however agreement that the Organization had an armed wing and that it advocated the use of violence, at least for defensive purposes (Qutb 1965; Abd al-Majid 1991, 96; Ramadan 1993, 318; Abdul Khaliq 2004, episode 15; Ashmawy 2005, 132).

The 1965 Organization was led by five commanders,[65] all of whom had been young activists at the grassroots level in 1954. In other words, they had had some training in organizing activities, but had no historical legitimacy or leadership experience. The constant problem that confronted those commanders, especially as regards recruitment, was their lack of a known spiritual leader who could bestow legitimacy on their organization. As a result, several released MB members refused to cooperate with them unless they got a clear authorization to initiate particular activities from al-Hudaybi (al-Ashmawy 2005, 132–133; Abd al-Majid 1991, 48–50; Issa 2004b, 8). The quest for legitimacy started at this point, with Abdul Fattah Isma'il asking Zaynab al-Ghazali to seek al-Hudaybi's approval for the reorganization. According to al-Ghazali, Ashmawy and Qutb, al-Hudaybi approved the reorganization attempt. However, Farid Abdul Khaliq says in his memoirs, as well as in interviews, that al-Hudaybi in fact gave conflicting signals (Abdul Khaliq 1989, 151; Abdul Khaliq 2004, episode 15).[66] In any case, the reorganization was underway, and the commanders asked al-Hudaybi to nominate a leader for organizational decisions. They suggested Abdul Khaliq, but he refused. Al-Hudaybi then suggested another candidate, Helmi Abd al-Majid, the former provisional commander of the SA between 1952 and 1953 (Issa 2004b, 8). He also refused however. The final candidate was Abdul Aziz Ali, a former minister of municipal affairs in the early days of the coup, as well as a former Patriotic Party activist. Ali was also versed in covert action, having co-founded an anti-colonial paramilitary movement called the Black Hand during the British rule of Egypt (al-Ghazali 1989, 60). Al-Hudaybi supported the nomination and Ali led the group for several months, before the release of Sayyid Qutb in May 1964.

In the period between 1957 and 1964, Qutb revised and produced several works on Islamic thought. Those works include *Fi Zilal al-Qur'an* (*In Shadows of the Qur'an*) and *Ma'alim fi al-Tariq* (*Signposts* or *Milestones*).[67] Qutb's works were generally popular in the Islamic world at this time, but *Milestones* in particular created a controversy among the imprisoned MB members,[68] at least until the works were endorsed by al-Hudaybi. The latter authorized the publication of the book, as well as including it in the curriculum of the MB in general and the 1965 Organization in particular.[69]

Given his image and the popularity of his works, the commanders of the 1965 Organization decided to choose Qutb as their new leader and to remove Ali in the summer of 1964. This move highlighted the leadership problems inside the Organization: in addition to the seemingly arbitrary removal and replacement of the leader, there were weak communications with the MB's leadership, and perhaps most importantly, al-Hudaybi's tenuous authority meant that it was unclear who set the objectives, determined actions, and indeed had the final say in the MB in general and the 1965 Organization in particular.

Contradictory stances on violence

Regarding violence, the initial plan of the Organization was to assassinate Nasser and thereby avenge what had happened to the MB in 1954 (Qutb 1965; Allam 1996, 139; Abd al-Majid 1991, 49–50; Abdul Khaliq 2004, episode 14; Ashmawy 2005, 142). Qutb however changed the objective to preparing a group of well-indoctrinated young men to lead a bottom-up societal change (Qutb 1965; Al-Ghazali 1989, 37; Abd al-Majid 1991, 50). In Qutb's plan, armed action was only to be defensive, in case the indoctrination process[70] was interrupted by the regime's forces. However, Ali Ashmawy, Abdul Fattah Isma'il and other commanders were more interested in rearming – thus the former started buying arms and smuggling them into Egypt via Sudan (Qutb 1965; Ramadan 1993, 319; Ashmawy 2005, 198).

Farid Abdul Khaliq, who was the official link between al-Hudaybi, the MB prisoners and the MB abroad, as well as being the one responsible for the MB in

Cairo (*Mas'ul*), was opposed to the whole idea of a formal organizational structure, and more fundamentally, to the use of violence at all (Abdul Khaliq 2004, episode 14; Qutb 1965; Issa 2004, 8). His idea was that the "best way to organize is without an organization" (Abdul Khaliq 2004, episode 14; Qutb 1965). Some of the MB's imprisoned leaders also held that position. Indeed, Salah Shadi, the former commander of UD, went so far as to ask his nephew to report the names of the 1965 Organization's commanders to the regime, in an attempt to stop them from reorganizing (Ashmawy 2005, 161).

Finally, al-Hudaybi did not himself provide any clear guidelines for action, nor indeed did he show that he had any influence on the actions of the Organization. When Abdul Khaliq and his faction started to criticize the Organization, the commanders of the latter sent to al-Hudaybi and asked him to order Abdul Khaliq to stop (Ashmawy 2005, 162). In response, al-Hudaybi was quoted as saying that he would not ask an active MB member to stop his activities. At the same time, he would also not ask an inactive member to start an activity (Ashmawy 2005, 162). He was also quoted by Ahmad Abd al-Majid, one of the five commanders, as saying to the faction of Abdul Khaliq, "leave whoever wants to attain martyrdom to attain it"[71] (Abd al-Majid 1991, 72).

Given that, it was clear that there was no strong leadership in the MB at this point in time, but rather each factional leader was pursuing his or her own policy. The official leadership refused to take a clear stance and continued to give conflicting signals and vague statements. The consequence was that each faction understood the leadership's statements according to its own circumstances, and based on their interpretation, claimed legitimacy for its actions. In this sense, it is not surprising that the leaders of these factions, such as al-Ghazali, Ashmawy and Abdul Khaliq, gave conflicting accounts of al-Hudaybi's position on the 1965 Organization in their memoirs (see al-Ghazali 1989, 16; Abdul Khaliq 2004, episode 14, 15). Ali Ashmawy sums up the conditions surrounding the MB's leadership in 1964: a hesitant *murshid* that offered vague statements (a reference to al-Hudaybi) and an indecisive leadership (a reference to Sayyid Qutb and Zaynab al-Ghazali) (Ashmawy 2005, 230).

The de-radicalization attempt

Given the leadership status, the de-radicalization of the MB at this point was less likely to succeed. Abdul Khaliq mentions that the commanders of the Organization did not even tell him that they had an armed wing (Abdul Khaliq 2004, episode 14). When Abdul Khaliq directly asked Abdul Fattah Isma'il[72] if they wanted to assassinate Nasser, the latter asserted that the aim of the Organization was to continue the *da'wa* activities of the MB (Abdul Khaliq 2004, episode 14). When al-Hudaybi and Abdul Khaliq discovered that they had an armed wing and that there was a plan for armed action, al-Hudaybi gave Abdul Khaliq an order to dismantle the Organization (Abdul Khaliq 2004, episode 15). The latter went to Sayyid Qutb and asked him to freeze the Organization in mid-1964 (Abdul Khaliq 2004, episode 15). According to Abdul Khaliq, Qutb was hesitant and did not give him a clear response (Abdul Khaliq 2004, episode 15). However, Ali Ashmawy mentions that he received an order from Qutb to stop any planning for armed action (Ashmawy 2005, 230). He received that order while the regime was in the middle of cracking down on the MB (in early 1965), with several members already having been detained. Therefore, the order contradicted the initial "defensive strategy" that Qutb had devised. Both Ashmawy and Ahmad Abd al-Majid describe the organization's internal status at this time as chaotic (Ashmawy 2005, 205, 211): "Everyone was giving orders and no one knew who was leading whom," Ashmawy wrote (Ashmawy 2005, 205).

State repression: intense, sustained, with mixed results

The period between 1954 and 1964 was of intense state repression directed against political opposition in general and the MB in particular. With regards to the latter, the years of 1954 and 1955 witnessed the aforementioned massive crackdowns, featuring mass-arrests, torture, military show-trials, long-term sentences, executions and then torture again in the prisons. In June 1957, the infamous Liman Turah Prison massacre occurred. The guards of Liman Turah prison opened fired, at the orders of the prison administration, on MB prisoners killing 23 and wounding 46 (Hammuda 1987, 130; Mubarak 1995, 47). The regime side of the story was that the massacre was in response to the MB prisoners' disobedience and refusal to go to the mountains for breaking rocks (the so-called "hard-labour" punishment) (Hammuda 1987, 130; Mubarak 1995, 47). The MB's version of the story was that the massacre was planned prior to the petition they sent to the prison's administration (to avoid doing the hard-labour) (Qutb 1965). According to Sayyid Qutb, the massacre aimed to liquidate some of them and intimidate the others (Qutb 1965).[73]

Regardless of which version is more accurate, this event in 1957 has affected the patterns of radicalization within the MB and other Islamist movements, both directly and indirectly for the decades to come. The wounded MB prisoners were transferred to the Liman Hospital where Sayyid Qutb was being treated (Qutb 1965). On their way into the hospital, the wounded prisoners were beaten by soldiers and Qutb witnessed that incident (Hammuda 1987, 130). The massacre marked the transformation of Qutb's Islamist political thought, from mainstream Muslim Brothers, upholding some modern ideas like electoral democracy, into a more radical version. In 1959, Qutb finished the third edition of *In Shadows of the Qur'an*. In this edition, the reinterpretations of the chapters (*surat*) titled *Yusuf* (Joseph), *al-An'am* (The Cattle) and *al-Tawbah* (The Repentance) can be perceived as laying out the foundations of Takfiri and Jihadi ideologies. *In Shadows* was published in 1962. In the following year, the first draft of *Milestones* was given to the members of the 1965 Organization as well as to other MB leaders. *Milestones* was published in 1964 (Issa 2004b, 8). Based on a selective reading, these two books became the forefathers of the Jihadi and the Takfiri literature of the 1970s and 1980s.

Milestones and *In Shadows* were produced by Sayyid Qutb. They were upheld by the *murshid* and the 1965 Organization under intense state repression. In this period, that repression has contributed not only to the radicalization process of the MB, but also to the birth of new types of radicals, who went further along the path of violence than the MB and its armed wings had.

Social interaction: attempts and failures (1962–1964)

Between 1962 and 1964, the writings of Sayyid Qutb led to an internal debate between the MB factions. The dividing line was between the supporters of Qutb's new thoughts that were outlined in *Milestones* and *In Shadows*[74] and the ones who argued that these thoughts were against the MB mainstream, and would probably lead to the concept of Takfir (accusation of unbelief/ excommunication).

The MB members in the late 1950s and early 1960s were either free inside Egypt, abroad or in prison. The prisoners were divided up among five prisons: al-Qanatir, al-Wahat, Military Prison, Liman Turah and Egypt Prisons (Qutb 1965). Qutb was in the hospital with only two inmates. Later on, other MB prisoners came mainly from al-Wahat and al-Qanatir prisons. Qutb was able to communicate his thoughts and to inspire some of the younger members of the MB (Qutb 1965). Qutb provides a survey in his memoirs, mentioning that out of the 98 MB prisoners with whom he discussed the new ideas, 35 were strongly supportive, 23 were strongly opposed and 50 were hesitant (Qutb 1965). When these detainees left the Liman Hospital and returned to al-Wahat and al-Qanatir prisons, they started discussing the Qutbian ideas with their fellow inmates. The discussion polarized the MB and led to severe tensions between supporters of the Qutbian ideas and those who rejected them (Qutb 1965; Issa 2004a, 8). This led Abdul Aziz Attiya, a member of the Guidance Office and the *Mas'ul*[75] of the political affairs of MB prisoners, to communicate with al-Hudaybi from al-Wahat prison and ask him for guidance (Qutb 1965; Issa 2004a, 8). Al-Hudaybi concluded that Qutb's ideas were Islamically correct but that the time was "too early to discuss [them] politically" (Issa 2004a, 8). He asked Attiya to tell the MB prisoners that they were free to adopt the Qutbian ideas or to reject them (Issa 2004a, 8; Abdul Khaliq 2004, episode 8).

Another type of internal interaction between MB factions occurred outside the prison. It aimed for behavioral and organizational de-radicalization rather than ideological change. In 1964, Farid Abdul Khaliq was tipped off by a former SA member, Wahba al-Fishawy, that the 1965 Organization had an armed wing. (Abdul Khaliq 2004, episode 14). Upholding the anti-violence stance and witnessing the consequences of the confrontation with Nasser's regime in 1954, Abdul Khaliq attempted to convince the leaders of the Organization to dismantle it. He first met with Abdul Fattah Ismai'l and Ali 'Ashmawy, and afterwards with Abdul Aziz Ali, who was still the leader of the Organization at that point. Abdul Khaliq pragmatically argued that it was impossible to succeed in toppling the regime because of Nasser's strength at that point. Ali refused the argument, and mentioned his experience in co-founding the anti-British Black Hand movement. Abdul Khaliq then offered the ideological argument, that toppling the regime through violence was not the "Islamically correct" way and that doing so would violate the teachings of al-Banna. That argument was also refuted on the basis of al-Hudaybi having sanctioned the Organization, and that he was the only legitimate MB leader at that time (Abdul Khaliq 2004, episode 15).

When Abdul Khaliq learned about the change of leadership in mid-1964, he went to the new leader, Sayyid Qutb, to try to freeze all activities of the Organization. However he failed to convince Qutb as well. In the end, the internal interaction process that had been led by Abdul Khaliq in support of de-radicalization had failed, mainly due to the patterns of interaction between state repression, lack of a charismatic leadership with a united stance supportive of de-radicalization and, finally, the lack of selective inducement.

The lack of selective inducements (1964–1966)

The period between 1958 and 1964 was also characterized by the lack of selective inducements. The regime, which was consolidated and thus more powerful following the "victories" over its internal rivals in 1954 and its external enemies in 1956 (the Suez Crisis), was more confident in using the "stick" and avoiding the use of "carrots." There was however one inducement initiative that took place. Zakaria Muhhiy al-Din, former head of the General Intelligence (1952–1953) and the interior (security) minister in 1961, met with al-Hudaybi and asked him to order the MB grassroots to join the Arab Socialist Union (ASU) (Ashmawy 2005, 220). The aim of Muhhiy al-Din was to counter the growing influence of the Left in the ASU. But al-Hudaybi refused the initiative (Ashmawy 2005, 220).[76]

The third attempt (1969–1973)

The third attempt to de-radicalize the MB began in prison, following the execution of Sayyid Qutb in August 1966. It started as a process of evaluation of the activities of the 1965 Organization, and was then transformed into a comprehensive de-radicalization process with ideological, behavioral and organizational dimensions. The highlight of the ideological dimension was the book *Preachers Not Judges*, which was allegedly authored by Hasan al-Hudaybi.[77] The book was a response to what al-Hudaybi and other mainstream leaders of the MB regarded as a misinterpretation of Sayyid Qutb's ideas and the misguided activities that resulted. The behavioral element of the de-radicalization process was led by other leaders in the prison, most notably Umar al-Tilmisani, Muhammad Hamid Abu al-Nasr, Salah Shadi and even Mustafa Mashhur[78] (al-Tilmisani 1988, 113; Abd al-Majid 1991, 253; Ashmawy 2005, 278–280). As demonstrated in the following sections, the de-radicalization attempt this time was successful. It put an end to the issue of using violence against the state through both ideological and organizational prohibitions. It also ended the existence of armed wings within the MB, at least within that generation.

Leadership: a unanimous anti-violence stance

As opposed to the divided leadership that existed during the previous de-radicalization attempts, this time there was unanimous agreement among the MB leaders that violence against the state, whether offensive or defensive, had led to disastrous consequence both within the group and outside it. As a consequence, it should be permanently stopped (Mahfuz 1988, 88). That view was shared between leaders from very different factional backgrounds, including the "elite" faction of al-Hudaybi,[79] SA and SO commanders (most notably Mustafa Mashhur, the fifth *murshid*, and Muhammad Mahdi Akif, the seventh and current *murshid*), Salah Shadi, the former head of the Units Department, and other Guidance Office members (Mahfuz 1988, 89–90; Abd al-Majid 1991, 253; Ashmawy, 2005, 278).

Preachers not judges: the ideological dimension of the MB de-radicalization

By 1968, the process of ideological de-legitimization of violence against the state had started. Initially, it featured several meetings between MB leaders, aimed at their taking a united stance against violence and excommunication of Muslims[80] (Mahfuz 1988, 90; Abd al-Majid 1991, 255). These meetings also aimed to produce a comprehensive theory that Islamically de-legitimizes two issues: violence against the state and excommunication of Muslims (see al-Hudaybi 1977). The first issue emerged later as the core of Jihadism, while the second is the core idea of Takfirism.

That research developed into the famous book *Preachers Not Judges*. Although al-Hudaybi is regarded as the author of the book, many sources mention that several other MB leaders either helped him or wrote major parts of the book (al-Tilmisani 1988, 138; Allam 1996, 219; Abdul Khaliq 2004, episode 15).[81] Those leaders included all the future *murshids* (from 1973 to 2008): Umar al-Tilmisani (the third *murshid*), Muhammad Hamid Abu al-Nasr (the fourth *murshid*), Mustafa Mashhur (the fifth *murshid*), Ma'mun al-Hudaybi (Hasan's son and the sixth *murshid*) and Muhammad Mahdi Akif (the seventh *murshid*); as well as several senior GO members like 'Abdul Aziz Attiyya and 'Abd al-Muta'al al-Gabry (Abdul Khaliq 2004, episode 14; Ashmawy 2005, 278). Also, General Fu'ad Allam claims in his memoirs that the "real" authors of the book were a combination of pro-regime Azhar Scholars and some of the MB leaders, including Ma'mun al-Hudaybi (Allam 1996, 222). He claims that the State Security Investigations, one of the multiple security agencies that dealt with the MB, had succeeded in "pushing al-Hudaybi to sign the book without his knowledge" (Allam 1996, 222). He does not elaborate on how they did this and, in general, his account seems farfetched, if not preposterous. Finally, other authors argue that the aforementioned MB authors, including al-Hudaybi, "had no specific training in Islamic Jurisprudence, so it is unlikely that they did the bulk of the research" (see for example, Zollner 2007, 424). The assumption is that to

produce a book like *Preachers Not Judges*, a specialist in Hanafi law had to par-
ticipate in the research. However, al-Hudaybis (both senior and junior), al-
Tilmisani and other leaders did have training in Islamic jurisprudence because of
their legal background.[82] In addition, there were several MB leaders from al-
Azhar imprisoned with al-Hudaybi who had helped with the book, most notably
Abd al-Muta'al al-Gabry (Allam 1996, 222; Abdul Khaliq 2004, episode 15).
Finally, the book in fact combines teachings from several schools of Islamic
jurisprudence rather than just being limited to Hanafi teachings. In fact, the dom-
inant teachings in the book are from al-Zahiri school of Ibn Hazm,[83] which al-
Hudaybi family strongly adhered to (al-Ghazali 1989, 17; al-Hudaybi 1977 132,
135, 140, 155, 163, 174).

In any case, whether al-Hudaybi wrote the book alone, was helped by other
MB leaders, or by the SSI and pro-regime Azhar Scholars, the name of al-
Hudaybi had to be on the book and his support/consent had to be granted to
provide organizational legitimacy for the ideological and theological arguments
presented. In other words, leadership was crucial to legitimize the transformations, regardless of who authored the book.

Mahmud Izzat, the current Secretary General of the MB, illustrates this point.
In a recent interview, Izzat recalls the controversy among MB prisoners after
reading Qutb's works in 1970 in the Qina Prison (Izzat 2007). This controversy
intensified after reading the first draft of *Preachers Not Judges*, sent to them by
the leadership form the Turah Farm Prison (*Mazra'at Turah*) (Izzat 2007, see
also Abd al-Majid 1991, 250–257). To settle the controversy, Izzat sent to al-
Hudaybi in the Farm to ask him whether or not the MB grassroots should read
Qutb's works. Al-Hudaybi told him that they could read it if they chose to, but
they had to keep in mind all the guidelines and the restrictions presented in
Preachers Not Judges (Izzat 2007). The message was clear here: Qutb's works
could be interpreted in various ways, some of which legitimized a violent confrontation with ruling regimes and non-Muslims, as well as excommunication of
Muslims. *Preachers Not Judges* clarified that this would not be the ideological
preference of the mainstream MB. The book also provided theological arguments to support that preference. The fact that it was authored, or was believed
to be authored, by al-Hudaybi provided the organizational legitimacy. In addition, the support from other leaders, whether behavioral through offering overt
approval, or ideological through the lack of any MB counterargument to *Preachers*, bolstered the process of ideological de-legitimization of violence.[84]

The organizational dimension: former SA commanders uphold de-radicalization

On an organizational level, the roles of Salah Shadi, Muhammad Mahdi Akif
and Muhammad Shakir were crucial in the transformation towards non-violence
(Ashmawy 2005, 278). The three had a history of struggle against the British,
the Egyptian Monarchy, and the Nasserite regime. Shadi was the former head of
the UD, and his roles in the MB's armed wings in the 1940s and 1950s have

been mentioned previously. Akif, the current *murshid*, was also a former SA commander who had a reputation for being a radical (Ashmawy 2005, 119). In 1965, he gave orders to the members of the Organization to fight until the end, and to use kitchen knives if they had to so as to resist arrest (Ashmawy 2005, 119). Shakir was another commander who had a well-known battle with the security forces in the Shubra district of Cairo in 1954. MB sources[85] describe his actions during this battle as "heroic." Outnumbered and outgunned, Shakir, along with other SA fighters, were able to resist Nasser's forces for a few days before their arrest (Abdul Ra'uf 1989, 194–195; Ashmawy 2005, 267–268). These two facts, that the former commanders could not be outdone in terms of having a history of violent struggle against the regime, and that they had subsequently become strong supporters of non-violence, bolstered the de-radicalization process. It made the job of non-SA leaders, especially those in the "elite" faction like al-Hudaybi and al-Tilmisani, much less difficult than it had been in previous attempts. Finally, Ali Ashmawy,[86] another former SA member and a commander in the 1965 Organization, acted as a liaison between the state security officers in charge of the MB file, most notably General Allam, and other MB leaders.[87]

A final point with regards to the characteristics of the MB leadership at this stage should be mentioned here: Ahmad Adel Kamal, the SA commander who along with several others was fired by al-Hudaybi in 1953, concludes in his memoirs that al-Hudaybi started his tenure in 1951 as a very controversial *murshid*. However, by the late 1960s "there was no controversy about him" (Kamal 1987, 254). The repression he endured, especially in the 1960s, made him a legend in the eyes of many MB members and leaders. Therefore, Kamal describes al-Hudaybi as a great *mujahid* who never gave in to the tyranny of Nasser and who kept the MB intact under incredibly adverse conditions (Kamal 1987, 255–256). That image of al-Hudaybi, as a strong leader who was never broken by Nasser's repression despite his age and ill health, was among the main factors that rallied the MB factions around him by the late 1960s and early 1970s, and that ultimately contributed to the success of the de-radicalization process.

State repression: once more intense, reactive and sustained

In the late 1950s and early 1960s, the faction led by Farid Abdul Khaliq[88] was staunchly opposing armed action against Nasser's regime. The stance of this faction was based on two arguments. The first was ideological and was centered on the idea that armed action is not the "correct" method of Islamic change, and moreover that it was not supported by al-Banna[89] (Abdul Khaliq 2004, episode 15; Ashmawy 2005, 161, 169). Their other argument was more pragmatic and less ideological: the consequences of an armed action would lead to even more intense state repression, and therefore the costs outweighed the benefits (Abdul Khaliq 2004, episode 15). Acting on the latter argument, Farid Abdul Khaliq met with Sayyid Qutb in his house in 1964 to attempt to convince him to dismantle the Organization before the regime discovered it and cracked down (Abdul

Khaliq 2004, episode 15). Abdul Khaliq argued that the SA and the SO were not able to confront Nasser in 1954. In the case of the Organization, he argued that the regime was currently stronger (1964), and that the commanders were young and inexperienced (Abdul Khaliq 2004, episode 15). In addition, he reminded Qutb that leading a secret paramilitary organization requires special training that the latter, as an intellectual, had not acquired. Qutb was not convinced however. Finally, Salah Shadi at some point in 1964[90] ordered some of his followers to report the activities of the 1965 Organization to the regime, to avoid another crackdown (Ashmawy 2005, 283).

The calculations of Abdul Khaliq's faction were correct. The Organization's paramilitary skills and resources were no match for the regime's strength and the experience of the security institutions. The "defensive strategy" that was adopted by Qutb and the five commanders did not materialize. In addition, Abdul Khaliq was also correct regarding the scope and the intensity of the regime's reprisals when it discovered the Organization. The regime's forces were able to arrest not only the members of the Organization, but also sympathizers, mainstream MB members who opposed the Organization,[91] as well as the families of leading figures like al-Hudaybi and Qutb (Abd al-Majid 1991, 107–108; Kamal 1987, 254). In addition, some of the MB strongholds, like the Kirdasa district of Giza, were attacked by paratroopers and the military police (Mahfuz 1988, 44; Abd al-Majid 1991, 109–117). The aim was to intimidate the population by showing the strength of the regime through a massive crackdown that included public flagellation and other forms of torture for suspected MB sympathizers (Mahfuz 1988, 45; Abd al-Majid 1991, 115–117). According to MB estimates, the number of detainees in 1965 reached 20,000, of whom about a thousand were court-martialled[92] (al-Tilmisani 1985, 135). Finally, the regime engaged in extra-judicial killings and extreme forms of torture that led to multiple deaths. The two most notable figures were Isma'il al-Fayyumi, one of Nasser's presidential body-guards recruited by the MB, and Rif'at Bakr, the nephew of Sayyid Qutb (Ashmawy 2005, 243).[93] The former was killed and the latter died under torture during the investigation (Ashmawy 2005, 24).

The memories of these experiences with the regime were still fresh in the late 1960s and early 1970s when the third attempt to de-radicalize took place. These collective memories were reinforced by the 1954 ones. As a result, the MB leadership and many of the group's followers were determined to put an end to violent confrontations and armed wings (al-Tilmisani 1985, 67; Ashmawy 2005, 284). According to Abdul Khaliq, al-Tilmisani and other MB leaders, the long, intense and sustained state repression contributed to that decision (al-Tilmisani 1985, 143; Abdul Khaliq 2004, episode 14).

There is one final consequence that should be mentioned with regards to the repression variable in 1965. That variable has led to the further radicalization of a group of young MB activists. And since the MB leadership was not interested in another confrontation, this group ultimately split from the MB and founded the first Takfiri organization in the twentieth century: *Jama'at al-Muslimiyn* (The Muslim Group, which is known in the media as *al-Takfir wa al-Hijra* or Excommunication and Migration) (al-Tilmisani 1985, 136; Mahfuz 1988, 88–89; Allam 1996, 141).[94]

Social interaction: counter-Takfirism

The period between 1968 and 1971 witnessed intensive activity within the MB. This was organized by leaders like al-Hudaybi, al-Tilmisani, Shadi, Mashhur, Akif and others, and had three objectives:

1 To counter the interpretations of Sayyid Qutb's works along Takfiri lines[95]
2 To stop the development of a Takfiri organization comprised of former MB members
3 To put an end to the legitimacy of armed wings within the MB.

The MB leadership failed to monopolize the interpretation of Qutb's works along relatively moderate lines, and therefore the first objective was not met. The second objective was partially successful however. Following two weeks of talks with al-Hudaybi, Ali Isma'il,[96] the leader of the newly born Takfiri group, decided to abandon the Takfir ideology and rejoin the MB in the summer of 1969 (Mahfuz 1988, 90). Although several members followed Isma'il, the group continued to exist under the leadership of Mustafa Shukri, another former MB member. Therefore, the MB leadership was only able to partially de-radicalize the first Takfir organization. The third objective, putting an end to armed wings within the MB, was met following intense deliberations whose final stages were held mainly in the Farm Prison in 1971 (Ashmawy 2005, 278). The deliberations aimed to convince the MB's grassroots that armed action against the regime is not Islamically sanctioned (al-Tilmisani 1988, 139–140; Ashmawy 2005, 275).

Externally, there were other types of interactions with various political and social groups. However, none of them directly impacted the de-radicalization process. One interesting type of external interaction should be mentioned here: that with Egyptian Jewish political prisoners. These interactions were described by al-Tilmisani in his memoirs. They featured dialogues with the members of the Jewish community who had been arrested following the 1967 defeat of Nasser (al-Tilmisani 1988, 137). Al-Tilmisani described the members of the group as being extremely polite and having good relations with the MB. He admitted that they helped the MB on several occasions, and shared their food and belongings with them (al-Tilmisani 1988, 137). Although he did not mention any effects of that interaction on the ideological/behavioral orientation of the MB,[97] al-Tilmisani was, relatively speaking, the most open MB *murshid* with regards to relations with the "other." He is credited for the consolidation of the de-radicalization process, for taking a hard stance against Salafi-Jihadi and Takfiri movements which were on the rise in the 1970s and 1980s, and for leading the group into a relative moderation process that reached its peak during his tenure with an Islamist-liberal (MB-Wafd) alliance in the parliamentary elections of 1984.

Selective inducements: al-Sadat and the Limited Accommodation Policy

In May 1971, President Sadat was able to consolidate his rule in what was known in the pro-regime media as the "corrective revolution." The opportunity presented itself for both the new regime and the MB, who had already developed a clear stance on the issue of violence against the state. The regime needed an Islamist movement to counter the influence of Nasserites and leftists from all factions. A few weeks after the "corrective revolution," al-Tilmisani, Zaynab al-Ghazali, Farid Abdul Khaliq and other MB leaders were released unconditionally (Abdul Khaliq 2004, episode 15, Ashmawy 2005, 275). In addition, the SSI began to hold talks with the MB prisoners, mainly the ones who led or belonged to the armed wings (SA, SO or 1965) (Ashmawy 2005, 275). The initial demand of the SSI was political "loyalty" (*wala'at*) or "support" (*ta'iyyd*) by the MB for the regime. However, both words were taboos within the MB ranks[98] (Ashmawy 2005, 276). After deliberations between an MB negotiating team led by the former head of the UD, Salah Shadi, and an SSI negotiating team led by Fu'ad Allam in 1971, both sides agreed to change the word "*ta'iyyd*" to "*nabdh al-'unf*" (rejection of violence) (Ashmawy 2005, 271, 284; al-Tilmisani 1988, 151–152). The final agreement included the ideological rejection of violence and the termination of any armed organization within the MB. In return, the Sadat regime decided to dismiss the case of the 1965 Organization and release all MB political prisoners. In addition, the released prisoners were allowed to go back to their jobs[99] and to perform peaceful *da'wah* activities, with restrictions on its political dimension as well on the location of the activity.[100] Another phase in the relationship with the Sadat regime began at this point.

Conclusion

Third time is a charm?

As opposed to the de-radicalization attempts of 1951 and 1964, the third attempt (1969 to 1973) was relatively successful. In 1951, the attempt failed disastrously. It not only led to deep divisions within the MB that culminated with the assassination of Sayyid Fayez, the SA commander in charge of the dismantlement process, but also to the cancellation of that process by the MB leadership, who opted for a less ambitious "reformation" process. The latter process led to the establishment of a new form of the SA: *al-Tanzim al-Sirri* or the Secret Organization (SO). The main objective[101] of that reform was to keep the SO under the direct control of the civilian MB leadership (al-Tilmisani 1985, 68). However, that objective was also not met, as demonstrated by the 1954 attempt on Nasser's life. Like its predecessor, the SO ended up being beyond the leadership's control.

In 1964, the second de-radicalization attempt took place, and involved some of the MB's leaders attempting to dismantle the 1965 Organization. The attempt failed again, mainly due to a combination of hesitant leadership giving conflicting signals/orders, multiple miscommunications, state repression and a lack of inducements.

Finally, the third attempt between 1969 and 1973 was relatively successful for reasons that were previously discussed, and which will be summarized in the next sub-section. As early as 1973, the MB had offers from various smaller groups to become their new armed wing, since the MB were perceived as the legitimate forefathers of Islamist struggle. In 1973, Karim al-Anadouly, the organizational leader of the so-called Technical Military Academy Group, approached the MB leadership and asked them to organize a new armed wing under their leadership. His request was declined by al-Hudaybi and other leaders (al-Tilmisani 1985, 146–147; Mahfuz 1988, 121).[102] Another request for armed action came from Yihya Hashim, one of the first Jihadist leaders in Egypt (al-Zawahiri [no date]). Ayman al-Zawahiri, al-Qa'ida's second-in-command and a friend of Hashim, mentions in his memoirs entitled *Knights under the Banner of the Prophet* that Hashim contacted the MB leadership in 1974 requesting support and seeking legitimacy for the establishment of a guerrilla movement based in Upper Egypt (al-Zawahiri [no date]). The MB declined the request and asked Hashim to sever contacts with Jihadists (al-Zawahiri [no date]). Finally, throughout the 1980s and 1990s, the MB and most of its branches outside of Egypt did not participate in violent action against ruling regimes.[103] In these decades as well as in the 2000s, the MB presented itself as an Islamist movement that upholds the "correct" form of Islam, which is anti-Jihadist and anti-Takfirist.

Why was the third time a charm?

The answer to the above question lies in the four previously mentioned variables as well as in the interaction between them. Table 4.1 summarizes the causal variables that affected de-radicalization.

As shown above, all four variables were present only in the last attempt. Leaders of all factions were united for the first time on the issue of the permanent abandonment of violence, behaviorally, organizationally, as well as ideologically. The latter dimension, presented mainly in *Preachers Not Judges*, had given an Islamic legitimacy to the process that was lacking in the previous attempts. In addition, the leadership was able to convince most of its grassroots and mid-ranking commanders to favor the de-radicalization process via internal interaction. Moreover, the MB's leadership was able to regain some of its grassroots members who had split from the group as a result of de-radicalization via internal interaction.[104] Both state repression and selective inducements were also geared towards supporting de-radicalization. Sadat's regime specifically demanded a complete abandonment of violence and secret armed wings. In return, he released the MB members from prisons and provided jobs and limited freedoms for *daw'ah* activities, as well as a channel to express the grievances of the MB.[105]

Table 4.1 Summary of the variables affecting de-radicalization

Variables/ de-radicalization attempts	Charismatic leadership	Social interaction	State repression	Selective inducements	The result
1951–1954	N/A: controversial; fragmented	Present: interacting partners are not supportive of de-radicalization	Present: radicalizing the moderates more than moderating the radicals	Present: co-optation of some radicals	Failure
1964–1965	N/A: hesitant; fragmented	N/A: miscommunications; few intermittent interactions	Present: causing radicalization, weakening leadership	N/A	Failure
1969–1973	Present: united leadership on issue of de-radicalization; ideological backing	Present: Mainly internal with the sole aim of de-radicalization	Present: in both current and historical perspectives	Present: new regime and new policies	Success

Is the de-radicalization of the MB a permanent result?

The answer to this question centers on three issues: generation, leadership and democratization. First, the MB as an organization had surpassed the de-radicalization phase (practical abandonment of violence, ideological de-legitimization of it and organizational dismantling of armed units) and had moved into the moderation phase (acceptance of and participation in the electoral process, as well as supporting democratization). It accomplished that transition under the leadership of individuals who are for the most part still active today. Those leaders have either lived through the confrontations in the 1950s and 1960s or have witnessed the consequences of Jihadist actions in the 1980s. The confrontations had disastrous consequences at the organizational, national and international levels. Therefore, the current leadership would not like to repeat that history again, even in reaction to intense state repression, especially given their current political victories and popularity as a non-violent Islamist movement.

However, the current leadership is composed of figures in their sixties, seventies and eighties. It is the younger generation (active in the 1990s and 2000s) that did not experience the consequences of armed action on the national level, that suffer constantly from repressive authoritarianism and that can easily access the messages and literature of Jihadists via the Internet and satellites television. This younger generation is still loyal to the older ones. However, the afore-mentioned factors of repression, inexperience and accessibility to Jihadism could initiate the historical cycle of repressive autocrats breeding violent theocrats. Historically, Jihadism and Takfirism were born in Egyptian political prisons, and the new recruits and some of the leaders of these two radical Islamist trends were formerly young members of the MB who were disaffected by the MB's transformation towards non-violence under state repression. Currently, the main difference is that the leaders of the MB from the older and the middle generations are in relative control of hearts and minds. However, given the conditions of political repression and the lack of a serious democratization process in Egypt, the younger generation of the MB grassroots could be pushed towards radicalization, thereby reversing both the de-radicalization and the moderation processes.

5 The de-radicalization of al-Qa'ida's allies

The Islamic Group and al-Jihad Organization[1]

Yes, the armed wing was permanently dismantled and its members will be paid pensions.

(Karam Zuhdi, Head of the Shura Council of al-Gama'a al-Islammiyya (IG), 2002)

Jihadists go back to the books of the salaf (predecessors) without understanding the changes of times and contexts.

(Sayyid Imam al-Sharif (alias Dr. Fadl), Former Ideologue of al-Qa'ida, 2007)

Two remarkable cases of de-radicalization are analyzed in this chapter. The first case is that of the Islamic Group of Egypt (IG). This group has co-assassinated President Anwar al-Sadat with al-Jihad Organization in 1981. It participated in the Afghan (1979–1992), Bosnian (1992–1995), and to a lesser extent, Chechen (1994–1996; 1999–present) conflicts. It also engaged in a violent confrontation with the Egyptian regime that started in 1989. That conflict featured a low-level insurgency between 1992 and 1997 and more than seven assassination attempts on President Mubarak.[2] In 1997, the IG became the first Salafi-Jihadi movement in the world to initiate a de-radicalization process. By 2003, the IG's de-radicalization process appeared successful: no armed operations since 1999, no significant splits within the movement and around 25 volumes authored by the IG leaders supporting their new ideology with both theological and rational arguments. Two of the volumes were critiques of al-Qaeda's behavior and a third was a critique of the "clash of civilization" hypothesis, arguing instead for cultural dialogue. The drafting of these volumes by the same movement that co-assassinated President Anwar al-Sadat for signing the Egyptian-Israeli Peace Treaty was a significant development. This process of de-radicalization removed more than 15,000 IG militants from the Salafi-Jihadi camp led currently by al-Qa'ida.

As for al-Jihad Organization, it also participated mainly in the Afghan conflict. It violently confronted Mubarak's regime between 1993 and 1995. Additionally, al-Jihad became closely associated with al-Qa'ida since the early 1990s. Compared to other armed Islamist movements, including the IG and the Taliban, al-Jihad Organization has the strongest ties with the al-Qa'ida. Arguably, al-Jihad figures are the co-founders and the main administrators of al-Qaʻida (al-Sharif 2007b, 8; Rashwan 2007, 13). Part of al-Jihad merged with al-Qaʻida in 1998.[3] Currently (2008), the commanders of al-Qaʻida in Afghanistan and Iraq are Mustafa Abu al-Yazid (alias Saʼid) and Yusif al-Dardiri (alias Abu Ayub al-Masri and also Abu Hamza al-Muhajir) respectively. Both leaders were former mid-ranking commanders in al-Jihad. In addition, al-Qaʻidaʼs second-in-command, Dr. Ayman al-Zawahri, was the former leader of al-Jihad between 1993 and 2000. In 2007, ten years after the IGʼs ICV, al-Jihad initiated its de-radicalization process.[4] By the end of that year, most of al-Jihad factions have joined the de-radicalization process (Jahin 2007, 11). The main exceptions are the faction led by Ayman al-Zawahri and two small factions in Egyptian prisons who mainly refuse the ideological component of the process.

The history of these two groups was discussed in the third chapter. In this chapter, the causes of the initiation of the de-radicalization processes are analyzed. These processes are analyzed according to the framework presented in the first chapter.

The causes of de-radicalization of the Islamic Group

As previously argued, four causal variables are proposed to explain the initiation as well as the relative success of the de-radicalization process of the IG: charismatic leadership, state repression, social interaction and selective inducement.

Leadership mattered

Although there is an abundant literature that emphasizes the controversial role of charismatic leadership in social movements in general, the issue is not sufficiently addressed when it comes to Islamist movements. Some exceptions include the works of Dekemejian and Wyszomirski (1972) on the Mahdi in Sudan, Brynjar (1998) on the leadership of the Muslim Brothers, and Gentry (2004) on the role of leadership in terrorism studies.

Here, it is argued that one of the main reasons behind the relative success of the de-radicalization process of the IG was the leadershipʼs charisma and the resulting influence and control over its followers. In this section, I demonstrate empirically how the leadership had a crucial role in the success of the de-radicalization process.

How did leadership matter?

Before the 1997 ceasefire declaration, there were at least 14 attempts to partially stop the violence between the IG and the state.[5] The most notable of these attempts are summarized below:

1   **1988–1994:** Several attempts are made by al-Azhar[6] scholars to convince the IG leaders and members that violence against the state and society is not sanctioned by Islam.

2   **1993:** The so-called "committee for mediation"[7] attempts to reconcile the regime and the IG. The mediation failed, mainly due to the fact that it was publicized as "negotiations with terrorists," and therefore embarrassed the regime.[8]

3   **1993:** General Abdul Raʼuf Salih, head of the Prisons Department in the Interior Ministry, suggests that the IG ceases violence against tourists. 'Abbud Al-Zummur, still on the IG *Shura* Council at that point in time, called in exchange for the regime to comply with the IG's six demands. The process failed as a result (al-'Awwa 2006, 226).

4   **March 1996:** Khalid Ibrahim al-Qusi, the former IG Emir in the southern city of Aswan, calls for cessation of violent activities during a military tribunal. The attempt was unsuccessful due to the lack of support from the historical leadership.

Al-Azhar and its scholars,[9] have tried to provide an Islamic-based counter-argument to the ideological preferences of the IG on several occasions inside and outside the prison (al-'Awwa 2006, 206; Ahmad 2002c, 6). Despite al-Azhar's recognition as a leading Islamic institution throughout the Sunni world, all of its attempts have failed to put an end to the violent behavior as well as to the legitimacy of the ideology that backs it. In addition, relatively peaceful and well-recognized Salafi sheikhs have made similar attempts in 1988 and 1989 only to have violent threats issued against them.[10] The most violent reaction, however, was when the Muslim Brothers attempted to criticize the IG's ideology and to relatively "pacify" them. The attempt led to several bloody confrontations and knife-fights between young members of the two groups in Assyut University campus in 1988 and 1989 (Umar 1994, 141; Student Union Leader 2001).

Two factors were constants in all of these ceasing violence attempts. First, before 1997, there was no consensus among the historical leadership about completely ceasing violence. Therefore, all of the attempts before that year lacked a supportive consensus. A related second factor is that all the attempts lacked an ideological justification from the historical leadership de-legitimizing the use of violence. Since *Fiqh al-'unf* literature was produced by that leadership, recanting the literature, providing a new literature that ideologically de-legitimize violence and then convincing the IG members and sympathizers to uphold that new ideology was a task that would be most likely to succeed if undertaken by the same historical leaders. In the eyes of their followers, that historical leadership was the only possible source that could bestow "Islamic legitimacy" on a comprehensive ideological de-legitimization of violence. Other sources were not credible enough and were usually dismissed as regime sympathizers or agents who have been co-opted (such as some of al-Azhar scholars) or have been weakened as a result of repression, like the case of Khalid Ibrahim.

From the IG members' perspective, the historical leadership is credible enough and beyond cooptation and weakening. This perception was made clear in several occasions. In June 2002, during a conference held in Wadi al-Natrun detention center, where more than 1,000 IG members were held, the followers showed signs of great respect to their leaders. This included kissing the hands and beards[11] of the leaders, as well as hanging signs and pickets on the walls of the conference site containing phrases like "Welcome Our Sheikhs, Delight of Our Eyes!" (Ahmad 2002b, 1, 12). In the Q&A session, almost all members started their questions with a welcoming and/or a praising phrase or a verse from a poem.[12] In another conference in August of the same year in the Istiqbal detention center, where around 2,000 IG members were held, the followers were only calling and referring to their leaders with the word *Mawlana* (our master/lord) (State Security Major 2002). This is despite the fact that most of those detainees could argue that they had spent years in detention and/or hideouts as well as being tortured, partially due to their leadership's policies, rhetoric and incompetence. Thus, rather than holding the leaders accountable for disastrous decisions, the members upheld and rallied around them.

Despite the signs of respect and evidence that the historical leaders are still in relative control of hearts and minds, convincing the followers that they have been wrong in the last two decades was not an easy task. To succeed in de-radicalization, the leadership had to convince its followers that they have to uphold the same arguments of their Islamist rivals as well as those of the official religious institution. This is the same leadership that have been harshly criticizing and mocking these groups for around 20 years. To limit potential dissent, the historical leadership had two tasks to perform. The first was to take a unanimous decision to stop the violence. The second task was to convince other segments within the IG to cease violence and uphold the new ideology. Those segments were mainly the leadership abroad, the imprisoned middle-ranking leaders and grassroots, and leaders of small units and grassroots in hideouts. The largest of those segments were the prisoners, more than 15,000 according to the semi-official sources (Ahmad 2002a, 7; Zuhdi *et al.* 2004, 237).

Hamdi Abdul Rahman, one of the historical leaders and a *shura* council member, explained in an interview that the conferences held in detention centers to convince the grassroots about the ICV were just the final stages of a long process that started in 1997 (Abdul Rahman 2002, 7). The historical leaders had been communicating and debating with their followers in political detention centers across Egypt from July 1997 until December 2002. The reactions in 1997 varied inside the prisons, mainly due to miscommunication and lack of direct interaction with the leadership. However, there were no reported splits inside the prisons as a result of the unilateral ceasefire declaration of 1997. In 2002, during the conferences, critical questions were raised that reflected the concerns of the IG members. These included questions about the reasons behind the delay of the ceasefire initiative, the fate of the deceased IG members, and the returns/compensations that the IG would get from the Egyptian regime (Ahmad 2002b, 7–17; Zuhdi et at. 2004, 116–129).[13]

The other two segments of the IG that the leaders had to convince about the ICV and ideological reform were the leaders abroad and the member in hideouts, both of which were important segments. During the years of confrontation, the leaders abroad were capable of training, funding, inciting and inspiring members to carry on violent operations. The IG members in hideouts were the ones who carried out operations or recruited new members, based on a confrontational ideology. If the de-radicalization process was to succeed, the historical leaders had to convince both segments.

Unlike the situation with the imprisoned members, I did not find many sources or details about how the historical leaders contacted and convinced their followers abroad and in hideouts. However, some elements of those interactions were made public. For example, following the ICV declaration, some of the leaders abroad issued statements refusing the ICV and promising new terror operations, most notably Rifa'i Taha. The latter, head of the *Shura* Council abroad at that point in time, went so far as to sign the 1998 declaration of Usama Bin Laden, announcing the foundation of the International Islamic Front for Fighting Jews and Crusaders. In a quick response, the historical leaders sent Taha a letter through one of their lawyers demanding his immediate withdrawal from the Front.[14] Taha withdrew one week after the declaration (Zuhdi 2002, 19; Dirbala 2006, 16; Ahmad 2002c, 19)[15] but the historical leaders sacked him from his position and appointed Mustafa Hamza, former head of the military wing (1995–1998), instead. The latter has unconditionally accepted the ICV. By March 1999, the *Shura* Council abroad had upheld the ICV.

However, three well-known leaders refused to accept the ICV and quit the IG. These were Muhammad al-Islambulli, former member of the *Shura* Council and the brother of Sadat's assassin; Usama Rushdi, former Emir of Assyut governorate; and Muhammad al-Hakaiyma, a middle-ranking leader from Aswan city who recently announced that he had joined al-Qa'ida network, together with al-Islambulli (see Al-Hakayima, 2006, 6). As for Taha, he was captured by the Syrian security forces and handed over to Egypt. He did not declare any support for the ICV or sign any of the new IG literature. However, in an interview with Karam Zuhdi, he insisted that Taha is still alive and that the historical leaders are attempting to convince him with the Islamic "legitimacy" of the ideological transformation.

As for members in hideouts, there was even less documentation about how the historical leaders contacted and influenced them. There were a few references, however. Karam Zuhdi and other leaders have mentioned on several occasions that those members have accepted the ICV and that there are ongoing talks to convince them to surrender to security forces (Zuhdi *et al.* 2002, 239). Some of those negotiations were successful, as Abdul Hamid Abu 'Aqrab, one of the senior commanders of the IG's dismantled armed wing, has surrendered to the SSI recently as a result. Since the Luxur massacre in November 1997, there has not been any incident of violence committed by the IG fugitives. Nor has any been committed by the thousands who were released from detention centers, many of whom became advocates of the ICV and the new ideological transformation (Ahmad 2002c, 18; State Security Major 2002).

Why did leadership matter?

In one of his books, Salah al-Sawy, a well-known Salafi Imam and a specialist on Islamism, has argued that many members of Islamist movements do not see except through the eyes of their leaders (al-Sawy 1994, 241).[16] While that can be an overstatement, there is one important question that has to be addressed when discussing the role of leadership in de-radicalization processes: why did the members follow them in opposing directions? In other words, Hamdi Abdul Rahman was asked once by a journalist: "the specialists who monitored the developments were shocked by the level and magnitude of obedience of the IG members ... how come there was no fury directed at the historical leaders by the followers who, carrying the orders of those leaders, spent their youth and/or teenage years fighting, on the run or imprisoned?" (Ahmad 2002c, 7). Abdul Rahman answered by elaborating on the strength of the theological evidences that was provided to convince the IG members. He also elaborated on the high level of trust between the leaders and the followers. In interviews with other leaders, the same factors were re-emphasized. They have also highlighted the importance of the conferences and the discussions with the members,[17] calling it a general assembly for the IG (Shu'ib 2002, 13; Abdul Rahman 2002, 13).

However, the "strength" of theological evidence only does not explain that level of obedience. As previously mentioned before, al-Azhar scholars and others have provided these same theological arguments before. At best, the IG dismissed these arguments and, at worst, they responded violently. Trust, however, could be a more plausible factor contributing to that level of obedience. Here, I briefly highlight two factors that have probably contributed to that level of trust, leading to full obedience.

To establish that level of trust, the historical leaders had to Islamically legitimize their new behavior and ideological stance, and explain this stance to their followers. That was done through meetings, conferences, lectures and literature production. In addition, although the members knew well the background of their leaders, the latter made sure to emphasize their "sacrifices" in media interviews and, briefly, in their meetings with their followers (Ahmad 2002b, 8). In other words, the leaders wanted to demonstrate to the members, and other monitors, that they did not send their followers to the frontlines while they have stayed in the back, that they have suffered as a result of their decisions more than many of their followers and that they cannot be "outbid" on the scales of dedication, endurance and sacrifice by their followers, or by the leaders abroad. In other words, they wanted to show to the followers that they are "true believers" and the decision for the ICV and the ideological transformation were "acts of faith," not mere strategic calculations to save themselves.

Another factor is equally important to explain the respect demonstrated in the conferences and the trust granted to the leaders by the followers. Both the respect and the trust levels can be seen as products of years of ideological indoctrination, or what Islamists like to call *tarbbiyah* (upbringing) (Khuwayra *et al.* 2004). The *tarbbiyah* is a process of soft indoctrination that involves different activities, ranging from regular prayers at specific IG mosques to biannual camping and weekly soccer playing.[18] This is in addition to direct ideological lecturing and, for selected IG members, paramilitary training. During these activities, there is an emphasis on the leaders' superiority, whether in performing rituals,[19] strategic thinking or religious knowledge[20] (State Security Major 2002). There is also an emphasis on the leaders' and senior members' "heroic" acts. For the IG these include the 1981 assassination of Sadat, the Assyut operation of 1981[21] and the participation in the Soviet–Afghan war in late 1980s.

Finally, the *tarbbiyah* process stresses versions of an Islamic concept: *al-ta'a* (obedience) (Ahmad 2002b 4; State Security Major 2002). *Al-ta'a*, is based on an interpretation of the Qur'anic verse "...Obey God, and obey the Apostle, and those charged with Authority among you..." (4:59). After convincing the new recruits that the IG leadership are Islamic leaders upholding the correct version of Islam and therefore "charged with authority," obedience for those leaders becomes a part of faith (Ahmad 2002b, 4). The end results of stressing the *ta'a* concept during the *tarbiyyah* process was demonstrated in 1997. Asked about his first reactions to the ICV declaration, Mamdouh A. Yusuf, former head of the military wing, said "I was not convinced at all, but in the end that [accepting the ICV] is an order form the [historical] leaders. I have no choice but to accept it" (Yusuf 2006, 202).

The *tarbiyyah* process was highlighted when the IG leaders attempted to explain to both members and journalists/researchers why some of their grassroots have "excessively" used violence during and before 1997 (al-'Awwa 2006, 130–133). The argument was that those grassroots did not undergo a comprehensive *tarbiyyah* process due to the absence of the historical leadership. As Yusuf puts it: "those members [who used excessive violence] were not 'brought up' in the school of Sheikh Nagih"[22] (Yusuf 2006, 133). Therefore, the argument goes, they were not "morally" prepared for a violent confrontation.[23]

Social interactions

As previously mentioned, I propose two types of interactions that have affected the behavior and the ideological transformations of the IG. The first is the interaction between the IG and other sociopolitical groups and individual activists (external interaction). The second interaction is between the historical leadership and its followers (internal interaction). I argue that external interaction has mostly affected the historical leadership's behavioral and ideological transformations, whereas internal interaction has mostly affected the members.

Interaction with the "other"

Externally, two factors should be highlighted: interaction with other Islamist movements and interaction with other political prisoners. In their conferences, interviews and new literature, the historical leaders have mentioned that among the reasons behind the ICV declaration in 1997 was their fear of an Algerian-like scenario (Ahmad 2002a, 17; Ahmad 2003, 193; Zuhdi *et al.* 2003, 123; Ibrahim 2005, 59–60), by which they meant the loss of control over their followers and the fragmentation of the IG during the confrontation period. The Algerian parallel was the loss of control over the armed factions by the FIS leaders.[24]

Another external interaction occurred in Egyptian political prisons between two very different camps, Takfiris and secular liberals. In one of his lectures, Nagih Ibrahim has referred to the phenomenon of "mixed cells" (Ibrahim 2003, 92). Since there were too many political detainees in the 1990s and early 2000s, the prisons' administrators decided to put detainees from different ideological backgrounds in the same cell. As a result, IG members and followers of different Takfir groups found themselves sharing the same cell (Ibrahim 2003, 93). Given that the IG members and Takfiris were under the same daily prison pressures, the IG leadership was worried that the more radical Takfir ideology would become attractive and more convenient to its members.

In addition, there were external interactions with detained secular liberals and human rights activists. Renowned pro-democracy activist and former political prisoner, Dr. Saad Eddine Ibrahim, has described some of those interactions (Ibrahim 2004; 2007). He mentioned that the leaders were first interested in knowing why the international community was outraged by his detention but not by the detention of thousands of Islamist suspects (Ibrahim 2004; 2007). That point started the debate about Islamism, democracy and human rights. The ideas expressed in the IG's new literature, as well as the references cited, reflect those debates and show a strong presence of modernism and post-modernism, albeit recycled in an Islamist framework. These ideas include upholding ideological and theological uncertainty over determinism (Ibrahim *et al.* 2005, 17), cultural and historical dynamism over rigidity (Ibrahim *et al.* 2005, 81), cultural dialogue rather than a clash of civilizations (Zuhdi *et al.* 2003, 236; Ibrahim 2005, 225–249), and the necessity for renewing religious rhetoric (Ibrahim *et al.* 2005).[25] Karam Zuhdi went as far as citing the controversy regarding the role of religion in the US foreign policy. He concluded that at least before 9/11 there was no Christian crusade against Islam led by the US as al-Qaʿida have assumed (Zuhdi 2002, 64).

Finally, I should mention that the IG leaders did not admit at any point that they have been influenced by secular intellectuals, literature or ideas. Despite that, they have expressed their gratitude for those secular intellectuals and politicians who supported the ICV, as well as their basic human rights (Hafiz and Abdul Majid 2002, 46). They have also condemned some of the leftist leaders[26] who refused the ICV and argued in favor of state repression. That stance by itself is a new development. Seculars in general, with no exceptions, were usually targets of the IG's harsh criticism, fiery rhetoric and, sometimes, its bullets.[27]

Interactions within the group

As mentioned before, the historical leaders of the IG toured all known political detention centers and prisons, from Damanhur in the north to al-Wadi al-Jadid and Assyut in the south, for a period of ten months in 2002 (Zuhdi *et al.* 2003, 21). Those tours and meetings aimed to illustrate the meaning of the ICV, to explain the new ideological perspectives,[28] and then to address the questions, comments and critiques of the members (Zuhdi *et al.* 2003, 23). The historical leaders would first hold meetings with the second-in-line commanders[29] to illustrate the general guidelines of the ICV and the new ideology. Then, there would be a "general assembly" where all the members would attend and meet with the historical leaders. The leaders would start with a discussion of the four new books, followed by an extended Q&A period. Afterwards, the leaders would meet with the members in their cells and in prison corridors to discuss the transformations directly in small groups (Zuhdi *et al.* 2003, 22).

In their book *A River of Memories* eight historical leaders considered the interaction with their followers during the meetings and conferences as being one of the main reasons for the relative success of the ICV (Zuhdi *et al.* 2003, 25). Before the long process of interaction, argumentation and discussion, there was not much support, if any, for the ICV among the middle-ranking leaders and the grassroots (Yusuf 2006, 202). Mamdouh A. Yusuf mentions that when the second-in-line leaders received the ICV-based orders, they were complying with it but without much conviction, if any. "We would ask the individual members to comply, but between us [second-in-line leaders], we still did not agree..." (Yusuf 2006, 202). In another interview, one of the grassroots members explained his initial reaction in 1997: "we carried arms based on God's orders ... we should not lay them down based on orders of humans unless they prove it to us [theologically], even if those humans were the Sheikhs [the historical leaders]" (IG member 2002).

Knowing about the opposition, Zuhdi called for transferring Yusuf and other second-in-line commanders from the Scorpion prison to the Liman hospital, where Zuhdi was held for treatment. "Hearing the [theological] evidences directly from the Sheikhs was different ... we heard these before from the Salafis and from al-Azhar ... we did not accept them ... we accepted them from the Sheikhs because we know their history..." Yusuf explained (Yusuf 2006, 206).

State repression: multiple effects

Whereas the role of the leadership and social interaction variables were evident in the de-radicalization process, the role of my third variable, state repression, is not as clear. Was repression a cause of radicalization, a hurdle to de-radicalization or a cause of de-radicalization? The empirical evidence that I gathered suggest all three. In the following sections, the multiple effects of state repression are discussed and then I attempt to reconcile these conflicting evidences.

Repression as a cause of radicalization

State repression as a cause of a radicalization is not a new idea to the literature. Several works have concluded that state repression can lead relatively peaceful movements to use violence and/or give the radicals within those movements the upper hand over the moderates (Dekmejian 1995; Esposito 1992; Nasr 2002; Hafez 2004). Examples supportive of this argument include the FIS in Algeria, the IRP in Tajikistan and the MB in Egypt (especially in the 1950s and 1960s as discussed in the fourth chapter).

In the specific case of the IG, that theoretical argument is supported by several empirical facts. The IG has always perceived its violent behavior against the regime as a defensive reaction to repression, not necessarily as an offensive act to topple the regime by force.[30] In most accounts written and told by the IG leaders and other Jihadi associates, the October 1981 operations were a direct response to the crackdown of September 1981, when 1,536 opposition leaders and activists, in addition to popular Azhar scholars, were detained by Sadat's regime (al-'Awwa 2006, 95, 99).[31]

When analyzing the violence of the early 1990s, the relationship between state repression and radicalization is clearer. According to the IG and several independent analysts, the violence of the 1990s was not aiming for the establishment of an Islamist state (al-'Awwa 2006, 99). Instead, it was aiming for pressuring the regime to revise its repressive policies and comply with the six demands of the IG, most notably releasing female hostages, uncharged detainees as well as ceasing torture. The violent tactics of the IG fired back, however. In response to a question by one of the IG members about the ICV, Karam Zuhdi said that they have started the "Jihad" in the early 1990s to release the 2,000 IG prisoners. However, as a result of that "Jihad," the situation deteriorated and the number of their detainees reached 20,000 by mid-1990s (Zuhdi 2003 *et al.*, 143).

Repression as a hurdle to de-radicalization

Another argument on the effects of repression is how it can become a hurdle for a movement to de-radicalize and abandon violence. All second-in-line commanders and the grassroots interviewed, and even one of the historical leaders, have mentioned that their opposition to the ICV in the beginning was a reaction to the state's repressive policies, rather than an ideological stance. Mamduh A. Yusuf mentioned that when the ICV was declared, he was suffering from malnutrition and kidney failure. He was denied any medical treatment and his mother, who had not been able to visit him for more than five years, had just died (Yusuf 2006, 145). He explained that if he had accepted the ICV in these conditions, the acceptance would have been interpreted by his followers as a sign of weakness and, possibly, betrayal.

Another second-in-line commander, Dr. Mahmoud Shu'ib,[32] explains in another interview that under repression, far from talking about ceasing violence, questioning the aims of the ongoing violence was a taboo within the IG (Shu'ib

2002, 12). "We had a lot of questions buried in us ... but everybody was afraid to be accused of defeatism or losing strength to prison conditions" (Shu'ib 2002, 12). Similarly, Usama Hafiz, one of the historical leaders, was held in the notorious al-Wadi al-Jadid (New Valley) political prison. In early 1997, he received a message from the rest of the historical leaders held in the Liman Turah prison in Cairo regarding the deliberations about the ICV. Hafiz mentions that since the conditions in al-Wadi were extremely repressive, he refused the ICV in the beginning. This is despite the fact that Hafiz, compared to Zuhdi, Ibrahim and others, is considered a "dovish" historical leader for his opposition to violence in the 1980s an 1990s.[33]

Repression as a cause of de-radicalization[34]

In several interviews, the historical leaders have referred to state repression as a cause for revising their behavior and their ideology. Repression forced the IG leadership to reassess the costs and the benefits of violently confronting the Egyptian regime. They have found the costs of the confrontation outweigh the benefits and, therefore, they came to the conclusion that Jihad is Islamically forbidden in this case (Abdul Rahman *et al.* 2002, 66). "Jihad is not an end by itself. It is just a mean to attain other ends. If you cannot attain these ends through Jihad, you should change the means" said Nagih Ibrahim to the IG members during the Wadi al-Natrun conference. Ali al-Sharif, another leader and co-author of *Shedding Lights on What Went Wrong during Jihad*, added in the same conferences that they fought for the IG's right to preach Islam,[35] as well as for their detained "brothers." What they received as a result was a complete ban on preaching, more detainees and incredibly repressive conditions.[36] According to the leadership's new perspective, since "Islam" was hurt by Jihad, the latter should be banned.

In addition, repression seems to have affected the worldview of some leaders. In an interview, Mamduh A. Yusuf discussed some examples and consequences of repression in prisons, including rampant tuberculosis infections, malnutrition, bad ventilation, bimonthly beatings of each political prisoner some of which resulted in deaths.[37] Outside prisons, the families of those detainees were suffering from economic deprivation, social alienation and systematic discrimination by the regime. Yusuf argued that if God was "on their side" these things would not have happened to the IG members and their families. Therefore, he concludes, there has to be something "theologically wrong" with the decision to confront the regime (Yusuf 2006, 245).

Reconciling the empirical evidences

Time-sequencing and the characteristics of repression are two important factors that should be addressed to reconcile the arguments on the relationship between the latter and radicalization/de-radicalization. In the specific IG case, indiscriminate, high-intensity repression contributed to the radicalization of the IG in the early 1980s and culminated in the assassination of Sadat and the production of *Fiqhul ʻunf* literature during the prison period. Outside prison, and starting in 1987, the same type of state repression has partially led to the continuation of the radical behavior. This was reflected locally in the attempt on General Badr's life in 1989, the assassination of Dr. al-Mahjub in 1990 and the further violence of the 1990s. Internationally, the radical behavior was reflected in seeking alliances with other extremist groups, as well as the inter-nationalization of the IG's violent operations, most notably the attempt on President Mubarak's life in Addis Ababa in 1995. Finally, long, indiscriminate and even more intense repression, especially in the prisons[38] starting in 1992, has contributed to the revision of both the behavior and ideology of the IG. As mentioned before, this was admitted by the IG leadership as among the causes for behavioral and ideological transformations, leading finally to the de-radicalization process.

There is a final note on the relationship between repression and de-radicalization. To contribute to a de-radicalization process, repression has to be calculated when applied to the historical (spiritual) leadership. The historical leaders were put under extreme physical, mental and psychological pressures. However, while several IG members have died under these conditions (al-Awwa 2006, 133), there was no attempt to liquidate the leadership, whether through forms of repression in prison or through executions in military and/or state security trials. This pattern continued even after the attempt on Mubarak's life by the IG in 1995 (Former Islamist leader 2002).[39] When I asked a former state security general in 2002 if he thinks that pattern was a deliberate policy or a mere coincidence, I received no clear answer. In the same year, I asked the same question to a former Islamist leader close to the IG. He argued that it was a deliberate policy. "If they killed us and then they wanted to talk, who will they talk to?... Who will order the grassroots to lay down arms?" he said (Former Islamist leader 2002).

The road to selective inducements

Another variable that contributed to the relative success of the de-radicalization process was *selective inducement*. Before discussing it, however, I have to mention that there were several developments preceding it. These developments can be classified into three categories: "de-repression" (1998–2001), coordina-tion (2001–2002) and then selective inducements (2002–present).

When the historical leaders declared the ICV in 1997, there was no coordina-tion with the state (Zuhdi *et al.* 2003, 135). Caught by this unexpected develop-ment, the regime initially gave several negative signals including apathy, rejection, hesitation and suspicion. By 1998, the state started interacting with the IG and this was the beginning of the "de-repression" period. The violence target-ing IG members inside most of prisons began to stop. Prison meals improved in both quality and quantity (Yusuf 2006, 144; IG member 2002). By 1999–2000, prison visits, which had been banned by the SSI since 1992–1993,[40] were gradually allowed, and the conditions of the visits gradually improved.[41] By December 2001, the regime's policies towards the ICV went to another level: coordination with the IG leadership.[42] This was reflected in allowing the historical leaders to tour and lecture in prisons and detention centers, in publishing and disseminating the new IG books, and in allowing the government media to cover and praise the ICV and the IG transformations. Finally, the selective inducements stage came later in 2002 and early 2003, when the regime started releasing IG members and leaders, initially in groups of hundreds and then in thousands (Salah 2006, 6). Karam Zuhdi himself was released in September 2003, followed by other historical leaders in the same month (Salah 2003, 1). In April 2006, an anonymous security official mentioned to *al-Hayat* newspaper that the there were only 2,000 IG detainees left in Egyptian prisons. He mentioned that the number had came down from 15,000, all detained under emergency laws (Salah 2006, 6). By April 2007, only IG members who were sentenced by military tribunals, state security or civilian courts were still left in prison. Their numbers are in the hundreds.[43] Moreover, the state has helped the group in publishing the rest of the books explaining their perspectives more comprehensively, criticizing al-Qaʻida and calling for dialogue with the state and the society. Also, Mubarak's regime allowed the IG to launch and administer their new website.[44] Finally, the leadership of the IG has announced that the members of the military wing will be discharged and will be paid pensions (Zuhdi 2002, 16).[45] Zuhdi declared that Nagih Ibrahim is in charge of paying them. However, he did not mention the source of funding. Since the overwhelming majority of the IG members were imprisoned for long periods, all funding options have to include assistance from, and/or cooperation with, the state. Therefore, the state will either provide direct funding or will allow IG activists to collect funds.

The causes of de-radicalization of al-Jihad Organization

Again, leadership mattered

Like the case of the IG, al-Jihad Organization struggled with its evolution towards non-violence. However, unlike the IG, whose leadership was remarkably able to adopt a united stance supportive of de-radicalization in less than two years (July 1997–March 1999) (Ashour 2007, 596–598), al-Jihad's de-radicalization took about a decade to be completed (July 1997–April 2007), and only substantively (lacking the organizational dimension). Two reasons accounted for that delay: the first has to do with the nature and the organizational structure of al-Jihad, a secret society by definition that emphasizes covert action. Organizationally, al-Jihad's cells did not know each other except in prison (Jahin 2007, 12; 'Ukasha 2002). Each group of cells, usually from the same town, city or prison, formed a faction with their own semi-autonomous leadership. In 2007, not counting those outside of the country, there was more than seven major factions inside Egyptian prisons. The most substantial differences between these factions involved their stances[46] on de-radicalization and their allegiances to different al-Jihad commanders.

Salih Jahin, a commander of one of al-Jihad's factions, explains how factionalism and the lack of charismatic leadership affected the de-radicalization process. He mentions that he had supported the de-radicalization process since the IG's unilateral ceasefire in 1997 (Jahin 2007, 4). However, he also explains that he had no authority over other factions and therefore he could not "order" or convince them to adhere to de-radicalization (Jahin 2007, 4). Similarly, Nabil Na'im, the commander of the largest faction of al-Jihad's prisoners, had the very same problem (al-Zayyat 2007, 4). He supported the IG's Initiative for Ceasing Violence (ICV) and the ideological component of it that was made public in 2002, but he could not speak on behalf of al-Jihad as a whole (al-Zayyat 2007, 4). Outside the prison, Usama S. Ayub, an al-Jihad commander who had participated in the Soviet-Afghan war, issued a statement from Germany calling for a permanent stop of armed operations in January 2000 (Ayub 2007, 5). His calls were ignored by the other factions.

Two factors characterized such calls for behavioral de-radicalization. The first is that it came from "equal heads:" factional commanders who had been operatives in the late 1970s and 1980s, none of whom was a leader of al-Jihad as whole.[47] The second factor is that none of these calls for non-violence was bolstered by theological/ideological literature, unlike the case of the IG whose leaders had published around 25 volumes to dismantle their previous ideological position and legitimize their new stance on Islamic basis (Ashour 2007, 613). Also, the commanders of these faction, like Jahin, Na'im, Ayub and others do not have high-level training in Islamic Jurisprudence that could allow them to undertake the task of theologically dismantling the Jihadist literature (Jahin 2007b, 5).

Given these factors as well as the de-centralized structure, al-Jihad's de-radicalization process stalled in 2005. However, the charismatic leadership variable was introduced to the process in 2007: the presence of al-Sharif, a former leader of al-Jihad Organization (1987–1993) and a highly regarded ideologue within the Salafi-Jihadi trend in general and al-Qa'ida in particular. In the eyes of al-Jihad members, al-Sharif possessed the theological credentials and historical legitimacy which commanders like Jahin, Na'im and others lacked. His books, *al-'Ummda* and *al-Jami'*, are considered to be "bibles" in Jihadist circles and some Islamists regard al-Sharif as the most influential ideologue in Jihadism after Sayyid Qutb (al-Zayyat 2007, 4; Rashwan 2007, 12). In addition, al-Sharif participated in the Afghan wars and many Jihadists also perceive him as a great *Mujahid*.[48] Having such a background, al-Sharif was an ideal mythical figure that al-Jihad factions can rally around to lead them towards successful de-radicalization. The alternative figures were not credible enough and were usually dismissed as figures whose leadership level is not "high enough,"[49] as regime sympathizers or agents who have been co-opted;[50] or as figures who have been weakened as a result of repression.[51] For most of al-Jihad members and leaders of factions, al-Sharif was beyond these accusations. Therefore, al-Sharif is an excellent candidate to produce new literature that ideologically de-legitimizes violence as well as to convince al-Jihad members and sympathizers to uphold that new ideology.

In addition, the impact of al-Sharif's new writings was not limited to al-Jihad activists. Members of small Takfiri groups and other Jihadists attended the lectures that al-Sharif had given in several prisons (al-Khatib 2007b). In December 2007, Majdi al-Safty, the commander of one of the small Takfiri groups which is known in the media as *al-Najun min al-Nar* (Survivors from Hell), issued a statement supporting al-Sharif's *Document* (al-Safty 2007, 1).[52] In addition, several small Salafi-Jihadist groups from the Sinai Peninsula, allegedly with links to al-Qa'ida, issued a similar statement (al-Khatib 2007b, 4).

State repression

As argued elsewhere, the state repression variable has multiple effects. It was an initial cause of radicalization in many cases, including those of the Muslim Brothers in Egypt, the Islamic Salvation Front (FIS) in Algeria, the Islamic Renaissance Party in Tajikistan (IRP) and many others.[53] However, as argued above as well as in the first chapter, long, intense and sustained repression can affect particular armed groups with defined structures and charismatic leadership and cause them to de-radicalize, rather than fragment, further radicalize and/or perish.

In the specific case of al-Jihad Organization, the prisoners and their families undergone the same repressive conditions that the IG, and before them the MB, had been through.[54] Some of these forms of repression were previously described.[55] Given that, some of al-Jihad leaders elaborated on the effects of repression on their behavioral changes.

Usama Ayub, one of al-Jihad leaders in Germany, mentioned that among the main reasons leading him to issue his statement calling for an end to violence in January 2000 was the sufferings of thousands of prisoners in Egyptian detention centers (Ayub 2007, 5). A similar argument was made by Salih Jahin, an al-Jihad commander who spent 26 years in prison, during 11 of which he was detained without charge (Jahin 2007, 5). Kamal Habib, one of the co-founders of al-Jihad Organization, mentions in an interview that Egyptian Jihadists during the 1980s believed that they had legendary powers (Habib 2007, 11). The repression and the prison experience made them realize that they are only humans and that "God's power" is not necessarily behind them (Habib 2007, 11).

In addition, state repression had repercussions even for al-Jihad members abroad. In 1992, al-Sharif gave Usama Bin Laden an advice: not to go to Sudan and to return back to Saudi Arabia (Ismai'l al-Sharif 2007b, 13). When Bin Laden asked why, al-Sharif simply answered: "you did not try exile before ... we [Egyptian Jihadists] did." (Ismai'l al-Sharif 2007b, 13). The statement reflected the impact of state repression on Jihadists abroad before the initiation of any de-radicalization process.

Social interaction

As mentioned in the first chapter, the term "social interaction" refers to the meetings, lectures and discussions held between the layers and factions of al-Jihad (internal interaction) or between al-Jihad and other Islamist or non-Islamist groups and figures (external interaction). Within the group, al-Sharif and other al-Jihad commanders have been touring Egyptian prisons to meet with their follower since February 2007 (Al-Sharif 2007b, 1, 8; al-Masry al-Youm 2007, 1). The tours featured small initial meetings with the commanders of the factions to organize a common stance. This was followed by lectures and Q&A periods between the al-Jihad's leadership, united this time under al-Sharif, and the grass-roots and middle-ranks (Jahin 2007, 12; al-Sharif 2007b, 8). This type of interaction was modeled after the IG leadership's ten months of discussions and meetings with their followers in 2002.[56] Moreover, the IG leaders were included in al-Jihad's meetings to share their experience and demonstrate their relatively successful case of de-radicalization. Karam Zuhdi, the head of IG's *Shura* (Consultative) Council, and Dr. Nagih Ibrahim, his deputy and the main ideologue of the IG, were present with al-Sharif in several internal al-Jihad meetings to encourage the process and answer questions (Abd al-Rasul 2007, 1; al-Masry al-Youm 2007, 1).

Another example of interaction was between al-Jihad members and secular liberals, most notably, again, renowned human rights activist and former political prisoner Dr. Saad Eddine Ibrahim (Ibrahim 2004; 2007). In 2002 and 2003, during his detention, Dr. Ibrahim held several discussions about Islam, democracy and human rights with detained Islamists, including al-Jihad members. He mentioned that following several months of talks with these members, many of them were ready to abandon violence and condemned the 9/11 attacks (Ibrahim 2007).

The interactions with secular liberals were not only reflected in the writings of former Jihadists, especially those from the IG, but also in the calls of some of al-Jihad leaders for the release of secular liberals who were detained by Mubarak's regime due to their political opinions (Hasan 2007, 1). In 2007, Usama Hasan (alias Abu Umar al-Masry), a former leader[57] who participated in the Bosnian conflict,[58] called on the regime to release Dr. Ayman Noor, a liberal politician and a former presidential candidate, and Tal'at al-Sadat, a secular politician and former MP (Hasan 2007, 1). Both politicians were imprisoned with Hasan and the stance, coming from a Jihadist leader, is a new development.[59]

Finally, some of al-Jihad's leaders attempted to form an alliance with some Egyptian Shi'ites and Copts (Isma'il 2006). The alliance was between 'Abbud al-Zumur's faction, the High Council of the Prophet's Descendants (Ahl al-Bayt),[60] and the Word Center for Human Rights.[61] The objective of the coordination was to bring about the attention of the international community to the plight of Egyptian political prisoners in general, and possibly to bring specific cases of Coptic, Shi'ite and Islamist prisoners in front of an international criminal court (Ismai'il 2006; Ahl al-Bayt Communiqué 2006, 1–2). Needless to mention that an alliance with Copts and Shi'ites was considered a "serious Islamic deviation" in the old Jihadist literature (Ibrahim *et al.* 1984, 37), not to mention bringing a case in front of a court in which the judges are "infidels" who do not rule by the "Shari'a laws."

Selective inducements

In the case of al-Jihad, the road towards selective inducements was modeled, again, on the IG's case. The approach adopted by Mubarak's regime can be called "incremental inducements." It started with an end to beatings and forms of torture and mistreatment in prisons, increasing the portion and quality of meals, providing medical treatment and allowing the prisoners' families to visit. Then the regime started to release al-Jihad suspects who had never been charged (al-Khatib 2007, 1). In addition, the regime signaled its will to comply with courts rulings that ordered financial compensation for the detainees who had been tortured and/or detained for years without charge (al-Minawy 2007, 6). As previously mentioned in the case of the IG, Karam Zuhdi declared at one of their conferences that the members of the IG's armed wing would be discharged and paid pensions (Zuhdi 2002, 16). It is unclear whether or not the same policy will be applied to al-Jihad members. Unlike the IG, al-Jihad is exclusively a paramilitary organization and all of its members receive military training (al-Zayyat 2007, 11). If the same policy was applied, all al-Jihad members will be paid pensions.

Also, semi-official figures like General Ra'uf al-Minawy, the former spokesperson for the Interior (Security) Ministry, called for the creation of a monetary fund to assist the former detainees by providing employment, financial compensations, and psychological and medical treatment (al-Minawy 2007, 6). Al-Minway's declaration came in reaction to al-Sharif's *Document*, although he insisted that there is no political deal with al-Jihad (al-Minaway 2007, 6). Finally, 'Abbud al-Zumur, the first leader of al-Jihad, has said that members of the group should be given a "political role" in Egypt (Rashwan 2007, 8). He declared his intention to establish a political party and participate in both parliamentary and presidential elections if the regime allowed him to (al-Zumur 2006, 1). However, it is unlikely that the regime complies with his demand at this point in time.[62]

Al-Jihad's de-radicalization: the effects on al-Qa'ida

As previously mentioned in Chapter 1, the phenomenon of de-radicalization is not limited to Egypt and it includes groups from various parts of predominantly Muslim countries. De-radicalized groups often interact with other radical groups, still upholding violence and in many cases, they do influence each other. The interactions between al-Jihad and the IG is just one example of how a de-radicalized group can influence the behavior of a radical Salafi-Jihadi one.[63] Given the strong ties of al-Jihad in general and its main ideologue, al-Sharif, in particular to al-Qa'ida, one question should be addressed here: will there be a domino effect? More specially, will the de-radicalization process of al-Jihad affect al-Qa'ida?

Although, it is still early to answer that question, two facts should be highlighted in any attempt to answer. First, Egyptian Jihad figures were the main organizers and administrators behind the establishment of al-Qa'ida. Those figures include al-Zawahri, Abu 'Ubayyda al-Panjsheiri, Abu Hafs al-Masry and many others. Al-Sharif argues in one interview that these Egyptian Jihad members are the "real" founders of al-Qa'ida (al-Sharif 2007, 8). The second fact concerns al-Sharif himself. He is considered to be one of the main "theological" ideologues of al-Qa'ida.[64] Given that al-Qa'ida leaders tend to legitimize their violent behavior to their followers and sympathizers on an Islamic theological basis, the de-legitimization of that behavior by al-Sharif's *Document* and other de-radicalized Salafi-Jihadist works, such as the IG's, might affect some of al-Qa'ida's members and sympathizers. The question then becomes: which of al-Qa'ida's layers is most likely to be affected?

Arguably, al-Qa'ida can be divided into three layers. The first layer is composed of a small core group that surrounds Bin Laden and al-Zawahri and receives direct orders from them. This layer is the least likely to be affected. Al-Zawahri has already criticized al-Sharif and mocked the ideas of revisions, publications and "fax machines" in Egyptian prisons (al-Zawahri 2007, 1). In addition, Bin Laden criticized the behavior of al-Qa'ida in Iraq after the media announced that al-Sharif was in the process of writing the *Document*, but before the *Document's* release. Bin Laden may have attempted to minimize the effects of the *Document* and send a preemptive message to his sympathizers that there would be changes in al-Qa'ida's violent behavior.

The second layer is that of al-Qa'ida's self-styled "branches" in Algeria, Iraq, Saudi Arabia and even Egypt. Of these "branches," the most likely to be affected is the Egyptian one because of the weight of al-Sharif in Egypt as well as the revisions of the IG. In the words, of Asim Abd al-Majid, one of the "historical leaders" of the IG, al-Sharif's *Document* is the final word in the "jurisprudence of violence" in Egypt (Abd al-Majid 2007, 12).

The third layer is that of the "internet militants:" mostly teenagers and young men who get inspired by al-Qa'ida's rhetoric, but have no organizational ties or contacts with its network. In other words, this is a layer of "self-recruited members." Probably aware that this layer has the weakest ties with the core of al-Qa'ida, al-Sharif dedicated a large part of his *Document* to warning young Muslim men about the Internet *Muftis* (al-Sharif 2007, 12). This layer is probably the one that will be affected the most, and its members could be discouraged from following Salafi-Jihadism in general and al-Qa'ida in particular due to the influence of al-Sharif's *Document*.

Table 5.1 The de-radicalization of the IG and al-Jihad

Variables/ organization	Charismatic leadership	Social interaction	State repression	Selective inducements	The result
IG (pre-1997 attempts)	Present: opposing de-radicalization	Present: limited, government-led	Present: high	N/A	No initiation
IG (1997–2002)	Present: supportive of de-radicalization	Present	Present: varying	Present	Success
Al-Jihad (pre-2007)	N/A: only some factional commanders	Present: limited, government-led	Present: high	N/A	Failure
Al-Jihad (2007– present)	Present	Present: mainly internal with the sole aim of de-radicalization	Present: varying	Present	Success (organizational dimension is still on-going)

Conclusion

To recap and summarize the argument, Table 5.1 shows the de-radicalization attempts of the IG and al-Jihad as well as the causal variables behind them.

This chapter has shown that two radical, armed Islamist movements have shown a remarkable ability to change. In the case of the IG, the Group was able to de-radicalize on the behavioral, organizational and ideological levels. Behaviorally, The IG shunned the path of political violence, ideologically de-legitimized it and its leadership was able to unite the organization to uphold the transformations. The Group called for reconciliation with state and society as well as for inter-cultural dialogue. Although its current stance is far from electoral or liberal democracy, this does not represent the end of the transformations. Several sympathizers and former members of the IG have participated in the 2005 Egyptian parliamentary elections (al-Zayat 2005, 5).[65] In an interview, Karam Zuhdi explained that the current IG position regarding democracy could change, based on the interests of the IG (Zuhdi 2006).[66] This indicated that pragmatism has a final say in the behavior of the IG.

In the case of al-Jihad, the smaller and more radical group, the Organization was able to follow the lead of the IG and de-radicalize on both behavioral and ideological dimensions. Unlike the IG, however, the organizational dimension of the de-radicalization process is incomplete. This is due to the fact there are a few factions within al-Jihad that still refuses to uphold de-radicalization. These factions refuse to leave the Organization and one of them is in alliance with al-Qa'ida. The process, however, did not end at this point.

Another factor can be highlighted in the case of al-Jihad. The lead of the IG and the interaction with its leaders has facilitated and influenced the de-radicalization process of al-Jihad, which stalled on several occasions. More-over, several Islamists argued that without the IG's de-radicalization process, there would not have been an al-Jihad one (Ibrahim 2007, 12; al-Zayyat 2007, 12). This suggests a "domino effect" hypothesis that can be a subject of future research: de-radicalization of one group can influence others operating in the same context under similar conditions. This hypothesis is supported by the cases of the small violent Takfiri and Salafi-Jihadi groups which joined al-Jihad's revisions in 2007 (Zinah 2007, 1), mainly in reaction to al-Sharif's *Document.*

6   De-radicalization in Algeria
Successes and failures

> We declared that ceasefire because the jihad was about to be buried by the hands
> of its own sons.
>
> (Medani Mezrag, Former Emir of the Algerian Islamic Salvation Army (AIS,
> 2005))

This chapter discusses the causes of de-radicalization among Algerian armed Islamist movements. As mentioned in Chapter 3, Algeria provides two cases of de-radicalization, one of which was successful while the other was a failure. The successful case was that of the Islamic Salvation Army (AIS), the self-declared armed wing of the Islamic Salvation Front (FIS). This process of de-radicalization took place between 1993 and 2000. The leadership of that organization was not only able to dismantle the AIS, but was also able to influence smaller armed organizations and factions to join the de-radicalization process. The AIS and its affiliates were also able to reintegrate into the Algerian civilian society. Currently, the leaders of that organization attempt to re-enter the political process peacefully through establishing a political party (Mezraq 2007, 1).

By contrast, the Armed Islamic Group (GIA) is a case that has seen mixed results. Whereas some of its affiliated militias joined the AIS-led process, the bulk of the group failed to de-radicalize. Instead, part of the GIA was completely destroyed by 2005. Another part broke away as early as 1998 and renamed itself in 1999 the Salafi Group for Preaching and Combat (GSPC). By 2007, a part of the GSPC was still negotiating laying down its arms and abandoning violence (behavioral de-radicalization), but the largest faction underwent even further radicalization by internationalizing their cause and allying with al-Qaʻida network. That splinter of the GSPC called itself al-Qaʻida in the Islamic Countries of al-Maghreb (QICM).

The AIS and the GIA started their armed action in the very same crisis environment that plagued Algeria after the 1992 coup. The two organizations however, ended up in very different positions. This chapter attempts to account for the discrepancy in the behavior of both organizations and to answer the question of why the AIS-led de-radicalization process was successful whereas the GIA failed to de-radicalize, despite being in the same context and subjected to similar influences. The argument in this chapter rests on the empirical fact that both organizations were subjected to intense state repression and were offered several types of selective inducements. However, the AIS had a consolidated, charismatic leadership that was willing to de-radicalize. That leadership was influential enough to disarm the 7,000 militants that made up the organization, without causing any splits, as well as influencing several hundreds militants from other smaller militias and factions. The GIA did not have this type of leadership at any point in its history (1992–2005). Additionally, the AIS was able to interact with other armed organizations, FIS factions, moderate Islamist figures and political parties to support de-radicalization and reconciliation. The GIA had very limited interactions with the "other," mainly due to its excessively violent behavior. The violence of the GIA was not only directed against the "other" but also against GIA figures and factions who were supportive of interaction.

Setting up the argument: ideology, controversial terms and missing variables

Did ideology matter?

Obviously, the AIS and GIA do not belong to the same ideological category of armed Islamists. The former was the self-declared armed wing of a political party that had won a landslide victory in the first relatively free and fair parliamentary elections in Algerian history. The AIS had a clear goal: to resurrect the electoral process that some of the army generals had cancelled in January 1992 (Mezraq 2005a, 6; Ben Aicha 2000, 8). Hence, the AIS Islamists were pragmatic militants[1] who participated in electoral democracy and were fighting for an Islamist state via that process. The GIA by contrast did not believe in that process to begin with. It equated democracy with apostasy and took pride in the fact that some of its affiliates fired shots at border guards before cancelling the electoral process in 1992 (GIA 1993, Communiqué no. 13). In 1994, the GIA declared that it was fighting the Algerian regime because of apostasy (*riddah*) and not for any other reason (GIA 1994, Communiqué in *al-Hayat* 15 September 1994, 6).

Common wisdom would suggest that these ideological differences might explain the decision to de-radicalize or not. After all, the AIS accepted electoral democracy and therefore was more inclined to compromises and accepting the "give-and-take" of politics. The GIA, on the other hand, upheld the infamous "Three No's" slogan: "no dialogue, no truce and no reconciliation" (Kertali 2000, 8; Ben Hajar 2000, 8; GIA Communiqué in *al-Hayat* 15 September 1994, 6). In a detailed communiqué from September 1994, the fourth emir of the GIA, Cherif Gouasmi, defended that slogan with theological and ideological arguments (GIA Communiqué in *al-Hayat* 15 September 1994, 6).

Although that argument seems attractive, it does not have much empirical support. First, ideological preferences did not necessarily reflect the groups' stance on de-radicalization and reconciliation. Many supporters of the electoral process and formerly elected MPs were against dismantling the AIS, most notably Anwar Haddam, the head of the FIS "Parliamentary Delegation," and Qamar al-Din Kharbanne, one of the FIS leaders (Haddam 1996; 2006; Kharbane 1998, 179). On the other hand, many radical leaders who still reject democracy upheld disarmament and de-radicalization. Those leaders include Abdul Haqq Layada, the founder of the GIA and a fierce critic of democracy, and Hassan Hattab, the former commander of the GIA's "Second Zone" and the founder of the GSPC (Ghimrasa 2005b, 6; Layada 2007, 6; Hattab 2007, 8).

In addition, both the GIA and the AIS[2] did not meet their ideological objectives. The AIS was not able to force the army to go back to the electoral process, or even to reinstate the "illegal" FIS. The GIA was not able to enforce Salafistyle Shari'ah laws in Algeria or even turn the country into some form of an Islamist state.

Finally, even if ideology had a role in influencing the decision of the AIS leadership to dismantle the organization and de-radicalize, the ideological factor does not explain why that process was successful and why other militias that were not necessarily supportive of democracy, had joined the AIS-led de-radicalization process.

Eradicators and reconciliators? The problem with dichotomies

Many former Algerian officials, opposition leaders and analysts divide the ruling generals in the aftermath of the 1992 coup into two factions: eradicators (*éradicateurs*)[3] and dialogists (also known as patriots, nationalists or reconciliators). As opposed to the dialogists, the eradicators are usually blamed for opposing negotiations, for undermining it in various ways if/when it starts and for preferring to "eradicate" armed Islamist opposition since 1992.

Whereas these terms "eradicator" and "reconciliator" can describe specific policies or political stances, they are misleading and inaccurate when applied to individuals (specific generals). The policies and the political attitudes of the generals were changing, like most of the other variables, throughout the civil war. For example, Liamine Zeroual, often described as a "patriot" and considered a leading figure in the "dialogist" camp[4] for his role in initiating negotiations in 1993, was constantly opposing dialogue with the FIS, the AIS and other armed opposition from 1995 until his dismissal in September 1998. Arguably, one of the causes of that dismissal was his stance on the AIS unilateral ceasefire, which he refused to accept or to even officially acknowledge (Boukhamkham 1999, 10).

Another example that shows the problem with applying these terms to individuals is that of General Isma'il Lamari, who is usually described as a leading eradicator, even by fellow intelligence officers who worked under his command, such as Colonel Mohamed Samraoui, by army commandos like Lieutenant Habib Souidia or by former officials like senior diplomat Muhammad Larabi Zitout (Samraoui 2002; Souaidia 2001; Zitout 1999). Despite being one of the coup plotters and despite upholding eradication policies in the early and mid-

1990s, in 1997 Lamari was the one who engineered the deal with the AIS. According to Mezraq, the national emir of the AIS, Lamari risked his career by upholding secret negotiations with the AIS, in the absence of guarantees for success (Mezarq 2004). He also risked his life by undertaking direct negotiation in the headquarters of the AIS in Beni Khattab Mountains in Jijel province (Mezarq 2004). Those direct negotiations ultimately became the basis for the de-radicalization and reconciliation processes. Thus, Lamari was an "eradicator" who risked his life and career for peace in Algeria in 1997.

Given this reality, the terms "eradicator" and "dialogist" are best applied to policies rather than to individuals. The adjectives can also describe factions within the regime, or even within the civilian opposition,[5] but it must be recognized that the members of those factions are constantly changing.

The lost opportunities for peace in Algeria (1992–1997)

Before 1997, the year in which the AIS declared a unilateral ceasefire in the mould of the IG in Egypt, there were at least three attempts to negotiate a peaceful resolution to the Algerian crisis with the FIS leadership. These three attempts took place in 1993, 1994 and 1995. They all had the following common characteristics. First, they were all negotiated by the political leaders of the FIS, and not by its military commanders. Second, there was a near-consensus among these political leaders that armed resistance to the junta should only be halted if the FIS was reinstated and the electoral process was continued on the basis of the 1991 elections. Third, there was a belief among the FIS political leaders that they could actually control or at least strongly influence the armed organizations that operated in the aftermath of the coup. That belief would be shattered later on in 1995 when the FIS leaders, Abbasi Madani and Ali Belhaj, were removed from the Consultative Council of the GIA (GIA 1995, Communiqué no. 36, 1) and when Muhammad Said and Abdul Razzaq Rajjam, the two former provisional leaders of the FIS, were killed by the GIA, on the orders of its leader Jamal[6] Zitouni. Finally, on the regime's part, there was no consensus about the idea of negotiating a peaceful settlement with the FIS (Mezraq 2005a, 8; al-Tawil 1998, 328–330). Until 1997, the so-called "eradication trend"[7] had the upper-hand in the decision-making processes and the internal bureaucratic wars.[8] Therefore, even when the negotiations with the political leaders of the FIS were ongoing, there were several acts that showed "bad faith" on the part of the regime.[9]

The first attempt for peace (1993)

The first attempt to de-radicalize armed Islamists and to reach a peaceful settlement in the Algerian crisis took place in the fall of 1993 in al-Blida Military Prison (Bou Khamkham 1999, 10). At that point, the defense minister appointed by the coup plotters was General Liamine Zeroual (al-Tawil 1998, 293; Madani 2004). The latter contacted Medani, Belhaj and other FIS leaders in al-Blida and asked them to call for a cessation of the violence perpetrated by armed Islamist organizations. In response, the FIS leadership demanded that the cancellation of the 26 December 1991 election results be revoked before they would call on supportive militias to put down their arms (al-Tawil 1998, 293; Madani 2004). That condition was not accepted by General Zeroual and the junta and as a result the talks had largely failed. They did however lead to the release of some of the FIS leaders, like Consultative Council members Ali Jeddi and Abd al-Qadir Bou Khamkham (al-Tawil 1998, 190; Bou Khamkham 1999, 10).

The second attempt for peace (1994)

The second attempt at achieving a cessation of violence took place in the summer of 1994, following the "unification" of several armed Islamist organizations and factions under the GIA's banner in May 1994.[10] That unification was completed under the leadership of Cherif Gouasmi (alias Abu Abdullah Ahmad). The latter was a local representative of the FIS in the Bi'r al-Khadim suburb of Algiers in 1990 and became a leading Jihadist after the coup (Ben Hajar 2000, 8). The strength of the GIA at this point had reached its zenith and the Group controlled several "liberated zones" in Central Algeria, especially in the *wilayat* (provinces) surrounding Algiers such as Ain el-Defla. Indeed, by mid-1994, there were rumours that the GIA was preparing to storm Algiers (al-Tawil 1998, 235; al-Suri [no date], 66–67).

In this context, the regime attempted to contact the leadership of the FIS for the second time in summer 1994. The contacts started following an address by General Zeroual, who then headed the High Council of the State, an unconstitutional entity that was set up by the coup plotters and that took over the political leadership of the country. Following the address that called for dialogue, Abbasi Madani sent two letters to Zeroual that were distributed widely by the regime-controlled Algerian News Agency. Madani agreed to initiate a dialogue based on the respect for democracy and getting the army out of politics. The regime took Madani's calls for reconciliation seriously. They released other FIS Consultative Council members from prison, including Kamal Goumazi and Abd al-Qadr Umar (al-Tawil 1998, 181, Madani 2004). Medani and Belhaj were also released, but placed under house arrest in one of the presidential mansions.

The GIA under Gouasmi, however, acted as a spoiler. The latter issued a GIA statement, refusing dialogue and upholding the slogan of "no reconciliation." However, what ended the talks this time was an interaction between Gouasmi and Ali Belhaj (Mehri 1998, 183; Sheikhy 2007, 6). The army forces killed Gouasmi in late September 1994 and found a letter from Belhaj with him (Mehri 1998, 184; Madani 2004). The regime distributed only the first paragraph of the letter, in which Belhaj praised the struggle of armed Islamists in Algeria (al-Tawil 1998, 190; Mehri 1998, 182; Bou Khamkham 1999, 10). The rest of the letter, which was not published at that time, contained a call for conditional cessation of violence, a theological argument to convince Gouasmi about the "legitimacy" of dialogue and truce, and a warning to the GIA's Emir not to turn

Algeria into another Afghanistan (Mehri 1998, 182; al-Tawil 1998, 190). Abdelhamid Mehri, former prime minister and chairman of the FLN who was advising
General Zeroual during these talks, concluded after describing the contents of
Belhaj's letter that the "eradicators" in the army were not interested in a genuine
dialogue and that Belhaj's letter to Gouasmi was being used as a pretext to end
what seemed to be a serious initiative (Mehri 1998, 184).

The third attempt for peace (1995)

The third attempt at achieving the cessation of violence came in the aftermath of
the Rome Accords (St. Edigio Platform), which were considered to be a political
victory for the FIS and the Algerian pro-democracy opposition. In January 1995,
the accords were signed by several major opposition figures and parties[11] in
Algeria including Islamists (FIS, al-Nahda Party, Contemporary Muslim
Algeria), Nationalists (National Liberation Front – Abdelhamid Mehri), Social-
ists (Socialist Forces Front – Hocine Ait Ahmad), Trotskyites (Workers' Party –
Lousia Hanoune), Nationalist-Democrats (Movement for Democracy in Algeria
– Ahmad Ben Bella), human rights activists (Algerian Human Rights League –
Ali Yahia) and even the anti-Islamist Rally for Culture and Democracy[12] (Hocine
Esslimani). The accords were brokered by the St. Edigio Catholic Community
and provided the basis for a peaceful resolution of the crisis via the establishment of common principals that all the co-signatories accepted and vowed to
respect. These included a commitment to the peaceful alternation of power based
on democratic elections, to rejection of violence, to political pluralism, to
freedom of religion and thought and to respecting international human rights
norms. By signing the accords, the FIS had shown significant political maturation especially when Ali Belhai, the most radical of the FIS leaders,[13] declared
his acceptance and support. The Rome Accords also robbed the military junta of
the raison d'être of the coup: that the FIS would not accept democracy and pluralism and would crack down on other parties.

Despite that political development, the military regime rejected the accords.
Its media launched a smear campaign on the participants, calling figures like Ben
Bella,[14] Hocine Ait Ahmad[15] and others "traitors" (al-Tawil 1998, 296–297). As
for the GIA, the regime's position was no less xenophobic and anti-democratic:
it called the participants "apostates who signed an infidelity accord under the
shadows of the Cross"[16] (GIA 1995, Communiqué no. 36).

After the regime's rejection of the accords, the media smear campaign and
the stagnant situation on the battlefield, the military commanders of the AIS
started their own initiative for the first time. Madani Mezraq sent a delegate to
Abbasi Medani, who was still under house-arrest (Bou Khamkham 1999, 8; al-
Tawil 1998, 298). Mezraq's delegate explained the conditions in the battlefield,
the fact that the GIA was a serious danger to the AIS/FIS and that the belief that
it could be controlled by the FIS leader was a myth. Mezraq's message to
Madani was clear in 1995: the situation in the mountains was far from being
controllable and therefore the violence had to be stopped at any cost, even if that

meant abandoning the demands to return to the 1991 election's results or reinstating/rehabilitating the FIS (Mezraq 1995a, 6–7; Mezraq 2008; al-Tawil 1998, 298).[17]

The meeting between the AIS delegate and Madani was followed by two communiqués from the AIS Emir to different segments of the Algerian society, most notably General Zeroual and the FIS leadership (Mezraq 1995a, 1995b). The two communiqués called for dialogue and a peaceful resolution of the crisis and they were widely interpreted as a green light from the military wing of the FIS to its politicians to initiate unconditional talks. The AIS emir called on the FIS leaders to take a common stance against the GIA in particular. Following these two letters, Abbasi Medani sent another letter to General Zeroual. Dated 9 April 1995, the letter delineated the general basis for dialogue, which included respect for democracy by all sides, a commitment to non-violence, and a demand for the withdrawal of the army from politics, as well as for the rehabilitation of the FIS (Madani 1995 qtd. in al-Tawil 1998, 308).[18] Following the letter, the talks with the FIS were re-initiated but subsequently failed again in July 1995 (Bou Khamkham 1999, 10; Medani 2004). The alleged reasons for the failure were differences over details like the members of the negotiating delegation of the FIS,[19] the venue for the negotiations,[20] the release of political prisoners,[21] and the rehabilitation of FIS.[22] By early June, all talks had stopped; then on 11 July 1995, Ahmed Ouyahia, the cabinet director appointed by General Zeroual, declared on national TV that the negotiations with the FIS had failed again "because the FIS did not renounce its ambition to turn Algeria into an Islamist state" (Boukhamkham 1999, 10).

More years of bloodshed

Following the failure of these talks and the electoral "victory" of General Zeroul in the presidential elections of November 1995, the violence rose to unprecedented levels. Between January 1996 and October 1997, there were three wars going on in Algeria. The first was between the armed Islamists and the regime. The second was between the AIS and other armed Islamists against the GIA. This latter war was intensified after the GIA's leadership started killing Islamist and Jihadist leaders as high-profile as 'Izz al-Din Ba'a (June 1995), Muhammad Said (November 1995), Abdul Razzaq Rajjam (November 1995), Abdul Wahab Lamara (January 1996), and even the former GIA emir Mahfuz Tijan (alias Abu Khalil Mahfuz) (January 1996) (al-Tawil 1998, 227–249; Ben Hajar 2000, 8; Ben Hajar 2007, 232; Kertali 2000, 8; al-Suri [no date], 64–66). The third war was declared by the GIA, and arguably, factions within the military establishment against Algerian civilians, especially the residents of the electoral districts that supported the FIS in the 1991 elections. The third war was described as "electoral cleansing" (Ait Larbi *et al.* 1999, 142).[23] It ultimately resulted in a series of massacres that took place between 1997 and 1998.

From the above overview, it can be concluded that two key variables were constantly missing in all the attempts to put an end to the violence. The first was a united leadership or a charismatic leader within the Islamist opposition who was influential enough to put an end to the violence. Whereas the FIS leadership in general was willing to call for a cessation of violence in exchange for political demands, it was unclear whether its calls for an end to violence in 1994, 1995 or even 1997 would have been accepted by the GIA or other non-AIS Islamists. Even within the FIS, a charismatic leadership – akin to the historical leadership of the Egyptian IG or al-Sharif in the Egyptian al-Jihad's case – was non-existent. As previously mentioned, the Front was not a consolidated, monolithic group with a long history of political activism. Hashimi Sahnoni, one of the FIS co-founders, and Mustafa Kertali, a leading member of the FIS[24] and the emir of al-Rahman Brigade, point out that the FIS was a front gathering together several Islamist groups with multiple ideological backgrounds and different leaders[25] (Sahnon 2000, 14; Kertali 2000, 8). In times of severe crisis, such a coalition was unable to hold together under a united command. The continuous splits that occurred following the controversial decision to go on strike in May 1991[26] showed the organizational volatility of the FIS, and the military coup of 1992 finally detonated what was left of its internal cohesion (Shahin 1997, 143; Waly 1994, 131). In the aftermath of the coup, each faction gave priority to its own ideological preferences and followed the orders of its own leader. "The majority of the FIS activists inclined to take up arms" joined the recycled Armed Islamic Movement (MIA) under "General" Chabouti,[27] despite the fact that Abdul Qadar Hachani, the provisional leader in 1992, "urged FIS's followers to remain calm, exercise caution and not to respond to any provocation from whatever sources" (Hachani 1992 qtd. in Shahin 1997, 151). Contrary to Hachani, Ali Belhaj urged his Salafi followers to join the ranks of Chabouti's MIA in 1992 (Shahin 1997, 156). Thus at best, the leadership of the FIS could not take a unified position after the coup. At worst, the leaders of the Front were giving their followers conflicting orders. In all cases, there was not one charismatic leader or a unified leadership that could bestow legitimacy on non-violent reactions. That continued until the regime finally decided to initiate talks with the AIS, whose leader, Madani Mezraq, was willing to negotiate and de-radicalize and was in control of his own armed men.[28]

In addition to the lack of a united, charismatic leadership, the policies of the regime were heavily tilted towards repression and therefore undermined the calls from within the FIS for dialogue, interaction and de-radicalization. The intense, indiscriminate repression, especially between 1992 and 1997, had shown that the so-called "eradicators" trend within the regime had the upper hand in decision-making.[29]

Also, the process of internal interactions between the FIS leaders, their armed followers and sympathizers was undermined due to the lack of charismatic leadership, the intensity of repression and non-cooperation from the regime. A few brief contacts took place under hazardous conditions, like the afore-mentioned letter from Belhaj to Gouasmi and the meeting between Madani and the AIS delegate.[30] But these brief interactions were not enough to support a de-radicalization process. Moreover, when these interactions became public knowledge, the regime usually cracked down and therefore undermined future attempts.

Finally, the only common variable in all these attempts to de-radicalize and reach a resolution to the crisis was the state repression variable, which alone led to disastrous consequences. Those consequences include the radicalization of the FIS, the creation of the AIS, the initiation of the civil war and at a later stage, the further radicalization of the GIA.[31]

The de-radicalization process of the AIS

The failure of the 1995 talks and the "victory" of General Zeroual in the presidential elections of November 1995 had several consequences for de-radicalization and reconciliation in Algeria. First, bolstered by the electoral victory, Zeroual and the presidential establishment felt that there was no need for dialogue with the political wings of the FIS (al-Tawil 1998, 330; Bou Khamkham 1999, 10; Mezraq 2004). The presidential establishment thought that the regime could militarily win the battle against the armed Islamist opposition, regardless of their objectives, backgrounds and orientations. In other words, it shifted from a dialogist to an eradication policy (Bou Khamkham 1999, 10).

The second consequence arising from the failure of these talks was that the AIS leadership arrived at the conclusion that the political leaders of the FIS had by then failed three times to negotiate a resolution to the crisis. In Mezraq's words, the FIS leaders "did not rise to the level of the crisis and its severity" and that they were acting as if they were "captives of the GIA" (Mezraq 2005b, 8; Mezraq 2008). Given that, the AIS took over the negotiation process and relegated the political leaders to a mere advisory role (Mezraq 2005b, 8; Mezraq 2008). In other words, the 1997 reconciliation/de-radicalization process was imposed by the AIS leaders on the FIS leaders.

As a result, the AIS readjusted its approach to the calls for negotiations. For the first time, it did not request any authorization from the political leadership of the FIS. Also, the AIS did not address the president, the presidential establishment or the leaders of the army – thus the negotiation attempt this time was a bottom-up process. The AIS sent a message to several mid-ranking officers in the military establishment's fifth zone (the eastern regions of Algeria), many of whom had blood ties with several AIS commanders from the east (mainly from Jijel province) (al-Tawil 1998, 329; Mezraq 2004; 2005a, 8). These contacts started becoming more significant, from the mid-ranking officers to the army commanders of the fifth zone, and finally ended up on the desks of the military intelligence generals. The meeting with the deputy-head of military intelligence, General Isma'il Lamari,[32] in the headquarters of the AIS in Jijel's Beni Khattab mountains was crucial to the initiation of the de-radicalization process and reconciliation in Algeria. It addressed the security dilemmas of both parties, built confidence measures and reassured both sides that there are at least two factions within the two warring camps who are committed to reconciliation and willing to take risks for a peaceful settlement.[33]

The AIS and FIS: complex relationship and distinct leaderships

Before discussing the leadership of the AIS and its impact on de-radicalization in Algeria, two issues should be clarified. First, several FIS leaders and former leaders, such as Abd al-Qadir Hachani,[34] Ahmad Marani,[35] Anwar Haddam,[36] Murad Dhina[37] and others, have pointed out that the AIS was not established, or ordered to be established, by the political leaders of the FIS. The FIS is a political party and the official stance of the aforementioned leaders is that political parties should not be armed (Dhina 2002; Marani 1999, 6). In addition, the only entity that could legitimately decide to establish an armed wing for the FIS was the Consultative Council, which in fact never met to sanction or to legitimize the AIS.

However, the AIS coordinated with several factions within the FIS, most notably the faction of Rabih Kabir, who headed the Executive Committee of the FIS abroad.[38] Also, all of the AIS' approximately 7,000 members are pro-FIS activists (Mezraq 2004; Unnamed AIS commander 1999, 14). Despite that, the AIS acted semi-autonomously throughout the Algerian civil war. Its soldiers were taking orders from its national emir, Madani Mezarq, and not from the political leaders[39] of the FIS. Those political leaders, mainly Madani and Belhaj, acted more as symbolic figures rather than as AIS leaders.[40] Both the AIS and the FIS leaders agree that the FIS did not engage in the 1997 Mezraq–Lamari negotiations (Bou Khamkham 1999, 10; Unnamed AIS commander 1999, 14; Mezraq 2008).

Second, regarding the leadership of the FIS, Ali Belhaj, Abbasi Madani and the other founders succeeded in gathering most[41] of the active Islamist groups under one umbrella, as was previously mentioned. Representation in the 40-member *Majlis al-Shura* (Consultative Council of the FIS) headed by Madani reflected the fact of the group's multiple leaders, with each ideological trend being represented by a different leader. Ali Belhaj and al-Hashimi Sahnoni represented two different factions of the Salafi trend.[42] More specifically, Belhaj represented the relatively hard-line, uncompromising faction, whereas Sahnoni represented the pragmatic wing, known for basing its *fatwas* (religious rulings) on the concept of *Maslahit al-Da'wa* (interest/welfare of the Islamic call).[43] Muhammad Said, Abdul Razzaq Rajjam and Abd al-Qadr Hachani represented *al-Jaz'ara* (Algerianization) trend[44] in *Majlis Al-Shura* (Shahin 1997, 118; Burgat and Dowell 1997, 317; Esposito and Voll 1996, 154). Abbasi Madani, the FIS' primary leader, represented the Islamist populist current that is characterized by its evasiveness, pragmatism and reliance on popular mobilization (street mobilization as opposed to partisan mobilization). Jihadists were also represented at the Consultative Council level by Said Makhloufi, a former intelligence officer who joined the Afghan *Mujahdieen* in their fight against the Soviets and then returned to Algeria as an Islamist Jihadist (Al-Tawil 1998, 110–111).

Given the conditions in which the AIS was born, the factionalized FIS leadership, and the lack of a charismatic leader around which the FIS factions could rally, it is not surprising that the AIS acted autonomously throughout the crisis.

The AIS and the making of a charismatic leader

As mentioned in Chapter 3, the first cells of the AIS were established in Western Algeria in 1993 with the help of Muhammad Shnuf and Abd al-Qadir Chabouti (Ben Aicha 2000, 8). In 1994, the AIS was mainly operating in the west and the east under the joint leadership of Ahmad Ben Aicha and Madani Mezraq respectively. Both figures were mid-ranking leaders in the FIS in 1991. Ben Aicha was an elected MP in el-Chelf district, who had turned to armed action after the cancellation of the elections, his subsequent arrest, and the two attempts on his life after being released (Ben Aicha 2000, 8). Mezraq was a former activist in al-Nahda Movement.[45] He had no leading role in the FIS except after the Batna Conference in 1990, in which he was appointed the FIS representative in the Jijel province and a member of the FIS' national committee for monitoring the elections (al-Sidawy 2002, 17; Madani 2004; Mezraq 2006, 8).

When the coup happened in 1992, the FIS had no leading figures to organize armed action, and no militias operating in its name.[46] In 1994, Muhammad Said and Abd al-Razzaq Rajjam, both former provisional leaders of the FIS, joined the GIA instead of organizing or leading the AIS cells. Others like Said Makhloufi, a former officer in the military intelligence, an experienced Afghan veteran and a former member of the Consultative Council of the FIS, had also joined the GIA.[47] In Ben Aicha's words, the armed men of the FIS became "orphans" after these leading figures joined another organization, which is different from the FIS[48] (Ben Aicha 1996, 8). However, Mezraq and Ben Aicha emerged as the new field commanders who upheld the "original line" of the FIS.[49] Their leadership was challenged on several occasions. The first challenge was in the aftermath of the "unity" agreement with the GIA, which the AIS had rejected in 1994. The second was during the negotiations of 1997 and in the aftermath of the unilateral ceasefire declaration. The third challenge came after January 2000, when the political leaders of the FIS, Madani and Belhaj, expressed their support for behavioral de-radicalization but their opposition to the terms of the agreement between the AIS and the regime. After each of these challenges, the leadership of AIS emerged stronger than before.

In one interview, Mezraq describes the reactions to the "unity" of 1994 within the AIS (Mezraq 2004):

> It was extremely difficult for any leader of an armed Islamist organization to stand up in front of his soldiers and tell them that he is against the "unity" because he was not consulted … especially when the GIA was at the peak of its strength.
>
> (Mezraq 2004)

However, Mezraq passed that leadership test, and most of his men obeyed his orders, without splits or factionalization (Mezraq 2004; al-Tawil 1998, 298). In March 1995, there were intense battles in the mountains of Ain el-Defla between the Algerian army (ANP) and the GIA. Several thousand GIA militants were killed by air strikes, and the backbone of the Group was broken (al-Tawil 1998, 335). Expecting a possible collapse of the GIA, the AIS declared that it chose Mezraq as a "national emir." The move was timely, as it consolidated the AIS under one commander. To capitalize on the situation, Mezraq issued a communiqué calling on the GIA members to join his army (Mezraq 1995b; al-Tawil 1998, 327). The GIA, however, survived the battles but never regained its 1994 status. The murders of Said and Rajjam, the two engineers of the "unity," as well as several other leaders by the GIA starting June 1995 had gained Mezraq a reputation of being a wise, charismatic leader for opposing the "unity" (Kertali 2000, 8; Ben Hajar 2000, 8). This was followed by several splits from the GIA and declarations of allegiance to, and coordination with, the AIS emir. Those splitting off included two of the GIA's largest brigades in Central Algeria. The first was al-Rahman Brigade in al-Blida province, whose commander Mustafa Kertali switched sides and became the AIS commander of the Center (Ben Aicha 2000, 8). The second was the LIDD in al-Medea province. It was headed by Ali Ben Hajar, who initially chose only coordination with the AIS, until he met with its emir.[50] Other groups and brigades joined between 1997 and 2000, including the FIDA organization[51] and al-Charrarba (Calitos) Brigade,[52] both of which operated in Algiers (Kertali 2000, 8; Mezraq 2005a, 8).

The second challenge for Mezraq's leadership and control over his followers was during the negotiations that started in 1997. Before the meeting between General Lamari and Mezraq, around 30 AIS detained affiliates, suspected sympathizers and relatives of members were summarily executed in the area of Umm al-Thalathin,[53] which is close to some of the hills controlled at the time by the AIS guerillas (Mezraq 2004). Mezraq interpreted this act as an attempt by other factions in the military establishment to "drive his followers crazy" before the talks (Mezraq 2004): "They wanted to tell us that the authorities have no intention to reach a resolution ... and possibly drive one of our men to kill their delegate [General Lamari]," Mezraq recalled (Mezraq 2004). Despite the incident, there was no violent retaliation on the part of the AIS and Mezraq was able to control his militiamen. On the other hand, Mezraq argued that the commanders of other armed organizations in Algeria were following the emotional and radical views of their soldiers: "Weak commanders in other organizations were leading their soldiers via the concept of 'whatever the listeners want' because these commanders loved leadership and fame ... that was a disaster for the [armed Islamist] movement"[54] (Mezraq 2004). Following that second challenge, the talks developed into a negotiation process that finally led to the dismantlement of the AIS and several other smaller organizations in January 2000.

Finally, the third test for Mezarq's leadership came from within the FIS. In 2000, Medani and Belhaj both approved a truce with the regime that permitted more dialogue and that aimed at a peaceful resolution of the crisis. However, they both refused the dismantlement of the AIS and other pro-FIS militias (Ben Hajar 2000, 8; Belhaj 1999, 6). Madani sent a letter to Ali Ben Hajar, the Emir of the LIDD and a formerly elected FIS MP in Medea. In it, he asked Ben Hajar to keep his arms and men, refused the details of the Lamari–Mezraq agreement and called for a resolution along the lines of what he (Madani) had proposed in 1994 and 1995 during the talks with the regime (Ben Hajar 2000, 8).[55] When asked directly if he thought that Madani approves the dismantlement of the LIDD, Ben Hajar answered: "I do not know ... but Sheikh Abbasi is a wise politician, he knows that we did not put down arms except for exigency[56] and that we did not abandon our duty..." (Ben Hajar 2000, 8). Ali Belhaj and Abd al-Qadir Hachani,[57] the provisional leader of the FIS who led the party to the electoral victory of 1991, had similar views. They both approved an end to the violence. However, they wanted better terms in the agreement with the regime, especially with regards to rehabilitating the FIS and allowing its members to be politically active (Ben Hajar 2000, 8; Hachani 1999, 6).

Despite that stance from the FIS political leaders, the dismantlement of the AIS and the de-radicalization of other groups and factions were successful. The AIS militiamen were following the orders of their direct commanders, who were in turn following the orders of the AIS' national emir, Madani Mezraq. The latter was also able to convince the emirs of other armed organizations to de-radicalize. In addition to that crucial role of leadership, the other three variables of repression, interaction and inducements contributed to the success of the de-radicalization process of these organizations.

Repression: between the state's hammer and the GIA's anvil

Algeria was plagued by several types of violence and repression following the cancellation of the elections by the army generals in January 1992. The costs of that violence were estimated by several parties. In 2005, Algerian President Abdelaziz Bouteflika estimated the war's toll at 150,000 fatalities between 1992 and 2002 (Bouteflika 2005, 1). Other estimates place the toll above 200,000 (Ait Ahmad 2002; Algerian League for the Defense of Human Rights 1998; Abdennour 1999, 18; Abdul 'ati 2002).[58] In addition, a group of researchers documented 642 massacres that occurred between 1992 and 1998 (Bedjaoui *et al.* 1999, 15–25; Aroua 2001).[59] Most of these massacres took place in districts that voted for the FIS candidates in 1991 elections (Bedjaoui *et al.* 1999, 25–30; Aroua 2001). Whereas the GIA took responsibility for some of those massacres (al-Zouabri 1999, 1–2), some researchers, opposition figures, and former Algerian intelligence officers and diplomats accuse the regime of being complacent or even directly responsible for others (Samraoui 2002; 2003, 10–12; Souaidia 2001; 2002; Bedjaoui *et al.* 1999; Abdennour 1999, 7, 9–11; Roberts 2001, 3).

In addition, following the 1992 cancellation of elections, between 30,000 and 40,000 FIS supporters, suspected supporters and sympathizers were detained, mainly in detention centers in the Algerian desert known as *al-Muhtashadat* (Concentrations). In 2006, a government committee appointed by President Bouteflika blamed the security services for 6,146 cases of "disappearances" between 1992 and 1998 (Cosantini, 2005, 1; Cosantini 2006, 19). According to the government, the total number of disappeared persons in this period was more than 10,000 (Oyahia 2006, 1), a number that exceeds the totals for any other place in the world other than Bosnia in the 1990s (Human Rights Watch 2003).[60] The same committee declared that the security establishment arrested more than 500,000 Algerians during the crisis as "terrorism suspects" (Costantini 2006). Finally, Prime Minister Ahmad Oyahia declared in 2006 that the security forces had killed 17,000 "armed Islamists," out of an estimated 25,000[61] operating between 1992 and 1997 (Oyahia 2006, 1; Cosantini 2006, 9). These figures, although slightly suspect because they come from one party in the conflict, still reflect the general level of state repression in Algeria in the 1990s. This section, however, focuses on a specific type of repression: that directed against the AIS and its affiliates, as well as how that repression affected the AIS decision to deradicalize.

Between 1993 and 1997, the AIS faced a double threat. First, there was a war against its guerrillas by the official National Popular Army (ANP), the pro-regime militias and the GIA.[62] The AIS dealt with that threat relatively better than the other two. Contrary to the GIA between 1994 and 1995, the AIS did not pose any significant threat to the ANP during the crisis. However, it was able to hold its positions in the face of the ANP strikes, and the latter was unable to destroy it (General Atayliyah 2000, 8; al-Tawil 2004). Also, the AIS was able to gain new ground at the expense of the GIA in 1996 and 1997 (Kertali 2000, 8; Ben Hajar 2000, 8). These gains were mainly due to the GIA's behavior under Zitouni and Zouabri, which alienated the affiliated militias as well as potential sympathizers. In a few cases in 1996 and 1997, the AIS gained new territory from the GIA via armed clashes (Kertali 2000, 8).

The second threat to the AIS came partially from the GIA and, allegedly, from factions within the military security establishment. That threat came in the form of the massacres that mainly targeted civilians in electoral districts that voted for the FIS in the 1990 municipal elections and 1991 legislative elections (Ait Larbi *et al.* 1999, 111, 412; Souidia 2001; Aroua 2001). The massacres became a regular phenomenon in 1997 as there was a massacre occurring almost every day in that year in Algeria (the total number in 1997 exceeded 300 massacres) (Aroua 2001; Ait Larabi *et al.* 1999, 64).

These massacres had a strong impact on the AIS decision to disarm and dismantle. On one hand, the AIS was a self-declared armed wing for the FIS. However, it could neither protect the families of its members nor the FIS supporters especially in Central Algeria (Ait Larabi *et al.* 1999, 75). For example, in 1997 the GIA claimed responsibility for the mass-killing of 31 "convicted apostates" in Ktiten village in al-Medea province (GIA 1997, Communiqué no. 13). The "convicted apostates" were mostly women and children from the extended family of Ali Ben Hajar, the emir of the LIDD, who was coordinating with the AIS and whose group assassinated Zitouni in 1996 (Izel *et al.* 1999, 412). In Bentalha, a small town south of Algiers whose residents overwhelmingly voted for the FIS in 1991, 417 civilians were massacred allegedly by the GIA in one night (22–23 September 1997)[63] (Yous 2007, 13). Many of those victims were relatives of AIS members. Awad Bou Abdullah (alias Sheikh Nur al-Din) was the AIS commander of the sixth zone, the nearest area to Bentalha in which the

AIS had a militia (Bou Abdullah 2006). In one interview, Bou Abdullah recalls that after hearing the news of the massacre, he sent an armed detachment to Bentalha to defend their relatives and supporters but it was "too late"[64] (Bou Abdullah 2006). In 1996 and 1997, it was clear that most of the mass killings were targeting areas that supported the FIS in 1990 and 1991.[65] The AIS, as a self-declared armed wing of the FIS, was unable to protect these areas, not to mention being unable to protect the relatives of its own members.

Answering a question in one interview about the causes behind the unilateral ceasefire, Mezraq mentions that the AIS declared it because the "Jihad was just about to be buried by its own sons" (Mezraq 2005a, 6). By this, he meant that the whole concept of Jihad in Algeria was being tarnished by the massacres and by the intra-Islamist fighting. There was consequently no point in continuing the fight against the regime, due to the waning in popular support (Mezraq 2005a, 6).

Mustafa Kabir, the AIS commander of the east and the brother of Rabih Kabir, argues that among the main reasons for declaring the unilateral ceasefire in 1997 was the on-going massacres. "We were used as an umbrella to hide the perpetrators of the massacres ... and therefore we had to remove this umbrella and dismantle our organization (AIS)" (Mustafa Kabir 2002, 8). Kabir was referring to the fact that many Algerians and non-Algerian monitors did not distinguish between the AIS and the GIA. They were all armed Islamists fighting against the regime, and the massacres hurt the reputation of Islamists in general. By declaring the unilateral ceasefire, the AIS wanted to send a message to Algerians and to the rest of the world that they were not behind the massacres and that they were putting down arms to "expose whoever is behind them" (AIS Communiqué 1997, 1; Mezraq 2005a, 6).

In addition to the "regular" forms of repression (imprisonment, torture, extrajudicial killings, media smear campaigns and other), the massacres had a strong impact on the AIS decision to de-radicalize regardless of who was really behind them. Whether it was the GIA practicing its Takfiri ideology, army factions using the massacres as a "counter-insurgency" tactic,[66] or a mix of both;[67] the massacres served as a main cause for the decision of the AIS to declare the unilateral ceasefire.

Interaction and the de-radicalization of the AIS

As discussed before in the third chapter, the AIS had nuanced differences in its ideology and behavior that separated it from the GIA and from other Jihadist groups. The main difference was its belief that armed Jihad is a last resort, defensive tactic to create an Islamist state after the failure of electoral politics. The AIS also believed that violence would not resolve the Algerian crisis (Mezraq 1995a, 1). Therefore throughout the civil war it attempted to negotiate a settlement, first via the FIS political leaders in 1995 and then via its own leadership in 1997. That political position was remarkably different from the "Three No's" stance that was upheld by the GIA from 1992 until its factionalization and partial destruction between 1998 and 2005.[68] The political position of the AIS can be considered as a partial product of interactions between the AIS figures and non-violent Islamists and secular groups.

The interactions between the AIS and moderate Islamists and non-Islamist factions (external interaction) were important in influencing the stance of the AIS on violence. First, the leadership of the AIS was influenced mainly by the ideas and works of the Egyptian Muslim Brothers, a group that had renounced violence against the Egyptian regime since the early 1970s. For example, when asked about the books that influenced his Islamist ideology and behavior, Mezraq mentioned *The Collection of Letters* of Hasan al-Banna, *The Muslim Brothers: Events that Made History* of Mahmud Abdul Halim[69] and Abu Hamid al-Ghazali's *Revival of Religious Sciences*.[70]

Second, throughout the Algerian crisis there have been calls from the Egyptian MB leaders for dialogue. The position of some of these leaders was quite different from that of the mainstream Algerian MB (HAMS or MSP); in general, they tended to be closer to those of the FIS/AIS rather than those of the military establishment. For example, Yusuf al-Qaradawi, a leading MB Islamic scholar who taught in Algeria for seven years, argued in one interview that the struggle of the AIS is a legitimate one (al-Qaradawi 1998). However, he urged on many occasions all armed Islamists to cease violence and negotiate a settlement and, at a later stage, to follow the AIS-led de-radicalization process (al-Qaradawi 1998).

In addition to the intra-Islamist interaction, the Rome meeting organized by the Catholic Community of St. Edigio was another chance for external interaction with other political forces in Algeria. Although there were not any AIS representatives at the meeting, Rabih Kabir, the head of the FIS Executive Committee abroad and the closest FIS leader to the AIS,[71] was among the signatories of the accords.[72] As opposed to the GIA and the regime, the AIS upheld the results of the talks and called for continuing negotiations based on them (Mezraq 1995b, 2).

Given this inclination to negotiate and the perception that armed Jihad is a mean to an end,[73] the internal interaction process to convince the AIS guerrillas to de-radicalize was less difficult as compared to those of other Jihadist groups. Medani Mezraq and Mustafa Kabir both mention that the internal interactions with their followers aimed at convincing them to de-radicalize were not easy, but were successful in the end (Mezraq 2004; 2006; Kabir 2002, 8). Indeed, there were no splits within the AIS. In fact, other factions from the GIA and the GSPC as well as independent armed organizations joined the AIS-led de-radicalization process.

Selective inducements

To support the de-radicalization process, the Algerian regime under Bouteflika had to address five major issues. These issues were political prisoners, the "disappearances," social reintegration, the political rights of the de-radicalized groups and individuals, and the role of the military in politics. Despite the activation of the Charter of Peace and National Reconciliation in 2006 (the legal framework that covers these issues),[74] most of the problems underlying the issues still remain unresolved due to their complexities and sensitivities. However, the inducements provided by Bouteflika's government with regards to these five issues were enough to bolster the de-radicalization process and make it attractive to thousands of militants.

Regarding political prisoners, the main demand of the AIS was the release of all its detainees, FIS leaders and other affiliates and supporters. The government complied with these demands, releasing high-profile prisoners like Ali Belhaj and Abd al-Haqq Layada, the founder of the GIA, in 2006 (Muqqadim 2006, 1). Tens of thousands of other political prisoners were released between 1999 and 2005.

Reintegration was another issue that the Bouteflika regime had to provide as an inducement. It was mainly centered on socioeconomic issues and safety concerns. The two socioeconomic issues were reemployment/employment and compensations for families who were victimized by the regime during the conflict. Although some of the AIS leaders became successful business entrepreneurs, others were still denied jobs due to their history (al-Sharq al-Awsat 2000, 1). In addition, many of the former militants were denied a passport and were continuously harassed by the security establishment. These conditions forced President Bouteflika to apologize and "ask forgiveness" from former guerrillas in a gathering at el-Chelf stadium, attended by thousands of former AIS members and other former militants (el-Chelf is one of the towns in western Algeria in which the AIS had a strong presence under Ahmad Ben Aicha) (Bouteflika 2005, 1).[75]

As for the safety issues, the state provided personal arms, mainly for the commanders of the AIS to protect themselves against the GIA and its splinters, pro-regime militias, and other potential threats. This, however, did not prevent various reprisals like the assassination of Ali Murad, a member of the AIS joint leadership staff, by one of the pro-regime militias in Souk Ahras province in 2006 (BBC Online 2001). This is in addition to the more recent attempt[76] on Mustafa Kertali, the former AIS emir of Central Algeria, in which he lost one leg in a car bombing orchestrated by QICM (Ghimrasa 2007b, 6).[77]

Another sensitive topic is that of political rights. On several occasions, the commanders of the AIS mentioned that they would not accept being "second class citizens" (Mezraq 2006), by which they meant the de facto ban on their political rights.[78] Mezraq, however, is presently in the process of applying for a permit to launch a political party, although he expects the Algerian authorities to deny his application request (Mezraq 2007, 4). The AIS leaders assert that the agreement with the regime upheld their political rights (Mezraq 2008; Ben Aicha 2000, 8; Kabir 2002, 8). However President Bouteflika mentioned on several occasion that he did not find "anything written" with regards to that (Bouteflika 2005, 1; Muqqadim 2005b, 6). Given that stance from the regime, Ali Ben Hajar, former emir of the LIDD, went so far as to refuse to call on the GSPC and the QICM militants to put down their arms (Ben Hajar 2005, 1). He argued in one interview that the regime did not honour its promises and therefore that he believed the reconciliation process to be "symbolic but not real" (Ben Hajar 2005, 1).

A more critical issue is the role of the military establishment in Algerian politics. After all, it was a group of incumbent army generals[79] who decided to cancel the 1991 elections and crack down on the opposition, thereby engendering the civil war. On the other hand, it was almost the same group who negotiated and supported the 1997 ceasefire and the subsequent de-radicalization process, and therefore reduced the status of civilian officials.[80] After the re-election of Bouteflika in 2004, it seemed that it was in the interest of both the Islamists and civilian "elected" politicians to limit the army's interference in politics. Powerful army figures like Muhammad Lamari who was the Commander of the Land Forces at the time of the coup and the Chief of Staff (1993–2004) had resigned (or was asked to resign) in 2004. Following his resignation, around 800 other senior officers were removed from their positions and given pensions, including Lamari's deputy Sherif Foudayl (Muqqadim 2005a, 6).[81] Those removals were widely regarded as an attempt by Bouteflika to professionalize and de-politicize the army (Muqqadim 2005a, 6).

The de-radicalization failure of the GIA

This section briefly discusses the de-radicalization failure of the GIA as an organization. Whereas some of the GIA's brigades and units have joined the de-radicalization process led by the AIS, a large section of the Group was destroyed by 2005.[82] A third part of the GIA, mainly the militias located in the "second zone"[83] comprising around 1,300–1,500 militants under the command of Hasan Hattab, broke away as early as 1998 in protest against the massacres and the transformation of the GIA from Jihadism to Takfirism. This subgroup of the GIA became known as the GSPC.

This section argues that the lack of a unified command and a charismatic leadership in the GIA, as well as limited social interaction, led to the failure of the GIA's de-radicalization process.

The lack of charismatic leadership

Since the Group's foundation, the GIA's leadership was characterized by several features. The first was the nearly constant quick elimination of most of its leaders. The table below shows a list of the GIA's leaders from 1992 until 2005.

As shown in Table 6.1, most of the GIA leaders had very short tenures, and were either killed or arrested in a matter of weeks or months. Regardless of their behavior and policies, the short periods of time that they led the group did not allow them to consolidate their leadership. The most successful and relatively charismatic of all of the GIA leaders was Cherif Gouasmi, under whom a faction from the FIS (al-Jaz'ara faction), the MEI, the MIA and other smaller groups were united under the GIA's command. The GIA's armed members in 1994 under Gouasmi numbered more than 10,000 fighters[84] and controlled several

Table 6.1 GIA leaders

GIA leader	Start date	End date	Period of leadership	Reason for termination
1 Abdul Haqq Layada (Abu Adlan)	September 1992	May 1993	9 months	Arrested in Morocco
2 Issa Ben Ammar	July 1993	August 1993	Less than 1 month	Killed by security forces
3 Murad Sid Ahmad (Ja'far al-Afghani)	September 1993	February 1994	5 months	Killed by security forces
4 Cherif Gousami (Abu Abdullah Ahmad)	March 1994	September 1994	7 months	Killed by security forces
5 Mahfuz Tajeen (Abu Khalil Mahfuz)	September 1994	October 1994	Less than 1 month	Removed by other GIA commanders – executed in January 1996 by the GIA
6 Jamal Zitouni (Abu Abdul Rahman Amin)	October 1994	July 1996	1.6 years	Killed by the LIDD
7 Antar Zouabri (Abu Talha)	July 1996	February 2002	4.5 years	Killed by security forces
8 Rachid Quqali (Abu Turab)	February 2002	July 2005	3.5 years	Executed by other GIA commanders
9 Nourredin Boudiafi (Hakim RPG)	July 2005	November 2005	4 months	Arrested by security forces

areas in Central Algeria (al-Tawil 2007d, 129). After Gouasmi, the GIA was constantly weakened due to leadership failures and successful ANP strikes.

The only three leaders that were able to lead the GIA for more than a year were Zitouni, Zouabri and Quqali. By no means were any of the three charismatic or successful. Zitouni was a former butcher from Algiers who did not complete his middle school education (Sheikhy 2007, 6). According to Umar Sheikhy, a co-founder of the GIA and one of Zitouni's close advisors, the latter's "religious" education was "average"[85] (Sheihky 2007, 6). His Arabic language skills, key for Arab Jihadist leaders to motivate their followers, were below average (Sheihky 2007, 6; Al-Tawil 1998, 222).[86] The lack of theological credentials and the weak educational background haunted Zitouni. According to Ali Ben Hajar, many in the GIA's grassroots were more inspired by figures like Mohammed Said and Abdul Razzaq Rajjam, who had more advanced theological training and an excellent command of Arabic.[87] These figures also upheld different ideological preferences (al-Jaz'ara) that Zitouni did not approve of.

Threatened by these figures and their relatively sophisticated background, Zitouni not only ordered their death but also lied about his responsibility for killing them even to GIA commanders and consultative council members (in addition to other national and international supporters and media outlets). Thus the GIA leader declared to al-Ansar Newsletter[88] that the security forces had killed Said and Rajjam, as he anticipated a possible revolt in the ranks of the GIA if he admitted his responsibility (al-Ansar 14 December 1995, 3; Sheikhy 2007, 8).

However, responsibility for murdering two provisional FIS leaders as high profile as Said and Rajjam could not be kept a secret for very long. After a few weeks, Zitouni had to declare that Said and Rajjam were "heretics" and announced that the GIA had executed them (al-Ansar 4 January 1996, 3). Tens of militias comprising thousands of GIA members split following the declaration. Also, most of the international Jihadist support for the GIA was withdrawn[89] (al-Zawahri 1996, 17 qtd. in al-Tawil 1998, 230–240; al-Suri [No Date], 50–56; al-Tawil 2007d, 238–240; Sheikhy 2007, 8). In less than a year, Zitouni was assassinated by the LIDD militants to avenge Said and Rajjam's murders (Hattab 1998, 6; Ben Hajar 2000, 8).

When Zouabri took over, his policies made those of Zitouni look less controversial and more peaceful. According to Zouabri's brother, a refugee claimant in the United Kingdom, Zouabri completed only the second grade in school, but did have some "religious" education (Ramadan Zouabri 1999, 7). Before becoming a Jihadist, Zouabri was a member of a criminal gang that operated in the impoverished town of Boufarik. After becoming the GIA emir, a result that was opposed by many GIA commanders, Zouabri expanded Zitouni's violent policies to include not only suspected Jaz'ra affiliates and their families but also Algerian civilians in general. Under Zouabri, the massacres started expanding and during his period of rule (1996–2002), other armed organizations and factions were at war with the GIA. Finally, Quqali followed the same policies of slaughtering, raping, looting and practicing mindless violence. By the time he was at the head of the GIA, its membership had dropped to less than 100 (Cosantini 2006). Far from being "charismatic," Quaqali was killed by GIA members who declared Boudiafi an emir. As noted, the latter was arrested and tried for participating in some of the massacres that the GIA under Zouabri took responsibility for (Muqqadim 2007, 6).

Another factor that contributed to the lack of the rise of a charismatic leadership within the GIA was its "specific type" of factionalization. As opposed to the FIS for example, most of the GIA's factions were prone to violence, perceiving violence against the "other" as *the* legitimate way to settle differences. The factions that can be seen as being "violence-prone" are the GIA's local Salafi-Jihadists, violent Takfirists and the Afghan veterans (or international Jihadists).[90] Because these violence-prone factions constituted the bulk of the GIA, and moreover that they were vying for the leadership while refusing to rise above factionalism, it was very difficult for a charismatic unifying leader to emerge, especially after the liquidation of Said, Rajjam and Tajeen.

These factors (short-term tenure, lack of theological training/background, limited education, excessively violent behavior and violent factionalism) combined together can explain the lack of a charismatic leadership in the GIA and the resulting impact on the failure of de-radicalization.

Limited interactions

In addition to the lack of charismatic leadership to initiate, legitimize and support a de-radicalization process, the GIA had very limited interaction with relatively moderate Islamists like the FIS or the MSP (HAMS), and almost no interaction with non-Islamists. Aside from the security risks and the ideological differences, the main issue that hindered interaction was the GIA's violent behavior and treachery.

Interaction with Islamists

One of the early reported "interactions" was with Sheikh Mohammed Bouslimani, a highly-regarded Islamic scholar and one of the leaders of the Muslim Brothers in Algeria (whose mainstream is represented by the MSP).[91] The GIA under al-Afghani had kidnapped Bouslimani in late 1993. The leadership demanded that Bouslimani issue a *fatwa* supporting their "Jihad" (Unnamed former GIA member 1998, 130). The latter demanded a debate first with the GIA commanders, including al-Afghani, about whether the violence in Algeria is a Jihad or not. Al-Afghani agreed to set up a debate. According to one of the attendees, Bouslimani was arguing that the current violence of armed Islamists was not a "Jihad" (Unnamed former GIA member 1998, 130). He presented a detailed theological argument and some of the attendees were showing signs of approval. Al-Afghani, however, decided to end the meeting prematurely and Bouslimani was taken to one of the GIA's stronghold near Algiers where he was executed (Unnamed former GIA member 1998, 130). When reported in 1995, this incident sent a warning that the GIA could not be trusted in debates, even if its leadership had initially approved them.

Another reported interaction was with Kamal Guomazi, a co-founder of the FIS and one of its leaders. That interaction came as part of the 1995 negotiations with the FIS leaders following the Rome Accords (Sheikhy 2007, 8). Whereas Ali Jeddi and Abdul Qadr Bou Khamkham were sent to the AIS in the east and the west to update them about the negotiation process, Guomazi was sent to the GIA, which was under Zitouni's leadership at this time. He conveyed a message from Belhaj and Madani asking the GIA to give dialogue a chance to resolve the crisis. Umar Sheikhy, one of the only two GIA co-founders who are still alive today,[92] attended the meeting and reported its details (Sheikhy 2007, 8). Probably learning from the prior interaction with Bouslimani, the GIA commanders[93] asked Guomazi an initial "control" question: is their fight a Jihad or not? According to Sheikhy, Guomazi said that it was a Jihad, but he still argued for negotiations and attempted to convince the GIA commanders about the legitimacy of the Rome Accords. In the end, Guomazi failed to convince Zitouni about the dialogue process (Madani 2004). Moreover, when he requested to return back to Algiers to report the results to the FIS leaders, some of the GIA commanders refused. They told him that as a Muslim, he should stay and perform Jihad as a *fard* (religious obligation) with them (Sheikhy 2007, 8). After a promise that he would convey the message and then return back to fight under the GIA banner, the GIA finally agreed to release him. Guomazi however never returned (al-Tawil 1998, 209).[94] Following the failure of this interaction, the GIA removed Madani and Belhaj from its Consultative Council[95] for supporting the Rome Accords (al-Tawil 1998, 208).

After the failure of that interaction, the GIA became less interested in any *fatwas* from Islamic scholars. A dialogue that was reported between Abu Bakr Zerfaoui, one of the consultative council members known for his theological credentials, and Zitouni illustrates that position. Zerfaoui suggested including some *'ulama* in the consultative council so as to guide the "Jihad" as well as to help ensure no "deviation" occurred in the leadership selection process. Zitouni refused, saying that the GIA "does not need 'ulama and if it did need their advice, it will consult them." Zerfaoui replied by saying "then, this is secularism!" (Ben Hajar 2007, 233). Zerfaoui was executed by the GIA in late 1995 along with Said, Rajjam and others (al-Tawil 1998, 166).

Interactions with non-Islamists

The interactions with non-Islamists were also very limited and were doomed to failure. The most importation of these interactions was with one of the French intelligence agencies,[96] which attempted to convince the GIA to stop any activity on French territories. Mahfuz Tajeen, the former emir of the GIA, led the negotiations with a high-profile French General in late 1995 (al-Ansar 11 January 1996, 1–2). Zitouni, however, denied that he knew about the talks and listed them as one of the reasons for executing Tajeen in January 1996, along with the rest of the negotiating team (Zitouni 1996, 1; al-Ansar 11 January 1996, 1–2).

In the end, the de-radicalization process of the GIA as an organization was unsuccessful. Part of the GIA was destroyed by 2005, another part de-radicalized starting in 1999–2000 and a third part split in 1998 to continue the fight against the regime. That last part underwent further radicalization in 2007 by joining al-Qa'ida. Unsuccessful de-radicalization can be explained in the GIA's case by the lack of charismatic leadership due to short term tenures, limited educational and theological backgrounds, excessively violent behavior and virulent factionalization. In addition, interaction was a very risky venture given that the GIA's leadership constantly liquidated the parties who engaged in it, whether from the GIA or from outside it.

The further radicalization of the GSPC

In 1998, following the continuous splits from the GIA under Zitouni and Zouabri, a large GIA militia located in the Second Zone (East Algiers) declared its autonomy, initially under the title of the "GIA-Second Zone." In April 1999, it declared its new name to be the "Salafi Group for Preaching and Combat" (GSPC). The third emir of the GSPC, Nabil Sahrawy, explains that the name "GIA" was tarnished by Takfirists and therefore the leadership had to change it (Sahrwy [No Date] qtd. in al-Tawil 2007d, 242). Initially, the GSCP was led by its principal founder, Hasan Hattab (Hattab 2007, 8), who perceived the GIA to be a deviant group (Hattab 1998, 6). Hattab argued for a limited number of targets, based on his insistence that the security and military personnel were the only legitimate targets (Hattab 1998, 6). This policy changed later after a large section of the GSPC joined al-Qa'ida and became known as QICM in 2007.

The reasons behind the de-radicalization failure of the GSPC are similar to those behind the failure of the GIA. This section argues that the lack of charismatic leadership and social interaction can explain such a failure.

Leadership status in the GSPC

The GSPC attempted to learn from the mistakes of the GIA. From the point of view of many GSPC members, one of the main reasons for the deviation of the GIA was that it was led by "theologically ignorant" commanders like Zitouni and Zouabri (Sahrawy [no date], 244). Although the commander who led the split, founded the GSPC and became its first emir was Hasan Hattab, the "elite council" (*Majlis al-A'yan*) of the GSPC chose Abdul Majid Dishu as the emir in April 1999, mainly because of his theological training.[97] The latter, however, was killed by the Algerian army in June 1999, less than three months after he was declared an emir of the GSPC. Hattab subsequently took over the GSPC again (Hattab 2007, 8).

The same sort of leadership crisis that plagued the GIA was recycled within the GSPC. Its leader and practical founder, Hattab, was marginalized due to several factors. The first was his stance on merging with al-Qa'ida, an option that seemed attractive to other Algerian Jihadists given the limited national support for their activities after the de-radicalization of the AIS and other armed groups. Hattab, however, refused the merge (Hattab 2007, 8; Ben Uthman 2007, 242). The second factor for the marginalization of Hattab was alleged negotiations that took place between him and the regime in 2000 and 2001. Moreover, President Bouteflika referred to these talks and distanced Hattab from other Jihadist commanders by saying in a speech that the latter "never targeted civilians" (al-Tawil 2007d, 373). That stance on al-Qa'ida and Bouteflika's referral added to Hattab's challenges for consolidating his leadership and by 2003 he had allegedly resigned or had been forced to resign.[98]

Nabil Sahrawy took over after Hattab but he was killed in June 2004. He was followed by Abdul Malik Drukdal. Both leaders were not interested in de-radicalization. They were also constantly challenged by other GSPC commanders. More specifically, Drukdal was frequently criticized by other commanders for his policies of expanding the conflict into the whole Magreb (mainly in Morocco and Mauritania) (al-Tawil 2007c, 6). At the same time, Hattab claims that he never resigned from the GSPC, and in fact still considers himself the emir (Hattab 2007, 8). However, he obviously does not control most of its members. This was made particularly clear when the GSPC changed its name to QICM, a position that Hattab had refused as early as 1999.

Limited interactions

The leadership problem was not the only factor negatively affecting the de-radicalization process, despite the presence of state repression and selective inducements. There were very few external interactions between the GSPC/QICM and the "other." Moreover those that did take place sometimes ended up a disaster, like the one that took place with an AIS delegate in 1998.[99] The AIS's version of that interaction is that their delegate was given an *aman* (security guarantee) from the GSPC commander of the Suknah region to talk to them about the de-radicalization process and to attempt to convince the GSPC to join the unilateral ceasefire declared by the AIS in 1997 (al-Tawil 1998, 8). But the GSPC acted treacherously and killed their delegate. The GSPC's version of the story was that the delegate never got this clearance and that he was not sent by the "common diplomatic channels"[100] (Hattab 1998, 6). According to the GSPC, the delegate was discouraging their militiamen and he died during a "questioning" session by the GSPC investigators (Hattab 1998, 6). In any case, the interaction failed. Hattab declared at the time that his group was fighting the regime because of "apostasy" and not for any other reason (Hattab 1998, 6). Therefore, he would only accept "reconverting to Islam" or a "humiliating surrender" from the regime (Hattab 1998, 6).

Other external interactions were relatively successful in influencing individual members and some factions, and even in changing the ideas of some commanders (al-Tawil 2007c, 6). These interactions involved Muslim scholars, mainly from Egypt (with an MB background like Yusuf al-Qaradawi) and Saudi Arabia (from non-violent Salafi backgrounds like Salman al-Audeh and Safar al-Hawali) (Qaradawi 1998; Unnamed Algerian Security Official 2007, 6). These scholars had supported the AIS-led de-radicalization and reconciliation processes in general. After presenting detailed theological arguments, these scholars issued *fatwas* that the conflict in Algeria was not a Jihad (al-Tawil 2007c, 6). According to a senior Algerian intelligence officer who worked on de-radicalization, the *fatwas* and the arguments of these scholars were transferred to the GSPC via "special delegates" between 1999 and 2003 (Unnamed Algerian Security Official 2007, 6). The official, who reported these interactions, argues that they were extremely important in de-legitimizing violence and that in the early 2000s, following careful readings of these theological arguments, several GSPC commanders abandoned their use of arms.

The GSPC faction that is still under Hattab's command took a middle stance: no perpetration of violence but at the same time they still kept their arms and positions in the mountains. This position can be seen as an attempt to hedge their bets so that they can see what will happen to the de-radicalized militias before abandoning their arms completely.[101] The "Protectors of the Salafi Call," a smaller splinter group from the GIA which did not join the GSPC and which is mainly composed of Afghan veterans,[102] has a similar position. Its commander, Salim al-Afghani, mentioned in one interview that he read the *fatwas* of the Saudi Salafi sheikhs who support de-radicalization (al-Tawil 2007c, 6). However, he did not say whether he supports these *fatwas* or not. Unlike the GSPC/QICM however, his militia has not engaged in combat since 2000, the year the AIS and other militias were dismantled. Commenting on that behavior, a security official said that the Algerian generals had "discovered the powers of Saudi and Egyptian sheikhs" and their potential impact on the de-radicalization process in Algeria (Unnamed Algerian Security Official 2007, 6).

Conclusion

The arguments presented above to explain the causes of successful de-radicalization in Algeria as well as the cases of de-radicalization failure can be summarized in Table 6.2.

In the first three years of the Algerian civil war, only state repression and very limited inducements to put down arms were available to support de-radicalization. These were by no means enough to definitively spur change. The state repression variable caused the initial radicalization of the FIS, whose dominant factions were willing to abide by electoral democracy. The selective inducements provided between 1992 and 1994 were not sufficient to bolster

Table 6.2 De-radicalization in Algeria

Causal variable/ organization	Charismatic leadership	State repression	Social interaction	Selective inducements	De-radicalization result
FIS-AIS (1993)	N/A	Available	N/A	Available (intermittent, usually in the form of "promises")	Failure
FIS-AIS (1994)	N/A	Available	N/A	Available (intermittent, usually in the form of "promises")	Failure
FIS-AIS (1995)	N/A	Available	Available (limited)	Available (intermittent, usually in the form of "promises")	Failure
AIS (1997–2000)	Available	Available	Available	Available	Success
GIA (1992–2000)	N/A	Available	N/A	Available	Failure
GSPC/QICM (1998–2007)	N/A	Available	Available	Available	Failure

de-radicalization. In 1995, there were some significant social interactions reflected in the Rome Accords as well as in the few talks between the FIS, the AIS and the GIA. Although these interactions prepared a fertile ground for a compromise and a resolution of the conflict, they were refused by the military regime as well as by the GIA. That refusal by the GIA underlined a significant problem within the larger armed Islamist movement in Algeria: the lack of leadership. Whereas the FIS leaders thought between 1992 and 1994 that they could control the GIA and other armed movements, that belief was shattered in 1995 after the murder of the FIS former provisional leaders by the GIA (Said and Rajjam). By then, it was apparent that only a part of this armed Islamist movement had a leadership that could control its followers and that was willing to compromise. The presence of this type of leadership within the AIS ultimately led, along with the three previously mentioned variables, to its successful de-radicalization.

In the cases of the GIA, GSPC and QICM, although they were the object of intense state repression between 1992 and 2008, and despite the presence of selective inducements after 2000 (following the de-radicalization of the AIS), there was a constant lack of charismatic leadership within these groups, and very limited interactions with the "other." As a result, there was continuous splintering and factionalization in all directions, whether toward radicalization, de-radicalization or even along apolitical paths (Kertali 2000, 8).

7   A world without violent Jihad?

The central theme of this book was the complex phenomenon of de-radicalization of armed Islamist movements. The research analyzed three types of de-radicalization processes (comprehensive, substantive and pragmatic) in Egypt and Algeria since the 1950s. These processes of abandoning political violence, prohibiting it ideologically and theologically, and/or dismantling armed wings started in 1951 with an attempt by the Egyptian MB leadership to dissolve their Special Apparatus. That first attempt failed, as did the next one; but the third attempt, between 1969 and 1973, was successful. Moreover the surge in the number of armed Islamist groups between the 1980s and the 2000s meant that contemporary cases of de-radicalization were suddenly being given significantly more attention, a trend that accelerated after the 11 September 2001 attacks. The case of the Egyptian IG became a de-radicalization model in which the leadership was able to control the followers and de-radicalize the Group on the behavioral, ideological and organizational levels. Three months after the IG's declaration of the unilateral ceasefire which started the process, the Algerian AIS also declared a unilateral ceasefire. That declaration started another de-radicalization process, this time in Algeria. Although that process lacked an ideological component (and hence has been labelled pragmatic de-radicalization in this book), it was able to attract several Islamist militias, as well as factions from armed groups whose leadership had refused to de-radicalize (like the GIA and the GSPC).

A decade later, al-Jihad of Egypt, the organization that both had and still has the strongest ties with al-Qaʻida network, followed the IG's lead. Also, many other armed groups and factions initiated de-radicalization processes in the 2000s. These groups and factions come from various parts of Muslim-majority countries including Libya, Jordan, Saudi Arabia, Yemen, Tajikistan, Malaysia and Indonesia.

The central hypothesis in this book is about the causes that might lead to such a process of de-radicalization, as well as the necessary conditions for its success. The argument made was that a combination of charismatic leadership in control of its followers, state repression directed against the armed movement, selective inducements proffered by state and other actors, and social interaction between the layers of the movement as well as between the movement and the "other" are the four variables that could explain the initiation and success of de-radicalization processes. The pattern of interaction between these variables is as follows: state repression and interaction with the "other" affects the ideas and the behaviors of the leadership of a radical organization. After updating its beliefs and worldviews, calculating the costs and the benefits and reassessing security dilemmas, the leadership initiates a de-radicalization process that is bolstered by selective inducements from the state, as well as by internal interactions (such as lectures, discussions, meetings between the leadership, mid-ranking commanders and grassroots in an effort to convince them to support de-radicalization).

The findings in comparative perspectives

This section is divided into two parts. The first part briefly restates the findings of the book, as well as elaborating some nuances and modifications. The second part is about the contribution to the existing literature on Islamist movements, security studies and Middle East politics.

The first proposition in this book was that four independent variables are necessary for the initiation and the success of a de-radicalization process within armed Islamist movements. These variables are charismatic leadership in control of its followers, state repression directed against the armed movement, selective inducements proffered by state and other actors, and social interaction between the layers of the movement as well as between the movement and the "other." As shown in the previous chapters, that was the case in Egypt and Algeria. The proposition can also explain the de-radicalization processes of other armed Islamist movements elsewhere and possibly the de-radicalization of armed, ideologically driven groups in general.[1]

On leadership

Several nuances should be added with regards to the leadership variable, however. One key finding is that the religious/spiritual leaders, as opposed to organizational leaders, have a crucial role to play in bestowing legitimacy on comprehensive and substantive de-radicalization. The impact of those theologically knowledgable leaders will be strongest if they are leading members within the organization which is attempting de-radicalization, as was the case of al-Sharif in al-Jihad or the historical leadership of the IG.[2] However, even if these religious leaders are non-members, they can still, to a lesser degree, influence de-radicalization attempts. Saudi Arabia, Yemen and Jordan provide cases were non-Salafi-Jihadi religious leaders and Islamist thinkers participated and were participating in, and influencing, de-radicalization efforts.[3] Additionally, the case of the IG's de-radicalization has influenced some of the leaders of the British Islamic Liberation Party, most notably Majid Nawaz the ideologue of the Party who spent time in Egypt interacting with the historical leadership of the IG (Nawaz 2007, 6).

In general, a leadership with theological credentials,[4] a history of "struggle,"[5] and a senior standing[6] in the organization would exert considerable influence in supporting de-radicalization processes. Also, a leader who has a history of rising above factionalism would be more likely to successfully influence de-radicalization efforts.

With regards to the relationship between leadership and de-radicalization, one finding of this book is that without a charismatic leadership that controls or strongly influences its followers, the initiation as well as the success of a de-radicalization process is less likely. As the case studies have shown, there were attempts to de-radicalize by non-charismatic leaders (such as the MB under al-Hudaybi in the 1950s and the GSPC under Hattab in the 2000s). Despite the presence of other variables (repression, inducements, interaction – albeit limited), these attempts were unsuccessful and were followed by factionalization, splintering and internal violence. Other case studies have shown the willingness of some factions within an armed organization to de-radicalize. The leadership, however, was opposed to the whole concept (such as the GIA in the late 1990s and early 2000s, as well as al-Jihad case between 1997 and 2007). In these cases as well, de-radicalization was unsuccessful despite the presence of the other variables.

Also, there were several regime attempts to "bypass" the leadership and de-radicalize the followers directly via repression and inducements. In Egypt under Nasser, the program of the *wala'at* (political loyalties), was an attempt to convince the MB members to declare allegiance to Nasser in exchange for limited inducements.[7] Under Mubarak, the program of *al-tawbah* (repentance) in the mid-1990s was very similar. The main difference was the request: to declare "repentance" rather than "political loyalty" to the ruling regime. Both programs failed to contain violence and were widely perceived as illegitimate by the members of the MB and the IG.[8] In Algeria, *Qanun al-Rahma* (Clemency Law) that was declared by Zeroual's regime in 1995 was also another attempt to bypass the leaders of armed Islamists by giving some inducements to the followers in a context of intense repression. As argued in Chapter 3, it failed to put an end to armed violence in Algeria. It was only when the regime directly negotiated a settlement with the leadership of the AIS between 1997 and 2000 that the pragmatic de-radicalization process began to be successful.

With regards to the position on violence, the only major difference between these programs (whether the *wala'at*, *al-tawba* or *al-rahma*) and the de-radicalization processes was that the leadership opposed the former and blessed the latter. The charismatic leadership of an armed Islamist organization seems to be the decisive factor in the success or the failure of any de-radicalization process.

On state repression

State repression, the second variable, is more problematic. Initially, it was a main, if not *the* main, cause of radicalization of not only the armed groups discussed in the book (MB, IG, al-Jihad, AIS and the affiliated militias, and the GIA and its offshoots), but also others operating under repressive authoritarianism (Tajik IRP, Uzbek IMU, Libyan FIG, Syrian MB and many others). In this sense, the findings on radicalization support the political strains approach[9] and the hypothesis that in Muslim-majority countries, repressive autocrats breed violent theocrats.

However, this hypothesis is time-bounded. Intense and sustained repression was one of the factors that led the leadership of armed organizations to rethink the costs of violent confrontations as well as the theological legitimacy behind it. Therefore, repression has partially contributed to the initiation of de-radicalization processes. Also, the experience and memories of these organizations under repression serves as a hurdle to reversals in the process. The history of these organizations under repression is usually highlighted by their leaderships, so as to legitimize de-radicalization and to show the members that their decisions to de-radicalize were correct (Zuhdi *et al.* 2002, 23; Ahmad 2002c, 13; Abdul Khaliq 2004, episode 14). Finally, all of the de-radicalization processes analyzed in this book were initiated under conditions of intense repression, except for the MB case of 1951.[10] Despite that, the cases analyzed had shown that state repression alone can result in the radicalization, destruction, fragmentation and/or further radicalization of an Islamist movement. It will not lead to a de-radicalization process without the four other variables.

In all the cases analyzed in the previous chapters, repression was the only variable which constantly existed throughout the periods under study (whether it was the MB in the 1950s and 1960s, the IG and al-Jihad in the 1980s and 1990s, or any of the Algerian organizations). Since intense repression was present in all of these cases and since the transformations in the behaviors and ideologies occurred only decades later, usually following the introduction of the other variables; repression alone could not explain de-radicalization. Indeed, intense repression has led to the destruction of some of the armed organizations,[11] or to the fragmentation which is usually followed by further radicalization either in behavior or ideology like the case of the Algerian GIA.

On interaction

External social interaction, if allowable and successful, usually affects the world-views of the leadership of armed organizations rather than the followers. If it did affect the followers, like in the Algerian cases (AIS' as well as Salafi Sheikhs' interactions with members of the GIA and the GSPC), de-radicalization of factions or individuals might occur, but the de-radicalization of the organization as a whole will not. This was the case in Egypt during the 1960s, 1980s and early 1990s, when the regime arranged several "debates" between MB and IG members and non-violent Islamists (usually pro-regime religious scholars from al-Azhar University). Saudi Arabia and Yemen also offer cases where external interaction have led to the de-radicalization of individuals and small factions loosely linked to organizations like al-Qa'ida. However, this type of interaction did not lead to the de-radicalization of organizations as a whole. Finally, factional de-radicalization usually leads to splintering and possibly internal violence.

De-radicalization efforts are much more likely to become successful when they originate from within the organization. Thus, internal interaction between a leadership supportive of de-radicalization and its followers is crucial, especially for containing opposition to the process. For example, in the IG's case, which is one of the most successful examples of de-radicalization, many of the followers did not support the process except after meeting with their "historical leadership" and intensely debating the "theological legitimacy" as well as the costs and the benefits of de-radicalization (Mamdouh 2005, 202; Ahmad 2002b; 10). Once that internal interaction was successful in the case of the IG (it featured a ten-month tour of Egyptian political prisons and detention centers by the leadership), it was replicated in other cases like the Egyptian al-Jihad one (in which the leadership undertook three months of tours in Egyptian prisons to communicate with their followers) and the Libyan FIG (al-Tawil 2007e, 6).

On inducements

Selective inducements serve as "carrots" to attract the attention of the members of armed organizations after periods of repression. They also bolster the position of the leaders who are supportive of de-radicalization relative to those who oppose the process. Additionally, like the memories of repression, selective inducements serve as disincentives to reversals in de-radicalization. In some instances, however, reversals could occur when the state reneges on its promises, as demonstrated by some cases in Algeria[12] and Tajikistan[13] (Ben Hajar 2005, 1; Olimov and Olimova 2001, 4).

Even in the Egyptian cases, in which there is a strong ideological/theological component prohibiting future violence, there have been several warnings from analysts, IG commanders and former officials regarding reneging on state commitments (Rashwan 2007; al-Minaway 2007, 7). For example, General Ra'uf al-Minaway, former spokesperson of the Interior (Security) Ministry, argued that the Egyptian regime has to abide by the court rulings regarding compensating victims of torture and administrative detention (al-Minawy 2007, 7). Moreover, since the compensations are merely symbolic, al-Minawy recommended the creation of a trust-fund that is administered by the regime and funded by Egyptian businessmen and possibly donations from Gulfian monarchs (al-Minawy 2007, 7). Al-Minawy's recommendations, as well as similar recommendations from others, were not aimed at addressing human rights abuses, but rather toward a preemptive security measure to avoid a potential cycle of violence in Egypt (Al-Minawa 2007, 6).

Finally, all of the de-radicalization processes analyzed in the book, in addition to others, had a "selective inducement" component. These inducements included freedom from prisons (in all cases), financial compensation (in Egypt, Algeria, Saudi Arabia and Yemen), permission to engage in political activism (for the Egyptian MB in the 1970s, and the Algerian AIS in the 2000s), employment/reemployment (for the Algerian AIS) and a power-sharing formula (for the Tajik IRP).

Comparative de-radicalization

Table 7.1 summarizes the important details of the de-radicalization cases that were analyzed in the book.

From Table 7.1, several conclusive points can be made. First, the longest de-radicalization process was that of the MB (22 years). This is despite the fact that the MB, as an organization, never subscribed to Salafi-Jihadism and never rejected electoral democracy. Therefore, ideology was not the reason behind the prolonged process. As discussed in Chapter 4, the reasons were a combination of contextual and organizational variables. Contextually, Nasser's regime was not interested in de-radicalization in the 1950s and 1960s (that changed later under the new regime of Sadat in the 1970s). Organizationally, the MB had a controversial leadership in this period. The number of MB members in the 1950s was in the hundreds of thousands with multiple polarized factions existing. That made the implementation of a de-radicalization program more difficult for an already weak and controversial leadership. Additionally, the SA was a well-established MB institution. Its members were in the thousands and they were

Table 7.1 De-radicalization case studies

Islamist organization	Political context	De-radicalization attempts	Total length of process(es)	Type of de-radicalization	End results
MB	Egypt (repressive)	Three attempts (1951–1954, 1964–1965, 1969–1973)	22 years	Comprehensive	Two failures, one successful
IG	Egypt (repressive)	One attempt (1997–2002)	5 years	Comprehensive	Successful
al-Jihad	Egypt repressive)	One *leadership* attempt (2007), three *factional* attempts (1997, 2000, 2004)	10 years	Substantive (organizational de-radicalization attempt is still ongoing)	Successful
AIS	Algeria (repressive)	One attempt (1997–2000)	3 years	Pragmatic	Successful
GIA	Algeria (repressive)	Several *factional* attempts (2000–2005)	5 years	Pragmatic	Failure
GSPC	Algeria (repressive)	Several *factional* attempts (2000–2007)	7 years	Pragmatic	Failure
QICM	Algeria (repressive)	N/A	N/A	N/A	N/A

only known to the SA leadership, not the leadership of MB. However, after the consolidation of leadership under repression and the changes in regime policy (mainly selective inducements following repressive period), the de-radicalization process became successful two decades later.

Time-wise, the IG's comprehensive de-radicalization process was the shortest (five years). This is due to the fact that the leadership exerted strong influence on its followers. The organizational commanders, mostly in Afghanistan, owed allegiance to their historical leadership in Egyptian prisons. Additionally, the estimated size of the armed wings of the IG was in the range of 800–900 members (State Security General 2002).[14] Because the number of members was quite low, it was relatively easy for the leadership to control them (particularly as compared to the unknown thousands of the SA).

As for al-Jihad, despite the small size of the organization, the de-radicalization process was a long and chaotic one. Again, the leadership and the structure of the organization mattered. Structurally, the organization was composed of secret cells who did not know each other and who were linked only to their direct commanders. This led to factionalism and mistrust between the cells. However, two leaders were known and had been respected by all commanders since the mid-1980s: al-Zawhiri and al-Sharif. The former was and still is strongly opposed to de-radicalization. The latter however upheld and legitimized it. Despite the fact that some of al-Jihad's factions had been supportive of de-radicalization since 1997, it was only when al-Sharif re-emerged as a leader of the group that the rest of the factions followed through with the process that he had initiated.[15]

As for the Algerian organizations, the AIS had the shortest de-radicalization process as compared to all the other case studies. The fact that the process was a pragmatic one, without an ideological/theological component, helped to speed it up. Ideological debates on the issue of violence within the same organization can often lead to factionalization. However, the caveat in pragmatic de-radicalization is that it lacks the ideological/theological arguments that de-legitimize violence whether in the past, present or future. The importance of the ideological/theological components lies in the fact that they represent one of the hedges against a future reversal towards violence.

Finally, the failed cases of the GIA and the GSPC have shown the crucial importance of a charismatic leadership supportive of de-radicalization. In both organizations, there were factions who were willing to de-radicalize. However, in the case of the GIA, the leadership opposed the process, while a few factions insisted on de-radicalization and joined the AIS.[16] In the case of the GSPC, the same scenario was replicated with one exception: the GSPC had a weak leadership that was willing to de-radicalize in 2005. By that time however, it was not in control of most of its followers and it was easily removed and ended up leading only one small faction.[17]

Research and policy implications

There are several issues pertaining to de-radicalization that could be researched and further developed based on the arguments provided in this book. First, there is a specific type of external interaction that merits attention: the "domino effect." De-radicalized Islamist groups often interact with other violent groups operating in the same context under similar conditions and, importantly, in many cases the former influence the latter. For example, the lead taken by the IG and the interaction with its leaders has facilitated and influenced the de-radicalization process of al-Jihad. Moreover, several Islamist leaders have argued that without the IG's de-radicalization process, there would not have been an al-Jihad process (Zinah 2007a, 1). Additionally, interaction between IG leaders and some of the leaders of the British Liberation Islamic Party have led to the latter leaders to renounce their radical ideology (Nawaz 2007, 6).

Also, following the publication of al-Sharif's *Document* and the interaction between him and other small Takfiri and Salafi-Jihadi autonomous groups, the latter groups joined al-Jihad's process (Zinah 2007a, 1). Recently, al-Zawahiri, who is al-Qa'ida's second-in-command, published a book entitled *al-Tabri'ah* (The Vindication) as a counterargument to al-Sharif's *Document.* Doing so shows that al-Qa'ida takes the new de-radicalization literature seriously enough to bother issuing a counterargument, thus showing the potential influence of a de-radicalized group on a violent one. Finally, the interaction between the AIS and factions within the GIA, the GSPC and other small autonomous organizations eventually led to their de-radicalization (Mezraq 2005a, 8). Given that fact, the details and the dynamics of this "domino effect" hypothesis can be a subject of future research.

Another research area that could be investigated in future research endeavors is comparing the importance of the causal variables, in an attempt to find a "dominant cause" behind de-radicalization. While this might be extremely difficult methodologically speaking, one way of doing it is to interview a sample of grassroots members and mid-ranking commanders from different de-radicalized organizations (if possible), and to ask them about the main cause behind their acceptance of different types of de-radicalization (leadership, repression, interaction, inducements or others?).

A third area of research could be the investigation of the international variables that might have influenced the de-radicalization of domestic groups.[18] Although the book touched on some of those factors,[19] it did not investigate de-radicalization cases in which a foreign military presence or some other strong external influence exists in the country under study. The prime example would be the Tajik case. Not only were the Russian forces present in Tajikistan and fighting for the Tajik regime of Emomali Rahmonov,[20] but also the peace negotiations/agreement that eventually led to the de-radicalization of the IRP were held in Moscow, not in the mountains of Tajikistan (like in the Algerian case).

In the International Relations tradition of the "second-image reversed," one objective for future research could be to asses the impact of foreign intervention on de-radicalization (or even moderation) of Islamist movements. More specifically, the research question could be: can international intervention be a cause of *de-radicalization* or *moderation* (as opposed to *radicalization*) of the behavior of particular Islamist movements, and if yes in some cases, what kind of Islamist movements, and under what conditions? The case studies that can be investigated include the US-EU interactions with the AKP in Turkey (moderation?), the Russian intervention in Tajikistan (de-radicalization?), the American intervention in Afghanistan, Iraq and Saudi Arabia (mixed results), French influence in Algeria (de-radicalization?) and Canadian–European interaction with the MB in Egypt (moderation?).

Another hypothesis that could be tested in future research has to do with the prospects of de-radicalization reversals: compared to moderation and radicalization, how likely is the reversal of a de-radicalization process? The testable hypothesis here could be: of the three processes (radicalization, de-radicalization and moderation), de-radicalization is the least likely to be reversed. Once Islamists de-radicalize after a violent confrontation, they are less likely to resort to armed violence again, and more likely to accept a form of electoral democracy (moderation). However, this hypothesis could be time-bounded, and only true for the generation that witnessed and bore the costs of violent confrontations.

Answering these research questions and testing these hypotheses in the future would further our understanding of de-radicalization processes within Islamist movements, and possibly in other types of armed movements and non-state violent actors. Also, this type of research could be valuable for policy purposes.[21]

With several armed Islamist movements in more than seven Muslim-majority countries having initiated de-radicalization processes, the question of whether or not this is going to be a trend in armed Islamism arises. In other words, will these processes of ideological, behavioral and organizational de-radicalization turn into an "end of history" for Salafi-Jihadism and armed Islamism, or will de-radicalization reversals and/or radicalization patterns dominate the future?

Despite the existence of several cases of de-radicalized armed Islamist movements, there are also trends of radicalization – most notably in Iraq, Afghanistan and Pakistan, where the contexts involve foreign military presence/influence, and where some of the previously mentioned conditions for de-radicalization are missing. Therefore, it is still too early to predict the dominant global trends in Islamist transformations. However, the IG's comprehensive transformation and the subsequent transformations of other groups that were modeled on the IG's case might be the initial signs of an "end of history" process for many Salafi-Jihadist groups and factions. Therefore, analyzing the cases is crucial for both academics and policy-makers.

The discussion and analyses provided in this book can be valuable for policy purposes. As argued before, external interaction aiming to influence Islamist leaders coupled with selective inducements can be key factors in de-radicalizing militant groups. Eliminating "spiritual" leaders (as opposed to organizational) of a militant movement could be perceived as a media/psychological victory for a government but would make a comprehensive or a substantive de-radicalization process less likely to succeed. Those leaders are necessary to legitimatize de-radicalization and initiate a genuine dialogue with their followers (internal interaction). While durable, intense and reactive state repression was correlated positively with the de-radicalization, the consequences of that type of repression were not limited to de-radicalization. Those consequences included the initial radicalization of some groups as well as the fragmentation and further radicalization of other militant groups.

As mentioned before, several governments have attempted to replicate the case of the IG with their own local militants, most notably in Libya and Yemen (al-Tawil 2007e, 6). Obviously, however, only parts of this formula can be replicated in Western democracies (especially with regards to state repression), such as the search for relatively less radical influential leaders, the promotion of the dynamics of social interaction, anti-terrorism laws, and the introduction of selective inducements.

A final point concerns the highlighting of very high profile de-radicalization cases such as those of the IG and al-Jihad. Because these groups' changes over a period of 20 years are quite remarkable, going from assassinating President Sadat to calling for a ban on armed wings in Islamist groups and inter-cultural dialogue, and because those changes were justified through quite extensive publication of Islamist literature, there is a strong potential educational effect. More specifically, highlighting these cases can send a powerful message to sympathizers and potential young radicals in Muslim communities: the pioneers of Jihadism and the authors of a large part of *fiqh al-'unf* (Islamic jurisprudence justifying violence) literature have admitted that they had misinterpreted Islam, have renounced violence both behaviorally and ideologically, have called for cultural dialogue rather than a clash of civilizations, and have Islamically justified all of these things in their published literature. Clearly, therefore, the productive future for political Islamic groups lies in a rejection of violence and a concurrent embrace of non-violent engagement. In the words of one of the IG leaders: "this [de-radicalization] literature is the final say in the Islamic jurisprudence justifying violence" (Abd al-Majid 2007, 13). In other words, violent Jihad was ideologically buried by the hands of its own sons and, therefore, there is hope for a world without that type of Jihad.

Notes

1 A theory of de-radicalization

1 These terms will be defined later in this chapter.
2 By early 2008, most al-Jihad factions had joined the de-radicalization process. The main exceptions were the faction led by Ayman al-Zawahri, which joined al-Qa'ida, and two small factions in Egyptian prisons whose refusals were based on their rejection of the ideological component of the process (see for example Jahin 2007, 12).
3 In general, I shall use the acronym by which an Islamist group is best known, regardless of which language it is based on. Especially in the cases of Algerian, Moroccan and Tunisian groups, the acronyms are based on their French initials. Otherwise, acronyms are largely based on English initials.
4 Now the GSPC is known as al-Qa'ida in the Islamic Countries of al-Maghreb (QICM).
5 The moderation processes started to be "institutionalized" in the late 1990s – most notably in Egypt with the official Brotherhood–*Wasat* split in 1996 and in Turkey with the Justice and Development Party breaking away from the Virtue Party in 2001.
6 Terms like radicalization, de-radicalization and moderation shall be defined in the following section.
7 The affiliated militias include Al-Rahman Brigade (RB), Islamic League for Da'wa and Jihad (LIDD), Islamic Front for Armed Jihad (FIDA), as well as factions from the GIA and GSPC.
8 Groups which fall under that section of the definition will perform *Ijtihad* (a process of independent reasoning to interpret the sources of Islamic jurisprudence like the Quran and Sunnah) by themselves, producing new teachings that can range from radical (e.g. *al-Takfir Wa al-Hijra* and the GIA's interpretations) to moderate (e.g. Hasan al-Turabi's *fatwas*, allowing the marriage of female Muslims to non-Muslim males).
9 Groups which fall under that section of the definition will recycle old interpretations of Islamic jurisprudence's main sources (Quran, Sunnah, Ijma' and Qiyas), based on their understanding of those interpretations.
10 *Electoral democracy* is contrasted here with *liberal democracy* (electoral democracy coupled with constitutional liberalism) (Zakaria 1997; Diamond 1999). Liberal democracy includes extensive provisions for protecting minorities against the tyranny of the majority. It also requires the absence of reserved domains of power for certain social groups (like the military in Turkey, the clergy in Iran or Jews in Israel).
11 That is "the institutional arrangements for arriving at political decisions in which individuals acquire the power to decide by means of a competitive struggle for the people's vote" (Schumpeter 1950, 269).
12 Most of the times, they emphasize it to the point of ochlocracy and tyranny of the majority.

13 Those include the rights of religious and ethnic minorities like the Copts in Egypt and the Berbers in Algeria.

14 For example atheists, gays and Baha'is.

15 Those include the MB in Egypt, the FIS in Algeria, IRP in Tajikistan, *Islah* (Reform) Party in Yemen, The Islamic Party, Supreme Islamic Council and *Da'wa* Party in Iraq and National Outlook Movement and its associated parties in Turkey.

16 The term "liberal-Islamist" could be even contradictory.

17 When compared to Islamist movements. Their policies will look much less liberal when compared to mainstream liberal-democratic parties.

18 Many of the radical Islamist groups use violent tactics. Others advocate violence as a method of change without using it. For example, the Islamic Liberation Party argues that a military coup would be the ideal method of Islamist change (Nawaz 2007, 5, Jabir 1990, 277–287). Their rhetoric and literature advocate sweeping changes but they do not participate in violent tactics. Instead, they call on the military to topple secular regimes, take over and impose Islamic laws.

19 The concept will be defined below.

20 A militant is defined here as a person who takes up arms in pursuit of a political, social or ideological cause(s).

21 Both movements fought for the reestablishment of the electoral process and additionally, in the IRP case, for the withdrawal of the Russian forces.

22 Ideologically, those movements define Jihad as mainly violent struggle and perceive it as a continuous sacred duty. For them, fighting seems to be an end in itself.

23 Although in several cases the Algerian AIS, for example, issued violent threats against civilians, most notably journalists (Hafez 2000, 583). No operations were carried out however and the AIS did not take responsibility for attacks on civilians (Mizraq 2006).

24 Examples of increasing the level of violence would be expanding the selection of targets to include civilians, indiscriminate violence and, in techniques, suicide bombings. After 1994, the methods utilized by the Algerian GIA exemplify increasing the level of violence.

25 The main example is the Egyptian Islamic Group which – based on their interpretation of Islam – still rejects democracy. However, their newly developed ideology delegitimizes violence and accepts "the other" – not necessarily as an "enemy."

26 Like the IG and al-Jihad in Egypt and the de-radicalized factions from the GIA and the GSPC in Algeria (see Chapters 5 and 6).

27 See Chapters 4 and 5 for more elaboration on these case studies.

28 See Chapter 5 for more elaboration on al-Jihad case. Also, the Indonesian Islamic Group and the Libyan Fighting Islamic Group can be viewed as potential cases of substantive de-radicalization. In the Libyan case for example, their de-radicalization literature has been published, but significant internal conflicts remain, with factions joining al-Qa'ida instead of de-radicalizing (Hasan 2008, 6).

29 In addition to AIS-affiliated militias like the LIDD and the FIDA as well as factions within the GIA and the GSPC. Also, the Tajik IRP is another example of pragmatic de-radicalization.

30 An example of a higher level of moderation is accepting liberal democracy as opposed to electoral democracy.

31 Subscribing to more than one ideological trend within the same armed Islamist movement is usually an indication of factionalization and potential internal violence.

32 The time period depends on the country. In Egypt, for example, these characteristics were established in the 1970s. In Syria, they were established in the late 1980s.

33 Hamas (Palestinian MB) is a main exception.

34 But not necessarily branches of the Muslim Brothers.

35 The mainstream autonomous MB branch in Algeria.

36 Currently the Felicity Party, and previously the National Order, National Salvation, Welfare and Virtue Parties.

37 This is in addition to the often conflicting understanding of Islam provided by these specific individuals.

38 For example, the Salafi faction within the Algerian FIS (led by Ali Belhaj and Hashemi Sahnoni) refused to participate in Algerian municipal (1990) and parliament-ary (1991) elections before getting a *fatwa* from the Saudi Mufti, Sheikh Abdul Aziz Ibn Baz and the Syrian Albanian Sheikh, Nasr al-Din Al-Albani. Both are leading figures in the transnational Salafi movements (Sahnoni 2000, 14; al-Qasim 2000).

39 Also known as Wahabism – although the term is unacceptable to Salafis since it implies that they are followers of Muhammad Ibn Abdul Wahab (father of contem-porary Salafism in Saudi in Arabia – 1703–1792) and not the *salaf.* Also the term Wahabi has a strong negative connotation attached to it in many parts of the Sunni-majority (like in Central Asia and the Caucasus) and Shi'ite-majority countries (like in Iran, Azerbaijan and Bahrain).

40 See Chapters 3, 4 and 5 for more elaboration.

41 The group was known by this name in the state-owned media and other outlets. The actual name of the group was the "Muslims Group." This group turned violent in the mid-1970s.

42 See Chapter 4 for more elaboration on this process and the role of internal interaction in bolstering it.

43 Also see the details in Chapter 4.

44 For a detailed analysis of the process of radicalization of that group see (Mahfuz 1988, 81–150; Ibrhaim 1980).

45 See Chapter 2 for details.

46 The term was coined by Mahfouz Nahnah, the leader of MSP, which represents the mainstream Algerian Muslim Brothers. He gave them that title to distinguish them from other Islamist movements with international connections like the MB and the Salafis (Shahin 1997, 120; Burgat, François and William Dowell 1997, 317). The title had a negative connotation in the 1980s but it was accepted by the adherents of this trend in the 1990s.

47 Ikhwanism has had a strong impact on al-Jaz'ara thought, although al-Jaz'ara affili-ates tend to deny it. For example, when asked about the books that influenced their ideas and behavior, al-Jaz'ara leaders cite MB books in addition to those of Bennabi (Mezraq 2006).

48 The other faction being the Salafis.

49 Since the book is concerned primarily with de-radicalization (not moderation), the MB are covered only from 1940 (when the SA was established) until the 1970s (when the SA was completely dismantled).

50 The "other" is defined here as any social actor or entity who/which is not Islamist or who/which is not recognized by the movement(s) under study as "Islamist."

51 In other words, external social interaction takes place between an Islamist movement and what it perceives as the "other."

52 Theological training and credentials and a history of issuing *fatwas* usually help in legitimizing the leader to the followers.

53 Usually armed action against "secular" national regimes or against a foreign military presence or invasion.

2 The good, the bad and the ugly: moderation, radicalization and de-radicalization in Islamist movements

1 As defined in Chapter 1.

2 Also referred to as "frustration–aggression" models.

3 Although relative deprivation theory explicitly addresses the issue of upper class expectations and discontents, the literature on Islamist radicalization tends to focus on lower classes, and therefore advances the notion that absolute deprivation and poverty

causes social alienation followed by radicalization (see for example Davis 1984, Dekmejian 1988).

4 This argument does not belong to structural–psychological approaches. I mention it here due to its relation with the identity-based "cultural defense" approach as well as due to the fact that it is common in the literature, media and sometimes political rhetoric.

5 This is the point where the two approaches differ. Whereas the cultural defense approach argues that radicalization occurs in reaction to cultural imperialism, the political culture approach argues that radicalism can be traced to, and legitimized by, classical Islamic scriptures.

6 Like SCIRI, *al-Da'wa* Party and, to a lesser extent, the Islamic Party (Muslim Brothers in Iraq).

7 Like the Islamic Society led by the former president as well as *Mujahidiyn* leader Burhannudin Rabbani and the Islamic Union in Afghanistan led by former *Mujahidiyn* leader, Abd Rabb al-Rasul Sayyaf. The Union is now known as the Islamic Call Organization. In addition, the Northern Alliance that collaborated with the US to overthrow the Taliban in 2001 was mainly an Islamist coalition.

8 The Egyptian MB is an interesting and rich case. Given 55 years of repression and exclusion, it passed through phases of radicalization (1954–1969), de-radicalization (1969–1973) and then moderation (1973–Present) (see Chapters 3 and 4, for a details on these transformations).

9 The pressures, however, were by no means equivalent to the pressure tactics employed in Algeria.

10 The different effects of political repression shall be further elaborated upon throughout the book.

11 The critique of this argument is discussed in the following section.

12 As mentioned in Chapter 1, the largest and the most popular of these movements belong to the "electoral" category. This means that they are unarmed and believe/participate in electoral democracy.

13 Ideology, however, is still a variable. Al-Jihad has followed the IG's lead and initiated a de-radicalization process in 2007.

14 Hamzeh followed this article 11 years later with a more comprehensive study of Hizbullah's transformations in his book *In the Path of Hizbullah* (2004).

15 In Chapter 1, I define *Moderation* as a process of relative change within Islamist groups that can take place on two levels. On the ideological level, the key transformation is the acceptance of democratic principles and the de-legitimization of violence against the state and/or national political rivals. On the behavioral level, the key transformation is participation in the democratic process and the practical abandonment of violence as a method to achieve goals.

16 Although Hudson's argument is nuanced. He argues for "limited accommodation" of Islamists a policy that was largely pursed in the Jordanian case (between the Hashemite Regime and the Muslims Brothers/Islamic Action Front) (Hudson 1995, 235–241). He does not recommend full inclusion of Islamists in a political process as a route towards moderation (Hudson 1995, 242–244).

17 Robinson's article did not distinguish between electoral and liberal democracy. Therefore, his conclusion about the MB/IAF being a force behind democratization is limited to the electoral dimension of the democratization process. The IAF/MB stances regarding women's issues for example is far from liberal (see Clark 2006, 541–553).

18 Schwedler (2006) also included the Yemeni case of the *Islah* Party.

19 There are also other reasons, mainly based on the independent variables the two authors chose to use. I will not discuss them here due to space limitations.

20 Clark points out that Islamists and secular liberals have different understandings of democracy, but she does not elaborate on their perspectives (Clark 2006, 542).

21 For example, Abdul Majid Zendani, the leader of the *Islah* Party, was the Emir of the

Arab-Afghans for a short period following the assassination of Abdullah Azzam, the "godfather" of the Arab-Afghans.

22 I also demonstrate this through the examination of the de-radicalization cases in Algeria and Egypt in the following chapters.

23 The Egyptian MB represents the spiritual leadership of the other MB international branches. The decision of the General Guide of the Egyptian branch is perceived as non-binding recommendations to the other branches (see al-Za'atra 2005, 6).

24 El-Ghobashy has overstated her case a bit here. It is true that the MB was secretive in the period between the mid-1950s and early 1970s, but this was mainly a reaction to survive under Nasser's repression. It is also true that the MB had a secret armed wing that primed in the 1940s. However, the organization as a whole did not adopt a secretive policy. In addition, their political behavior can hardly be interpreted as "antidemocratic." Hasan al-Banna, the founder of the MB, has participated in parliamentary elections as early as 1942 (Mitchell 1969, 307). In most of their history, the MB was neither "highly secretive" nor "antidemocratic."

25 The volume investigates the reasons behind the AKP electoral victory in 2002 and assesses the possibilities for another victory in 2007. Most of the contributors predict a 2007 electoral victory if the AKP continues its relentless pursuit of the EU membership as well as if it continues to moderate its Islamist discourse.

26 Since I have outlined the approach and its critique before in the section on radicalization, I shall move on directly to the case study here: the *Wasat* Party.

27 I define de-Radicalization as a process of relative change within Islamist movements, in which a radical group reverses its ideology and begins to de-legitimize the use of violent methods to achieve political goals as well as accepting gradual social, political and economic changes within a pluralist context. A group undergoing a *de-radicalization* process does not have to abide by democratic principles. De-radicalization can occur on the behavioral level as well. On that level, de-radicalization means abandoning the use of violence to achieve political goals without ideological de-legitimization.

28 Although, Karam Zuhdi, the head of *Shura* Council of the IG, said in an interview on al-Jazeera Network that the IG's leadership will reassess its position on democracy and if it finds that its interests coincide with participating in elections, it "might" participate (Zuhdi 2006).

29 Also see Chapter 1 for the theoretical argument/framework and figures.

30 The talks with al-Jihad Organization and the debates within the movement date back to 1997. However, the activation of the de-radicalization process has started recently in 2007.

3 Historical overviews of de-radicalization cases

1 Chapter 6 demonstrates the reasons behind that failure.

2 In general, the SA is a translation of *al-Nizam al-Khass* (can be also translated as the Special Regime or Structure). The SA is also referred to as *al-Jihaz al-Sirri* (Secret Apparatus), *al-Tanzim al-Khass* (Special Organization) and *al-Tanzim al-Sirri* (Secret Organization) (Mitchell 1969; Ramadan 1993; Lia 1998). Ahmed Adel Kamal, a senior commander in the SA, mentions that the post-1953 armed wing that was restructured under the second General Guide Hasan al-Hudaybi and led by Yusuf Tal'at was called *al-Tanzim al-Sirri* (Kamal 1987, 290, 331). Ramadan mentions that only the leadership of SA was referred to as *al-Jihaz al-Sirri*, although he uses the two aforementioned terms interchangeably throughout his book (Ramadan 1993).

I use *al-Nizam al-Khass* (Special/Private Apparatus) to contrast and separate it from *al-Nizam al-'Amm* (General/Public Apparatus), the term used by MB leaders to describe the public bodies of the organization including the administrative, consultative and executive bodies as well as the non-secret paramilitary bodies like the Rover Scouts and the Battalions (Lia 1998, 101; Abdul Khaliq 2004, episode 2). Also, *al-Nizam al-Khass* is usually the term that the MB leaders use when referring to their armed wing (see for example the commentary of Salih Abu Ruqqayq, one of the MB leaders, on Mitchell 1979, 189; see also Abdul Khaliq 2004; Akif 2004).

3   Known in Arabic as *Qism al-Wihdat*, the UD was mainly responsible for propagating the ideology of the MB (*da'wah*) in the army and the police force. Unlike the SA, armed operations were not assigned to the UD as an institution (Shadi 1984, 29–34; Kamal 1987, 183). However, some of its members engaged in violent operations in 1948 as well as in the early 1950s, following orders from its commander, Police Major Salah Shadi (Shadi 1984, 34–40; Kamal 1987, 185).

4   The dearth of impartial studies in the Arabic language was commented on by General Salah Nasr, the former head of the Egyptian General Intelligence (1957–1967). The latter mentions in his memoirs that the history of the MB and their confrontations with successive Egyptian regimes deserves impartial and intensive study away from political/ideological biases and journalistic propaganda (Nasr 1984, 118). Nasr is hardly an impartial (or a less controversial) figure, given that he spent most of his tenure cracking down on the MB. Coming from him, however, the statement is significant. I should also note here that studies of the MB in the English literature are generally less biased and not as politically/ideologically motivated as the ones in Arabic. Examples include the two excellent works done by Richard Mitchell (1969) and Brynjar Lia (1998).

5   See for example the memoirs of Salah Shadi, former head of the UD and one of the main links between Nasser and MB (Shadi 1981) compared to those of Ahmad Adel Kamal, a leading commander in the SA (Kamal 1987). The memoirs of the latter were written as a reaction to those of the former (Kamal 1987, 17). Also, see the memoirs of Zaynab al-Ghazali, a leading figure in the so-called "1965 Organization" and the former head of Muslim Sisters Society (al-Ghazali 1989), which mainly contradict those of Farid Abdul Khaliq, al-Banna's assistant and disciple and one of the very influential figures in the MB history (Abdul Khaliq 1987; 2004).

6   Tariq al-Bishri is a historian and a former constitutional court judge. He was perceived in Egypt as a leftist until the late 1970s and early 1980s. Currently, he represents the relatively moderate Islamist *Wasatiyya* trend close to the *Wasat* Islamists.

7   Muhammad Abduh (1849–1905) was an Egyptian jurist, religious scholar and reformer. He is considered by many scholars to be the founder of, or a main contributor to, Islamic modernist thought.

8   Sometimes it is translated as the "Nationalist Party."

9   In Islamic jurisprudence, *al-bay'a* is understood to be a conditional oath of loyalty to the new ruler, mainly to obey and defend him as long as he upholds and follows Islamic injunctions. In the case of al-Banna and his followers, it meant a vow/ promise to struggle for their understanding of Islam. In his memoirs, al-Banna used that strong term (*al-bay'a*) to describe the vow given to him by his disciples (al-Banna 1966, 87).

10 Part of the funding for that mosque came from the Suez Canal Company (al-Banna 1966, 110) and that created the earliest controversy about the MB. The company was owned by British and French shareholders and was perceived as an "embodiment of imperialist domination in Egypt" (Lia 1998, 41). Many Egyptian historians perceive this funding as "evidence" that the MB was a British creation or pawn (Mubarak 1995, 28–33; Sa'id 1990, 90). In defense of accepting that funding, al-Banna says in his memoirs that "the canal is our [Egyptian] canal, the sea our sea and the land is our land..." therefore he does not perceive the funding as problematic (al-Banna 1966, 111).

11 The building of the girls' school was finished in 1932.

12 *Al-Nadhir* can be translated more accurately as the "Alarming Harbinger."
13 The MBN folded due to an internal conflict between its editor-in-chief and al-Banna (Lia 1998, 97).
14 I show below the contradictions in the ideology, rhetoric and behavior of al-Banna with respect to the issues of violence and democracy.
15 The MB has had seven General Guides since its establishment. Those were Hasan al-Banna (1928–1949), Hasan al-Hudaybi (1951–1973), 'Umar al-Tilmisani (1973–1987), Muhammad Hamid Abul Nasr (1987–1996), Mustafa Mashhur (1996–2002), Ma'mun al-Hudaybi (2003–2004) and Muhammad Mahdi Akif (2005–present). There were also two provisional Guides running the MB's daily affairs during the selection processes: Ahmad H. al-Baquri (1949–1951) and Muhammad Hilal (2004–2005).
16 This significantly changed in 2004 after the death of Ma'mun al-Hudaybi, the sixth Guide. The "selection from above" process was among the main reasons that caused the famous MB-Wasat split in 1996, as well as internal factionalization.
17 Most of these characteristics are vague and contradictory. It can be argued here that al-Banna's heritage is more organizational and less ideological/ideational.
18 Also, behaviorally, the MB supported the decision of the Revolutionary Command Council (RCC) to dissolve all political parties in January 1953. Many historians perceive this action as the MB's contribution to the destruction of the nascent democratic process in Egypt (Ramadan 1993, 134; Mubarak 1995, 41). In 1954 however, the MB's leadership realized that this was a mistake and insisted on the reinstallation of civilian leadership and the return of the army officers to their barracks (Abdul Khaliq 2004, episode 9, 10). Hence, the MB's position on democracy fluctuated pragmatically without a clear ideological preference, at least until the 1970s.
19 Depending on the source, the SA was established between 1938 and 1940 (see the next section for more details).
20 Although there is ample evidence that al-Banna wanted to avoid a confrontation with the British, at least until the end of World War II in 1945 (See for example Ramadan 1993, 42–44).
21 The *al-Wafd* (The Delegation) and *Misr Al-Fatah* (The Young Egypt) Parties both had armed wings that were disbanded in 1938 (see Jankowski 1970 for a detailed account).
22 All accounts agree that the SA was established before al-Banna's internment. If Ramadan's argument was correct, the SA should have been established after al-Banna's internment. Moreover, in 1947, one of the MB student leaders, Mustafa Mu'min, asked al-Banna to have an SA section responsible for protecting university students from police brutality, after two incidents in which the police used excessive violence. Al-Banna denied the request twice. Mu'min established his own armed group but it was dismantled later by the SA (Kamal 1987, 149). This gives more credit to the argument that the purpose of the SA, at least in al-Banna's vision, was more related to anti-colonial struggle. However, the SA, once strong and institutionalized, was operating almost autonomously on the national level, especially under the charismatic leadership of Abdul Rahman al-Sanadi (1944–1953).
23 Islamic obligation/duty required to be performed by every individual Muslim like prayers.
24 Islamic obligation/duty for the whole community of believers (*ummah*). The Muslim individual is not required to perform it as long as a sufficient number of community members fulfill it.
25 Oath of allegiance given by an MB member to the MB leaders.
26 The operation was known in the media as "New Year's Eve Bombs."
27 The SA had an intelligence unit that was responsible for gathering information on Egyptian political parties, paramilitary groups and the Egyptian-Jewish community (Kamal 1987, 129). That unit started gathering information on pro-Zionism Egyp-

tian Jews starting in 1944 (Kamal 1987, 122). They also gathered information and studied the movements of leading Egyptian politicians (Kamal 1987, 127). Also, the UD was responsible for bombing other Jewish civilian targets including the Jewish Alley in June 1948 and the Jewish-owned Chikoreil Company in July 1948 (Kamal 1987, 185).

28 This is despite the fact that Kamal is staunchly defending al-Sanadi in his memoirs. Kamal described al-Sanadi as a true commander and a hero of Islam (Kamal 1987, 17, 121). He has a whole section in his memoirs titled "Saluting the Special Apparatus," in which he honours the SA and its leadership (Kamal 1987, 121).

29 The highest court of appeal in Egypt.

30 Al-Hudaybi was a man of few words and was not a talented and eloquent speaker like al-Banna. Abdul Khaliq mentions that the MB members were disappointed when their weekly lecture (The Tuesday Talk) given by al-Hudaybi lasted only a few minutes in a time of a severe crisis (Abdul Khaliq 2004, episode 8). Kamal mentions that al-Hudaybi's personal behavior was perceived as arrogant by many MB members (Kamal 1987, 251).

31 Fayez was the provisional commander of the SA in 1948–1949, after the arrest of al-Sanadi in the so-called "The Jeep Case." The case was based on several important SA documents that were being transported in a Jeep car that fell into the hands of the Egyptian Political Police on 15 November 1948. Therefore it led to the arrest of several SA leaders and operatives. The case is important as it sheds light on the internal structure, policies, training, divisions and plans of the SA between 1941 and 1948 (al-Sisi 1986, 216; Kamal 1987, 269–287).

32 A former top-level commander in the SA who wrote his version of the history of that organization in two books (al-Sabbagh 1989; 1998).

33 Abdul Nasser, Abdul Hakim 'Amir, Salah Salim, Khalid Muhydin and other members of the RCC gave the *bay'a* to the MB and even to the SA under al-Sanadi at different points in time. Nasser and others also trained the SA members before and during the Arab-Israeli war in 1948 (Shadi 1980, 3; Shadi 1984, 123–131; Hamruch 1974, 109, 118, 145; al-Ashmawy 1991, 91; Muhyidin 1992, 45; Abdul Khaliq 2004, episode 9).

34 This is despite the fact that Nasser's coup was not an Islamist one.

35 Farid Abdul Khaliq and other MB leaders called this action a disastrous mistake and political naivety on the part of Audeh, since the latter dismissed the demonstrators without any guarantees from Nasser (Abdul Khaliq 2004, episode 12). Audeh was arrested the very same night and was executed with other MB and SA leaders in January 1955 (Ramada 1993, 137–139).

36 He was also a former Patriotic Party activist who co-founded an anti-colonial paramilitary movement called the Black Hand during the British rule of Egypt.

37 Farid Abdul Khaliq mentions that he met with Qutb in 1964 based on the orders of the *murshid* to dissuade him from leading the reorganization attempt (especially its paramilitary dimension). He told Qutb that he had no training in covert action and that the *murshid* and himself were ideologically opposed to subversive activities (Abdul Khaliq 2004, episode 14; Ramadan 1993, 313).

38 It is useful to mention here that Salah Nasr, the head of the intelligence then, said to Nasser that there was no reason to execute Qutb and the rest of the activists. He also warned Nasser of possible consequences. According to Nasr, Nasser replied by saying that he did not sleep at night because he had the same argument with his wife, who asked him to stop the executions. However, Nasser told Nasr that preemption was necessary. "I have to eat them for lunch before they eat us for dinner" he said to Nasr (Nasr 1984, 119–120).

39 As opposed to pieces of literature written by a poet. Also, Farid Abdul Khakiq claims that Qutb had written elaborate notes to clarify *Milestones* and to distance himself from potential Takfiri ideologies during the military investigations of 1965.

When asked about the location of those notes, Abdul Khaliq replied "ask the security services" (Abdul Khaliq 2004, episode 15).

40 I will discuss the causes behind the lack of organizational resistance to al-Hudaybi's decision in Chapter 4.

41 The latter thought was not fully developed in the late 1960s and early 1970s when *Preachers Not Judges* was written.

42 The book's title is *Ma'alim fi al-Tariq* and it is usually translated as *Milestones* or *Signposts*. It can also be translated as *Signs on the Road*.

43 The concept denies any human the right to legislate. It attributes this right exclusively to God. Following from that, any human who legislates, especially if his/her legislation is contrary to what God has "ordered," is an idol (*Taghut*). Therefore, the concept legitimizes a confrontation with any human/regime perceived as a legislator. Two decades later, the IG picked up the argument and recycled it in *Another God with Allah? Declaration of War on the People's Assembly* [Parliament] (IG Research Unit 1990).

44 General Fu'd 'Allam, former head of the Egyptian State Security Investigations (SSI), claims that the SSI is the "true" author of that book and al-Hudaybi just "agreed" to put his name on it. Al-Hudaybi died in November 1973 and cannot comment on the claim. But other MB leaders mock that claim and consider it to be ludicrous. Allam's claim was not supported by any other source (Allam 1996, 118).

45 Moreover, Karim al-Anaduly, the leader of the Technical Military Academy group – a small group that attempted to overthrow Sadat's regime in 1974 (see more details in Ibrahim 1980) – visited al-Hudaybi in 1973 and offered his allegiance to the MB as well as a plan to reorganize an armed wing. Al-Hudaybi declined the offer and severed contacts with al-Anadoly. Zaynab al-Ghazali for her part, connected al-Anaduly with Salih Sariyya, a Palestinian professor who latter became the principal ideologue and the spiritual leader of the Technical Military Academy group (Mahfuz 1988, 21; Ukasha 2002; Abdul Khaliq 2004, episode 14).

46 The MB still support "anti-colonial" armed struggles like those in Palestine, Lebanon, Chechnya and Kashmir. However, these particular cases are widely perceived in Muslim-majority countries as fair and legitimate struggles. Therefore, the support of these struggles is not limited to the MB only and includes other political groups, both Islamist and secular.

47 The author wishes to thank the *Middle East Journal* for the permission to use the following article: Ashour, Omar. "Lions Tamed? An Inquiry into the Causes of De-Radicalization of the Egyptian Islamic Group." *Middle East Journal* vol. 61, no. 4 (Autumn 2007): 596–625.

48 *The Death of the Pharaoh of Egypt* authored by Tal'at Fu'ad Qasim (alias Abu Talal al-Qasimi), the former spokesperson of the IG (Qasim 1992) and *A River of Memoirs* authored by eight members of the IG's Consultative Council (Zuhdi *et al.* 2003). The latter book only addresses some of the history and the dynamics of the de-radicalization process.

49 These were Abdul Mun'im Abul Futuh, Issam al-Aryan and Abul 'ila Madi respectively. Issam al-Aryan is currently the director of the Political Bureau of the Muslim Brothers. Abdul Mun'im Abul Futuh is a member in the GO of the MB. Abul 'ila Madi was a leading activist in the MB. In 1996, he resigned from the MB and co-founded the *Wasat* Party.

50 A derivative of the word *salaf* (predecessors or ancestors), Salafism is a school of thought in Sunni Islam that attributes its beliefs to first three Islamic generations: the *sahaba* (companions of the Prophet) and the two succeeding generations. Salafism believes that pure Islam was practiced by these first three generations. "Innovations" in religious matters are unacceptable to Salafis. Vaguely and broadly defined, the term "innovations" could range from modern ideas like democracy and to different understandings of Islam like mystical Islam (Sufism) and Shi'ite Islam.

51 According to the *Mithaq* (Charter of the IG), Jihad (defined here as armed struggle) is one way to achieve sociopolitical change. The other two means being *da'wa* (proselytizing) and '*amr bil ma'ruf wal nahyi 'an al-munkar* (ordering virtue and preventing vice – OVPV) (Ibrahim *et al.* 1984, 16). The latter method could be violent or non-violent.

52 Al-Zumur was the most senior military officer in the group, a major in the military intelligence. Later on, he held several leading positions in the broader Egyptian Jihadi movement, including the leadership of the Jihad organization and membership in the *Shura* Council of the IG. During the meeting of September 1981, he staunchly opposed the assassination of Sadat. His opposition was mainly due to pragmatism (Hafiz 2005).

53 The most famous of Sadat's assassins and practically the leader of the group that carried out the assassination.

54 Abdul Rahman was sentenced by a US court for his role in the 1993 World Trade Center bombing.

55 Mostly from Cairo and al-Sharqiyya Governorate in the Delta region.

56 'Issam al-Qamary is credited for bringing up this theological argument as well as for most of the work in that document (al-Siba'i 2002, 11).

57 It has to be mentioned that in most cases the IG did not practice that ideological preference. IG members have engaged in killing soldiers during the confrontation with the regime in 1981 and between 1992 and 1997. They still however give verbal support for that ideological preference (Yusuf 2006, 125). When it came to organizational alliances, however, ideological preference mattered. Al-Jihad has attempted to ally itself with Takfiri groups which do not uphold the *al-'uzr* concept. The IG on the other hand did not consider these groups as Sunni and therefore avoided allying with them due to their stance on the *al-'uzr* concept.

58 Sometimes they are also referred to as "second-generation leaders."

59 Abdul Ghani was also one of the main defendants in the trials of the assassination of Rif'at al-Mahjub, the former speaker of the Egyptian parliament in 1990.

60 By *da'wa*. I mean calling for and propagating IG ideologies. IG activists usually interpret that kind of *da'wa* as a call for the "true" Islam.

61 Hence, according to S. Abdul Ghani, it was called *Qism Himayat al-Da'wa* (Protection of the *Da'wa* Unit) (Abdul Ghani 2005, 124).

62 Al-Islambulli is a middle-ranking leader in the IG and the brother of Khalid al-Islambulli, Sadat's assassin. He had recently joined *al-Qa'ida* with other IG members who were disaffected with the ideological and behavioral transformations.

63 That violence was mainly exercised when IG members were trying to change "vices" by "hand" (force) in areas where the IG had a strong presence. The most notable example was preventing belly-dancers and female singers from performing in weddings – an action that clashed with traditional Egyptian customs and led to brawls with the wedding organizers. One of those brawls ended up in a gunfight in which one of the wedding organizers was shot in 1987 (al-'Awwa 2006, 116).

64 Civilian courts as opposed to military and state security courts – both are emergency courts that are widely perceived as unfair and illegitimate.

65 This was a policy that General Zaki Badr introduced in the late 1980s. The emergency law allows the state security forces and the police to detain suspects for two months without brining them to court and formally charging them. After two months, the detainee has to be brought before a court or released. To avoid that, the state security agency would issue a report every two months saying that the detainee was released but he/she resumed his/her "illegal" activities and therefore was re-detained. The reality was that the detainee was released "bureaucratically" but not practically. Some detainees stayed in prison based on this bureaucratic cycle for more than ten years.

66 With the exception of the period between January 1991 and June 1992, which was

relatively peaceful compared to the high-profile assassinations before and afterwards.

67 Dayrut is a small town located in the Assyut governorate in Upper Egypt. The Dayrut events started as a dispute over a 200LE ($40 US) financial loan between a Muslim and a Copt. The dispute led to a violent clash that left two Muslims and one Copt dead. Thinking in traditional vendetta terms – which are widespread in Upper Egypt – IG members interfered to avenge the two Muslims by killing one more Copt. Instead, the intervention led to multiple clashes leaving 17 Copts dead. The security forces responded with a wide-scale crackdown that included assassinating the IG Emir of Dayrut, Sheikh 'Arafa al-Gami, in front of the mosque in which he had just given his Friday sermon. The situation kept on escalating in Upper Egypt until the notorious Luxur massacre of November 1997 (State Security General 2002, Hafiz 2005, 137).

68 In which 58 tourists were gunned down by IG terrorists.

69 As opposed to systematic torture in state security building, mainly during investigation or as a form of revenge.

70 To force possible guerrillas from their hideouts inside these cultivated lands.

71 Most notably Rifa'i Taha, who headed the *Shura* Council abroad at that time. As result of Taha's condemnation, he was fired from the position and was replaced by Mustafa Hamza, a supporter of the ceasefire.

72 Most notably Ayman al-Zawahri, currently the second man in al-Qa'ida network (Hashim 2000, 1).

73 The reasons will be addressed in detail in Chapter 5.

74 Mainly to avoid violence and intimidation during the process of "ordering virtue"!

75 Even some of the former militant leaders refuse to support the continuation of the de-radicalization of other armed Islamist movements, most notably Ali Ben Hajar, the former commander of the dismantled Islamic League for Da'wa and Jihad (LIDD) (see interview in *al-Sharq al-Awsat* 2007, 6).

76 During their high-school years in the mid-to-late 1960s, al-Zawhiri, Isma'il Tantawy, Nabil al-Bura'i, Essam al-Qamary, Sayyid Imam al-Sharif and other future Jihad leaders used to take religious lessons in the house of an Azhari Sheikh. One day the Sheikh cancelled the lesson as he was sad for the execution of Qutb in 1966. They took an oath back then to avenge Qutb's execution (al-Zayyat 2005, 135–136; 'Ukasha 2002).

77 For more elaboration see the subsection "Jihadi Splits and Distinctions" in the section discussing the background of the IG.

78 Al-Zawahri was the Emir of al-Jihad organization from 1993 till 1998. He is also known as Abdul Mu'iz and Dr. Ahmed (al-Siba'i 2002b, 10).

79 Al-Sharif was the Emir of al-Jihad from 1987 till 1993. He led the de-radicalization process in 2007. He is also known as Abdul Qadir Ibn Abdul Aziz and Dr. Fadl.

80 Al-Sharif is a medical doctor by training. However, he is considered by many in the Jihadi trend as a *'alim* (scholar of Islamic Jurisprudence) who can issue *fatwas*. He is also considered a principal ideologue by groups like al-Qa'ida, al-Jihad and others. Two of his books were taught in al-Qa'ida, al-Jihad and other Jihadist camps in Afghanistan: *Talab al-'ilm al-Sharif* (*Pursuing The Noble Science*) and *al-'umda fi I'dad al-'udda* (*The Pillar in Preparing the Equipment*) (al-Siba'i 2002b, 10, Ibrahim 2007). The latter book represents detailed theological arguments supporting Jihadi ideologies.

81 In a later stage, al-Masri became one of Bin Laden's deputies and a leading figure in al-Qa'ida network. He was killed in 2001 during a US air strike.

82 Later on, in early 1995, al-Panjsheiri became the military commander of al-Qa'ida. He is credited by other Jihadists for establishing al-Qa'ida's links and units in East Africa, especially in Somalia. He drowned in Lake Victoria in Kenya in 1996.

83 Al-Qamary was a Captain in the Armored Vehicles Unit in the Egyptian armed

forces. He participated in the October 1973 war and received several medals. He is considered to be one of the few military experts in al-Jihad organization prior to the experiences learned in Afghanistan.

84 This was inaccurate and misleading since there was not an independent existing organization by the name of "Tala'i' al-Fatih." Some of the persons detained in these sweeps were members and middle-ranking leaders of al-Jihad Organization.

85 Composed of 25 leading members, the Constitutive Council represents the *Shura* Council of the Jihad. It is the main body in which deliberations take place before decision-making.

86 Al-Jihad's organizational body which is in charge of issuing *fataws*. It is composed of leading members who have theological training.

87 Other movements that belong to Salafi-Jihadi current uphold the same ideological concept most notably the IG in Egypt until 1997.

88 In the Jihadi literature, they usually mean by that the "secular," national regimes.

89 In the Jihadi literature, this term usually means states that are perceived as "enemies of Islam" by Jihadists' most notably Israel.

90 Azzam and Zendani had no particular interest in fighting Arab regimes, and criticized that behavior in some of their writings.

91 The causes of the ideological shift are not that clear, despite voluminous speculation by specialists on Islamist movements (Gerges 2000; Rashwan 2002), former Jihad leaders (al-Siba'i 2002d, 11; Habib 2006), security experts (Allam 1996; Scheuer 2005, 7) and even journalists like CNN's Christiane Amanpour (Amanpour 2006). Although Bin Laden is not as ideologically sophisticated as al-Zawahiri, he might have influenced the ideology of the latter. Other potential causes include the defeat of al-Jihad Organization on the national level and therefore the lack of activism in Egypt, as well as the international arena's ripeness for a confrontation with the "other" in that period, due to the Qana massacre in 1996, the Israeli raids on Gaza and the West Bank, and the US air strikes against Iraq in 1998.

92 Five other Jihadist leaders signed that declaration with Bin Laden: Ayman al-Zawahiri representing the Egyptian Jihad, Rifa'i Taha representing the Egyptian IG (which later withdrew), Mawlawi Fadul Rahman representing the Pakistani Society of Scholars, Mir Hamza representing the Pakistani *Ansar* (Protagonists) Movement and Abdul Salam Muhammad representing the Bangladeshi Jihad Movement.

93 'Ukasha is a well-known commander in al-Jihad who was in charge of attacking the state-owned TV and Radio HQ in 1981 and declaring an Islamic revolution from there. He was also in charge of maintaining and nurturing foreign contacts, mainly with the Iranian Revolutionary Guard in 1980–1981 (Ukasha 2002).

94 Na'im was a co-founder of the first nucleus of al-Jihad Organization in 1968 with al-Zawahiri and others.

95 More elaboration on the causes of successes and failures of de-radicalization attempts of al-Jihad Organization are found in Chapter 6.

96 The latter was handed over from Yemen in 2004 and then "disappeared" for three years, before the Egyptian regime declared that he is still alive and present in the Scorpion prison south of Cairo in 2007 (al-Tawil 2004, 6; Zinah 2007, 1).

97 As mentioned before, the book was authored mainly to educate militants in Jihadist camps. It is considered an ideological/theological guide for groups like al-Jihad and al-Qa'ida.

98 "The Land of the Quiver" is an old poetic term in the Arabic-Islamic literature that refers to Egypt.

99 A commander close to the former Emir of al-Jihad Abbud al-Zummur.

100 One of al-Jihad leaders who was the deputy of al-Zawahiri in the mid-1990s.

101 Like Hani al-Siba'i (See al-Siba'i 2007).

102 Not necessarily from the FIS, but also from other Islamist groups.

103 Chabouti was a leading member of an armed Islamist movement that operated in

the 1980s under the leadership of Mustafa Bouya'li. The latter is perceived to be the founder of the first Jihadist movement in Algeria.

104 Makhloufi was a former pilot in the Algerian air force and an Afghan veteran during the war with the Soviets. Also, there is some controversy regarding the leadership of the MEI and the MIA centered on "who led what and when?" Several Algerian Islamists claim in published interviews that Chabouti led the MEI along with 'Ezzedin Ba'a and Makhloufi in 1992. They do not mention the MIA (see interviews in al-Tawil 1998, 59–62; 107–108). However, other interviews with Algerian Islamists who fought during the war claim that the two movements were separate, with Chabouti leading the MIA, Makhloufi leading the MEI and Ba'a, at a later stage, led an autonomous armed band operating in the center of Algeria and coordinating with the AIS (Hattab 1998, 6; Kharbanne 1998, 175; Sheikhy 2007, 7; Layada 2007, 6).

105 He is also known as Moh Levilly and he is from the Algerian Berber minority, like many of the leading figures in the Algerian armed Islamist movement (contrary to the common belief that the movement is dominated exclusively by Arabs).

106 Hence, Layada is usually referred to as the founder of the GIA in the literature on Algerian Islamist movements.

107 A small town between the provinces of Medea and Blida.

108 Although the GIA declared several times in the mid-1990s that it aims to establish an Islamic state and a caliphate, the rhetoric of its founder has changed significantly in 2007. In a recent interview with Layada, he claimed that he founded the GIA and fought the regime "in defense of the Algerian people" (Layada 2007, 6), rhetoric that is very similar to that of the AIS in the 1990s.

109 According to Ben Aicha, in 1993 there were AIS cells in Ain al-Defla, al-Chelif, Oran, Tissemsilt and other western regions (Ben Aicha 1996, 6).

110 Central Algeria was the domain of the GIA. The AIS did not want to confront the GIA on its turf. In an interview with Qamar al-Din Kherbanne, a FIS leader and an Afghan veteran, he described operating in central Algeria without the GIA's approval in that period (1992–1995) as a "death sentence" (Kharabnne 1998, 175).

111 Both the MIA and the GIA reject the ideas of democracy and electoral politics as un-Islamic.

112 That would be Rabih Kabir's faction, who heads the Executive Committee of the FIS abroad. This faction is known for its pragmatism, its relative conciliatory rhetoric and its continuous calls for a political solution. It upholds ideological elements from both *al-Jaz'ara* (Algerianization) trend and the MB's ideology. Also, both Kamal Qumazi and Ali Jeddi, co-founder of the FIS and members of its FIS Consultative Council, supported the faction on several occasions.

113 The GIA, for example, takes pride in that its affiliates attacked a border post before the cancellation of elections in November 1991 (GIA 1993, 6). The group perceived armed struggle (Jihad) as an eternal Islamic duty that should be carried out against "secular" regimes, regardless of their stance on democracy.

114 On 13 May 1994, the GIA considered itself the only legitimate Jihad organization in Algeria (GIA communiqué 1994, 2). It declared that all other Jihadist groups and individuals must join its ranks and give the *bay'a* to its Emir (Cherif Gousmi, alias Abu Abdullah Ahmad, at this point).

115 Said's real name is Belqasim Lounis (Boukra 2002, 197). In addition to his position in the FIS, he is also considered to be the uncrowned leader of *al-Jaz'ara* trend (Shahin 1997, 144–145; Anas 2001). Said, Rajjam and Abdul Baqi Sahrawi, a cofounder of the FIS, were the highest profile Islamist victims of the GIA.

116 Al-Zouabri only finished his second grade in elementary school (al-Zouabri 1999, 7). Only members of the post-1995 GIA (after Zitouni) considered him qualified theologically to issue *fatwas* (Kertali 2000, 8).

117 Several parties launched that third war. These include the GIA (al-Zouabri 1998, 1;

Hattab 1998, 6), segments within the Algerian military establishment (see Souidia 2001; al-Samraoui 2001; Aroua 2001) and government-sponsored militias (al-Samraoui 2003, 202–205).

118 The AIS declaration followed the IG's unilateral ceasefire in July 1997 and was produced in a very similar fashion (see the IG declarations in Zuhdi *et al.* 2003 and the AIS declaration in al-Hayat 1997, 1). However, Madani Mezraq strongly denies that the AIS's decision was influenced by the developments in Egypt (Mezraq 2005b, 6). The IG leaders in Egypt however do not deny that the Algerian case has influenced their decision to declare a ceasefire and de-radicalize (See for example Zuhdi *et al.* 2003, 123; Ibrhaim *et al.* 2005, 59–60).

119 Those three groups are affiliated ideologically with the *Jaz'ara* trend. They hold highly regard for Muhammad Said, who was killed by the GIA. His murder and the GIA's behavior drove them closer to the AIS.

120 Isma'il is also written in some literature as "Smain." Lamari is one of a few powerful generals who strongly influenced the Algerian political scene from 1992 until the present day. The others were Khalid Nazar, the incumbent Defense Minister at the time of coup; al-Arabi Belkhair, the incumbent Interior Minister at the time of the coup; Muhammad Lamari, the incumbent Commander of the Land Forces at the time of the coup and chief of staff from 1993 to 2004; Lamari's deputy General Sharif Fouaydal; Muhammad Médiène (alias Tawfiq) head of the military intelligence (DRS) (1988–Present); and to a lesser extent Generals Boughaba and Abdul Salam Bousharib (Razaqi, 2000a, 8; Hafez 2000, 590; Samraoui 2001; Ben Bella 2002; al-Saydawy 2002, 17).

121 Before the LCC, there was the so-called "Clemency Law" (CL) adopted by General Liame Zeroul, who became a president with the support of the army after the assassination of President Muhammad Boudiaf in 1993 and who won a very controversial presidential elections in 1995. The CL mainly limited itself to potential punishment of former guerrillas who surrendered and/or cooperated with the regime. The CL was unsuccessful in de-radicalizing militants however as only 500 militants surrendered their weapons to the regime based on it (this figure is acclaimed by the regime and unverified by independent sources) (see al-Sidawy 2007, 7). Also, there was a surge in violent tactics in the period between 1995 and 1998, including more than 200 massacres (Aroua 2001).

122 Full amnesty was given to militants who did not rape women, commit murder or place bombs in public places. The ones who committed any of those aforementioned crimes could be sentenced to a maximum of 12 years.

123 Depending on the source, the number of armed militants operating post-2000 ranges from 800 to 4,000 individuals (Ghimrasa 2006, 1). Most of them are operating under the banner of the GSPC, now QICM (Ghimrasa 2006, 1).

124 Except for crimes of rape and murder as well as placing bombs in public places.

125 The second zone is located in the Eastern part of Algiers. It includes its suburbs and the neighbouring towns and villages (Ghimrasa 2005, 6). Since Mustafa Buya'li's movement in the mid-1980s, the leaders of armed Islamists have tended to divide Algeria into zones of influence and have appointed an emir for each zone (al-Hayat 1994, 6; Hafez 2000, 576). Bouya'li's movement, the AIS, the GIA, the QICM and others followed the same organizational strategy. To a large degree, these divisions are similar to the way the Algerian army divides Algeria into military districts.

126 *Majlis al-A'yan* (The Elite Council) of the GSCP distributed a statement in August 2003, confirming that Hattab has resigned. However, in a recent interview, Hattab denies that he resigned and challenged the new leadership of the GSPC (Abu Mus'ab Abdul Wadud) to prove his resignation (Hattab 2007, 8).

127 As they appear in the literature of these groups and statements of their leaders during confrontation periods.

128 IG affiliates and sympathizers were implicated in the 1993 bombing of the World

Trade Center in New York City. However, the leadership never took responsibility for terror acts against the US and it stressed in the 1990s that it does not target the United States (see for example Zuhdi *et al.* 2003, 18). Also, there was an assassination attempt in 1995 against an Egyptian diplomat (or an intelligence agent) in Geneva, Switzerland. The Egyptian regime blamed the IG, but the leadership did not take responsibility.

4 The untold story: the de-radicalization of the armed wings of the Muslim Brothers

1 All these attempts were led by the same General Guide, Hasan al-Hudaybi and his "elite" faction.
2 As demonstrated later, the consequences partially include an attempt to assassinate Gamal Abdul Nasser in October 1954 and another one to topple his regime in 1964. This is in addition to the development of the Jihadi and Takfiri trends in the late 1960s.
3 Umar al-Tilmisani consolidated the de-radicalization process and led the MB into a moderation process that featured the permanent abandonment of violence and an endorsement of electoral democracy, with the aim of establishing an Islamic state through electoral methods (see for example the interviews with al-Tilmisani in al-Qa'ud 1985). The MB still upholds the non-violent and pragmatic legacies of al-Tilmisani, not only in Egypt but also in other countries like Algeria, Jordan and Kuwait.
4 Those variables are: charismatic leadership, social interaction, state repression and selective inducements.
5 Farid Abdul Khaliq, al-Banna's close associate, disciple and a long-time GO member, mentions in an interview that al-Banna thought that dismantling the SA could lead to its secession from the MB and therefore the birth of an independent armed Islamist organization in which al-Banna would not be the leader. Therefore, he did not want to dismantle the SA (Abdul Khaliq 2004, episode 5). Both Abdul Khaliq and Abu al-'ila Madi, a former MB leader and co-founder of *al-Wasat* Party, argue that al-Banna, in his last years, thought that establishing the SA was a "mistake" (Madi 2004; Abdul Khaliq 2004, episode 4).
6 As mentioned in Chapter 3, violent operations were not assigned to the UD as an institution (Shadi 1984, 29–34; Kamal 1987, 183). However, it was another armed institution within the MB whose members were either military men or policemen and it was headed by a police officer, Major Salah Shadi. In any case, some of the UD members engaged in armed operations (Shadi 1984, 34–40; Kamal 1987, 185).
7 In reference to al-Azhar University and Schools, since the leading figures in this faction and many of their followers graduated from there.
8 Mitchell mentions that Dallah's membership in the MB was "described as an introduction into the movement of 'Cadillacs and aristocracy'" (Mitchell 1979, 184).
9 Not to be confused with Salih al-'Ashmawy or, later on in the 1965 Organization, Ali 'Ashmawy. There are no blood relationships between these three figures.
10 Other sources also refer to the meetings of al-Hudaybi with the King in 1951 as "evidence" of the Palace's support. For example, al-Banna tried to meet the King several times in 1948 and 1949 before his assassination, but the King refused (see for example Mitchell 1979, 184; Abdul Khaliq 2004, episode 8).
11 According to Farid Abdul Khaliq and Hasan al-'Ashmawy, only two leading figures knew about al-Hudaybi's ties to al-Banna, given his sensitive position as a judge and the laws forbidding judges to be affiliated with political groups. The two figures were Munir Dallah and Hasan al-'Ashmawy (Abdul Khaliq 2004, episode 8, Al-'Ashmawy 1977, 41).
12 Al-Baquri describes some of the sentiments of the MB leaders following al-

Hudaybi's selection. When he was told he should give *al-bay'a* to al-Hudaybi, he was quoted as saying that any of the previous candidates ('Ashmawy, 'Abdin, al-Banna or himself) would have been a better choice.

13 In general, the position of the MB's "elite" faction was consistently anti-violence and anti-SA. However, my argument differs from that of Mitchell (1969), Ramadan (1993), Khattab (2001) and other researchers, as I show later that al-Hudaybi has supported, at least, the rearmament and the reorganization of the SA (it was then called the Secret Organization – SO) in 1954 and, partially, in 1964, mainly in response to state repression.

14 Although that was inaccurate since the MB's leadership in al-Isma'iliyya declared Jihad against the British in the same year (see for example Mitchell 1979, 191; see also the commentary of Abu Ruqayq on Mitchell 1979, 192). Also, the involvement of the SA/SO and its future commander, Yusuf Tal'at (1953–1954) in the Canal Zone has been well-documented (see for example Naguib 1955; al-Sharif 1957). Mitchell mentions that at least 300 MB and SA members participated in the Canal fighting in 1951 (Mitchell 1979, 193).

15 Al-Sabbagh mentions that he replied back by saying that "your honour [addressing al-Hudaybi] talks about the SA as if you were Ibrahim Abdul Hadi [Prime Minister of Egypt between December 1948 and July 1949, who cracked down on the MB and who the SA attempted to assassinate following al-Banna's assassination]" (al-Sabbagh 1998, 93).

16 As noted in Chapter 3, *al-Nizam al-'Amm* (General/Public Apparatus) is the term used by the MB leaders to describe the public bodies of the organization, including the administrative, consultative and executive bodies, as well as the non-secret para-military bodies like the Rover Scouts.

17 Al-Sabbagh says that this was the argument of Abdul Qadir Audeh, upheld later by Al-Hudaybi (see al-Sabbagh 1998, 92). He also argues that the idea of dismantling the SA initially started from within the SA ranks (al-Sabbagh 1998, 67–73). His argument will be discussed in the section on state repression and its consequences.

18 There is a controversy regarding the issue of whether or not al-Hudaybi knew about the existence of the SA before accepting the leadership of the MB. Mitchell (1979) and Ramadan (1993) argue that he did not know. However, Ramadan's argument is based on official "confessions" during the military tribunals of 1954, which are not credible given the conditions of torture and repression under which those "confessions" were extracted, as well the regime's forgery of those "confessions," as described by Ramadan himself, in addition to Mitchell and others. In his commentary on Mitchell (1979), Abu Ruqayq argues that al-Hudaybi knew about the SA before accepting the leadership (Mitchell 1979, 190). Abdul Khaliq (2004) supports that argument as well (Abdul Khaliq 2004, episode 8).

19 Al-Sanadi meant by that the fact that al-Hudaybi was selected by the members of the Guidance Office and not by three-quarters of the votes of the Constituent Board's members, as required by the MB's laws (see the laws in Mitchell 1979, 186, 299–302).

20 Those were Abdul Aziz Kamil, Muhammad Khamis Himmida and Hussein Kamal al-Din (Al-Sabbagh 1998, 117).

21 *'Usra* (pl. *'usar)* means "family" in Arabic, and it is the name that Hasan al-Banna chose for the smallest, constituent cells of the MB Organization. An *'usra* is usually composed of three or four Brothers and their commander (see Society of Muslim Brothers – 'Usar Unit 1953).

22 Before that, the *'usar* of the SA received their orders from the leadership of the SA. Theoretically, the latter should take their orders from the *murshid* directly, but that had not been the case since the late 1940s (see for example Kamal 1987, 236; Abdul Khaliq 2004, episode 4, 5).

23 Which usually required specific characteristics in the candidate, including following

orders without questioning them, as well as having a high level of physical conditioning.

24 In his extensive interview on *al-Jazeera*, Abdul Khaliq mentions a clear example of the problems emanating from the cult of secrecy surrounding the SA. Abdul Majid Hasan, al-Nuqrashi's assassin, was a member of the MB's Students Department headed by Abdul Khaliq. The latter did not know that Abdul Majid, the student under his command, was an SA operative (Abdul Khaliq 2004, episode 5). In the late 1940s, noticing the activities of the SA within the student ranks, Abdul Khaliq complained to al-Banna that the SA was recruiting students behind his back (Abdul Khaliq 2004, episode 5).

25 Different accounts of what happened inside the house exist. These accounts range from pushing al-Hudaybi around and verbally abusing him to putting a gun to his head to force him to sign his resignation (al-Tilmisani 1985, 101–102; Shadi 1981, 104–106; al-'Ashmawy 2005, 100; Kamal 1987, 284–285).

26 Given what happened in al-Hudaybi's house, the second account is more likely to be closer to the truth.

27 Later on, al-Ghazali became a leading scholar in Islamic thought. His ideas are widely regarded as anti-Salafism.

28 Kamal mentions that around 40 armed SA members were gathering in a house near the HQ of the MB where al-Hudaybi's supporters were making the decision to fire the dissidents. Kamal says that he dismissed them before they stormed the HQ with arms (Kamal 1987, 288).

29 Although Kamal challenges that by arguing that Tal'at was a good soldier, but that he was not suitable leadership material (Kamal 1987, 290).

30 As mentioned in Chapter 3, he is an army colonel and a co-founder of the Free Officers Movement. He is considered to have been the most experienced military commander in the MB in the 1950s.

31 Old SA guards like Kamal mock the new organization by saying that there was nothing "secret" about it. Kamal claims they he collected the information about the SO's men from the "streets of Cairo" (Kamal 1987, 290–291). Ashmawy, an SA foot-soldier at this point in time, supports Kamal's claims by saying that the new MB leadership (al-Hudaybi and his faction) did not know how to administer/control a secret, armed organization (the SO) (Ashmawy 2005, 224). After mocking the SO, both authors agree that its leadership's experience was no where near that of the former SA commander, al-Sanadi (Ashmawy 2005, 224; Kamal 1987, 290).

32 Kamal mentions that despite the fact that he is a strong supporter of al-Sanadi. The former dedicated most of his memoirs to staunchly defending the latter (see Kamal 1987, 121).

33 The point of departure onto the track of rivalry and hostility was a meeting held on 29 December 1952 between Nasser, RCC members and the MB leaders in which Nasser refused the ideas of holding elections and withdrawing the army from politics. Faird Abdul Khaliq, who attended the meeting and negotiated with Nasser in private, mentions that since then the relationship with the new regime had been rapidly deteriorating (Abdul Khaliq 2004, episode 10).

34 However, as discussed in Chapters 1 and 3, the relationship between state repression, radicalization and de-radicalization is more complex. In addition to al-Hudaybi's effort to dismantle the SA in 1951, al-Sabbagh mentions that the idea of dismantling the SA originated from within its ranks during the prison period of SA members in 1949 and 1950 (al-Sabbagh 1998, 71; 88–91; also see al-Sisi 1987, 236). Al-Sabbagh also refers to the interaction of those members with elite Islamic scholars like Sheikh Muhammad Abu Zahra as a reason for their changing their ideas and demanding the dismantlement of the SA (al-Sabbagh 1998, 68).

35 In that regard, Umar al-Tilmisani, the third *murshid*, mentions in an interview that from the very beginning two politicians warned that Nasser's intentions regarding

political reform could not be trusted: al-Hudaybi and Fu'ad Siraj al-Din (one of the prominent leaders of al-Wafd Party and interior minister of Egypt in the early 1950s) (al-Tilmisani 1985, 95).

36　The latter was a strong supporter of Nasser and perceived Nasser's coup as an Islamist-nationalist one (Hamrush 1974, vol. 1, 397; al-Tilmisani 1985, 67; al-Sabbagh 1998, 359; Ramadan 1993, 120; Abdul Khaliq 2004).

37　A former member of the Free Officers, who was the commander of the UD cells in the army.

38　Also a former member of the Free Officers, an MB commander in Palestine and another leading figure in the UD cells in the army.

39　As briefly mentioned in Chapter 3, 25 March was a crisis following the dismissal of Naguib on 25 February 1954. The Cavalry Army Unit, some of the Free Officers and massive civilian demonstrations called for the return of Naguib, reinstalling the political freedoms and releasing political detainees. By 25 March 1954, under the pressure of the demonstrations mainly organized by the MB and al-Wafd Party, Nasser was forced to issue the "six decisions" that included disbanding the RCC, allowing political parties to exist, reinstalling Naguib as president, releasing detainees and holding elections by July 1954 (see al-Baghdady 1977; Ramadan 1993; Hamrush 1974).

40　He refers to al-Hudaybi as "the father" in his memoirs.

41　That was dismissed by Abdul Qadir Audeh, and was considered a tragic mistake by other MB leaders (see for example Abdul Khaliq 2004, episode 12).

42　Al-Ashmway was a Legal Consultant in the State's High Council, a supporter of al-Hudaybi and a member of the "elite" faction. His transformation towards the upholding of violence can be seen as a direct consequence of state repression (see al-Ashmawy 1977; Mitchell 1979; Ramadan 1993; Abdul Khaliq 2004, episode 7).

43　Although documented during the military tribunal of 1954, Yusuf Tal'at's alleged statements and actions confirm that conclusion by al-Ashmawy. Tal'at said that he was "working [by which he meant operating/rearming] against his conscience" since he believed that violently confronting the regime was not the way of al-Banna (Tal'at qtd. in Mahkama 1954, vol. 7, 1478–1488). It should be mentioned that Tal'at was arrested at one of the MB's weapons depots, where he had enough arms and ammunition to put up a fight. Instead, however, he surrendered peacefully, although he probably knew what his destiny would be (that is, execution), as he mentioned in the tribunal (Tal'at qtd. in Mahkama 1954, vol. 7, 1488).

44　It is unclear whether that was the aforementioned al-Sanadi-Nusayr's suggested plan of assassination or another one.

45　At this point in time, the leadership was mainly blamed for lacking initiative (see Abdul Ra'uf 1989, 114–115, 148–149, Mansur 2004, episode 12).

46　By September 1954, the repressive policies included asking headmasters of schools to give the names of the MB-affiliated students so that they could either be expelled from school or denied access to universities (Mansur 2004, episode 13).

47　The attempt took place three days before the MB-planned demonstration to topple the regime (29 October 1954).

48　The sentence was later reduced to life-imprisonment due to his age. Al-Hudaybi was released later in 1957 due to his medical conditions.

49　Another member of the elite faction whose positions were consistently anti-violence and pro-democracy, it was Audeh who dismissed the February 1954 demonstration that surrounded Abdin Palace, thereby saving President Naguib, Prime Minister Nasser and other RCC members who were present in the Palace (See Naguib 1955; Ramadan 1993, 138; al-Shaf'i 1999, episode 6).

50　Estimates of MB detainees following the assassination range from 17,000 to 24,000 (al-Qa'ud 1985, 121).

51　The Blue Shirts of *al-Wafd* (The Delegation) and the Green Shirts of *Misr al-Fatah*

(The Young Egypt) were disbanded in 1938 (see Jankowski 1970 for a detailed account).

52   Some of these interactions were described previously in this chapter and in Chapter 3.

53   For more discussion on this point, see Chapter 1.

54   The IG case in 2002 provides an excellent contrast. One of the keys to the success of the IG's de-radicalization process was the internal social interaction between a consolidated historical leadership, middle-ranking commanders and the grassroots (see Chapter 5, also see Ashour 2007).

55   The principal anti-democratic faction in the Free Officers was that of Nasser.

56   A member of the Free Officers who is credited for the decisive action that led to the success of the 1952 coup. Since the coup attempt was uncovered, Siddiq moved with his troops earlier than had been planned so as to neutralize the pro-monarchy army officers before they could crackdown on the coup leaders (See for example Hamroushe 1974, vol. 1; Mansur 2004, episode 10).

57   He became the leader of Egyptian *al-Tajammu'* (Rally) Party (a leftist group) in the 1980s and 1990s, and a strong critic of the MB during that period.

58   He later became the Information/Media Minister and is currently the Deputy Chief of the regime's High Council for Human Rights.

59   The former is a supporter of al-Hudaybi and the latter is a supporter of al-Sanadi.

60   For example, al-Sabbagh describes Nasser as a good SA soldier, and Ashmawy mentions that al-Sanadi perceived Nasser's regime as being the great fruit of the SA struggle (al-Sabbagh 1998, 359; Ashmawy 2005, 166).

61   This faction was characterized by elitism and political conservatism. They were the ones who called for the dismantlement of the SA.

62   This section covers the period between 1955 and 1966. However, the second de-radicalization attempt occurred only between in 1964 and 1965.

63   In addition to the SA, the UD and the SO.

64   Ashmawy is a former SA foot-soldier and the Commander of Cairo in the Organization. He switched sides later on and became a critic of the MB. MB leaders accuse him of becoming an informer for the security services after the 1965 arrests.

65   Those were: Ali Ashmawy (Commander of Cairo), Abdul Fattah Isma'il (Commander of Eastern Delta), Ahmad Abd al-Majid (Commander of Upper Egypt), Awad Abdul 'Aal who was succeeded by Sabry al-Kumy (Commanders of Western Delta) and Magdi Abd Al-Aziz (Commander of Alexandria) (Ashmawy 2005, 147, Abd al-Majid 1991, 51–52; Ramadan 1993, 317).

66   Abdul Khaliq, Munir Dallah and others were opposing the idea of reorganization form the very beginning (Abdul Khaliq 2004, episode 14, 15; Ramadan 1993, 318).

67   The first book led to his release in 1964 due to the intervention of Abd al-Salam 'Arif, the Iraqi President who was a fan of Qutb's works (Qutb 1965; Abd al-Majid 1991, 94; Issa 2004, 8). The second book was the main reason for his execution according to General Allam (Allam 1996, 171).

68   Especially the prisoners in al-Wahat (Oases Prison) (Qutb 1965; Issa 2004b, 8). The controversies will be discussed in the following sections.

69   In that regard, Farid Abdul Khaliq says that he told al-Hudaybi that *Milestones* could be misunderstood by MB members as a collection of *fatwas* with practical implications. He mentioned in particular the young age of many MB members/prisoners and the conditions of state repression as factors conducive to "misunderstandings." However, al-Hudaybi approved and authorized publishing it (Abdul Khaliq 2004, episode 15; Issa 2004b, 8).

70   The indoctrination process was called *al-da'wa* (preaching/proselytizing) and the ideology here was perceived as "the correct version of Islam" (Qutb 1965).

71   Al-Hudaybi was referring to the possible execution of the MB's younger members by Nasser's regime in response to the activities of 1965 Organization.

72 A co-founder and one of the five commanders.

73 For more details about the Liman Massacre see Mahfuz (1988), pp. 17–25.

74 The core of these thoughts is related to the concept of *Hakimiyyat Allah* and a bottom-up change of society to impose the concept (Qutb [no date], 27–34; 82–92). The concept of *Hakimiyyat Allah*, as mentioned before in Chapter 3, denies any human the right to legislate. It attributes this right exclusively to God. Following from that, any human who legislates, especially if his/her legislation is contrary to what God has "ordered," is an idol (*Taghut*). Therefore, the concept legitimizes a confrontation with any human perceived as a legislator. The ones who will lead that bottom-up change are supposed to be a group of indoctrinated young men (part of the vanguard).

75 *Mas'ul* is an Arabic word meaning "responsible person." The MB uses the term to denote a leader rather than using *Emir* (leader/commander), a more common word in Islamist movements.

76 Ashmawy mentions in his memoirs that Muhhiy al-Din's initiative might have been a personal one, and thus lacking the regime's support. He mentioned that meeting between al-Hudaybi and Muhhiy al-Din to Shams Badran, the Head of the Military Criminal Investigations, in 1965. Ashmawy said that Badran was surprised, and that he immediately called Nasser to inform him about that incident (Ashmawy 2005, 221).

77 As mentioned in Chapter 3, there is a controversy about who authored the book. Most likely it is Hasan al-Hudaybi with the help of other MB leaders, most notably his son Ma'mun al-Hudaybi, who became the *murshid* in 2002.

78 A former SA commander with a militant reputation that prompted General Allam to describe him in his memoirs as "the hawk of all hawks" (Allam 1996, 175–176). Mashhur became the *murshid* in 1996.

79 Composed mainly of members from the legal profession (judges and lawyers).

80 At this point, Takfiri thought was gaining some ground in the prisons of Liman Turah, Qina and Abu Za'bal (Mahfuz 1988, 88–92).

81 Umar al-Tilmisani mentions that there were seven MB leaders/Islamic Jurisprudence specialists helping al-Hudaybi with his book (al-Tilmisani 1988, 138).

82 Judges and lawyers in Egypt do receive training in *Shari'a* law. Hasan al-Hudaybi, Ma'mun al-Hudaybi and Umar al-Tilmisani in particular were specialists in Islamic Jurisprudence (Ashmawy 2005, 270). Also, the most comprehensive study done to counter Takfiri ideologies was that of Salim al-Bahnasawy, a legal consultant with expertise in Islamic Jurisprudence. It was entitled *The Judgment in the Case of Muslim Excommunication (al-Hukm fi Qadiyat Takfir al-Muslimyin)* (al-Bahnasawy 1977).

83 Considered by some Sunni Scholars to be the fifth school of Islamic Jurisprudence.

84 These conditions can be contrasted with those that led to the factionalization of the 1950s, especially when al-Sanadi and other SA commanders were challenging the argument for dismantling the SA.

85 Including the memoirs of Abdul Mun'im Abdul Ra'uf, 'Abbas al-Sisi, Ali Ashmawy, Mahmud al-Sabbagh and others (al-Sisi 1986; Abdul Ra'uf 1989; al-Sabbagh 1998; Ashmawy 2005).

86 The Commander of Cairo in the 1965 Organization, who was in charge of giving paramilitary and guerrilla training to the members based on his expertise in the SA.

87 Ashmawy had helped security officers in the case of the 1965 Organization (Abd al-Majid 1991, 105; Allam 1996, 130, 145; al-Ghazali 1987, 88), and therefore many MB members consider him a "traitor." However, Umar al-Tilmisani mentions that he helped the security forces mainly due to coercion (al-Tilmisani 1985, 134). Because of Ashmawy's relationships with both sides, he was able to act as a liaison between them (Ashmawy 2005, 283).

88 As mentioned before, this faction was primarily collecting funds for the families of

the imprisoned MB members and attempting to find employment for released members. Their activities were confined to countering the consequences of the regime's socioeconomic discrimination.

89 Al-Banna gave many statements in various situations at different points in time. His speeches and writings can be read selectively to both oppose and support violent action.

90 It is unclear from the source whether this point was before or after Abdul Khaliq's final attempt to dismantle the Organization and his meeting with Qutb.

91 Including Farid Abdul Khaliq and al-Hudaybi.

92 An overwhelming majority of them are civilians.

93 For a detailed list and an estimate of deaths, see Ra'if (1986).

94 For the discussion of the multiple effects of state repression see Chapter 1.

95 As opposed to some arguments in the literature, the mainstream MB did not abandon or distance itself from Qutb's works at any point in time. In their writings and interviews, MB leaders and members describe Qutb as a martyr, and his works as a great contribution to Islamic political thought. Their argument however is that Qutb's works were misinterpreted by Takfirists and Jihadists. The MB uphold a similar argument with regards to other controversial figures like Abdullah Azzam (that is, they uphold his works and believe in his martyrdom, but argue that Jihadists misinterpreted him).

96 He is the younger brother of Abdul Fattah Isma'il, one of the five commanders and a co-founder of the 1965 Organization. Abdul Fattah was executed in 1966 with Sayyid Qutb. Both Abdul Fattah and Ali were young Azhar Sheikhs.

97 Especially given the fact that the SA and the UD had attacked several Egyptian Jewish civilian targets in 1948.

98 Ashmawy quotes Hamid Abu al-Nasr, the fourth *murshid*, as saying that the MB members who declared support for Nasser's regime in exchange for their freedom were beaten up in al-Wahat Prison and socially alienated in other prisons (Ashmawy 2005, 281).

99 Most of them lost their jobs as a result of the Law for Political Dismissal that was enforced under Nasser. The law denied employment to political opposition members.

100 For example, universities and factories were out of the question in the beginning.

101 Other objectives were previously discussed in this chapter.

102 Zaynab al-Ghazali however connected al-Anadouly with Salih Sarriya, who became the spiritual leader of the group (Allam 1996, 200–201; al-Tilmisani 1985, 146–147). Both men were executed by the Sadat regime following a failed coup attempt in 1974.

103 Hamas of Palestine and the Syrian MB in the early 1980s are two main exceptions. However, the Iraqi Islamic Party for example cooperated with the United States when it intervened in Iraq in 2003 and 2004, and participated in the American-sponsored elections in 2005. In Algeria, the MB (Movement for the Islamic society – MSI or Hams) chose to side with the military junta in 1992, despite the anti-democratic nature of the coup and the fact that it was against another Islamist movement (FIS).

104 The most notable case is that of Ali Isma'il, who was the leader and the main ideologue of the first Takfiri movement in modern history. He went back to the MB after deliberations with al-Hudaybi, as discussed above (Mahfuz 1988, 90).

105 That was *al-Da'wah* Magazine, which began publication in 1976.

5 The de-radicalization of al-Qa'ida's allies: the Islamic Group and al-Jihad Organization

1 Parts of this chapter were originally published in *The Middle East Journal* in the article "Lions Tamed? An Enquiry into the Causes of De-Radicalization of Armed

Islamist Movements: The Case of the Egyptian Islamist Group" The Middle East Journal, (Autumn, 2007) pp. 596–626.

2 Most famous of these are the Sidi Barrani airport attempt in 1993 and the Addis Ababa attempt in 1995.

3 Some of al-Jihad commanders opposed that merge since it changed a basic concept in their ideology: fighting the nearby enemy given priority over fighting the faraway enemy.

4 There were multiple attempts to initiate a process before 2007, especially between 2004 and 2005. They all failed mainly due to the lack of leadership. The reasons behind the success will be discussed in details later in this chapter.

5 I mean by "partially" that those attempts were not aiming to stop the violence completely like the ICV. More specifically, those attempts either aimed to stop a specific operation, or to stop "excesses" in using violence, leading to killing or hurting bystanders or neutral civilians. Those attempts aimed as well to cease regime-sponsored violence against the IG and its affiliates.

6 Al-Azhar is a world renowned Islamic institution, mosque and university. It is considered by many Sunni-Muslims to be the most prestigious school of Islamic learning, despite the fact that it was established by the Shiite Fatimid dynasty in the tenth century.

7 The committee was led by the late Sheikh Muhammad M. al-Sha'rawy, a leading popular cleric from al-Azhar. The committee members were mainly from the Muslim Brothers and other independent moderate Islamists. The lack of secularists in the committee made them take a hostile stance from the mediation process. State-owned and leftist media outlets criticized the attempt and called on the state to stop negotiating with Islamist terrorists.

8 This led to the sacking of General Abdul Halim Abu Musa, the interior minister who was behind the process.

9 The IG shows respect to many of al-Azhar scholars, going as far as choosing an Azhari Sheikh, Dr. Umar Abdul Rahman, as their Emir in the early 1980s. They have also praised al-Azhar and some of its scholars in their poems and literature (Qasim 1995, 81). Still they have criticized and mocked many of the pro-regime Azhar scholars.

10 One notable example was in 1989 in Shubra, an impoverished area near downtown Cairo, where members of the armed wing of the IG threatened a well-known Salafi Sheikh, Dr. Muhammad Abdul Maqsud, not to speak against their ideology or he might suffer a beating. One of Abdul Maqsud disciples was beaten (Islamist leader 2002).

11 A traditional way to show great respect.

12 Another traditional way to show respect to the leaders.

13 Also at some points, the discussion stalled. In an interview with one of the attendees of the *Istiqbal* conference in August 2002, he mentioned to me that the members were so critical of the ideological reform that Essam Dirbala, one of the leaders and a *Shura* Council member, said "OK brothers, should we cancel the initiative?" There was a moment of silence, until one of the IG members from Assyut broke it by saying "carry on *Mawlana*, we are listening."

14 Zuhdi *et al.*, *Istratijiyat wa Tafjirat*, 19; Essam Dirbala, "Al-Ahram Yuhawir Essam Dirbala (Al-Ahram Interviews Essam Dirbala)," Interview by Ahmad Musa, *Al-Ahram*, 26 August 2006, 16.

15 Taha told the historical leaders that what he really signed was a declaration for supporting Iraq against the UN–US sanctions, not an alliance with Ibn Laden and his Front (Dirbala, *al-Ahram*, 16; Ahmad, *Ahmad Yuhawir al-Qiyadat*, 19; Zuhdi *et al.*, *Nahr al-Zikrayat*). Two of the historical leaders, Zuhdi and Dirbala, described that situation as a "trap" planned by their rivals from al-Jihad (who signed on as constituent members of the Front) to ruin the ICV and drag the IG into a confrontation (Dirbala, *al-Ahram*, 16; Ahmad, Ahmad *Yuhawir al-Qiyadat*, 19).

16 Sayyid Imam al-Sharif, the former ideologue of al-Qa'ida and former commander of al-Jihad Organization (1987–1993), echoed that argument in 2007 (Al-Sharif 2007c, 11).
17 I will further discuss this factor in the section titled *Social Interaction*.
18 It is worth mentioning that the IG has imported its *tarbbiyah* methods from the MB.
19 This is understood by IG members as an evidence of sincere piety, suggesting the possibility of having a special relation with God. This understanding supports the aura around the historical leaders, leading the members to kiss their hands and to ask them for their prayers (Ahmad 2002b, 11).
20 In an interview with a former middle-raking IG leader, he referred to the historical leader as the "most knowledgeable men in Egypt." This is despite the fact that he defected from the IG in the late 1980s (IG former leader 2002).
21 The operation is usually highlighted by the IG since almost all of the historical leaders have participated, and a few got injured, in it (al-Zayyat 2006). Following the assassination of Sadat, on 8 October 1981, 35 IG militants have attempted to control Assyut governorate, initially with only six Kalashnikovs (al-'Awwa 2006, 101; IG member 2002). They have attacked the City Hall, the main Police Station and the General Security HQ. Despite being outnumber and outgunned, they have killed 129 officers and soldiers and controlled the buildings for a few hours (al-'Awwa 2006, 102; IG member 2002). The part that is not usually highlighted by the IG was that most of the soldiers were poorly trained and did not try to fight back. Most of them attempted to flee or hide under their trucks and were ruthlessly killed in that situation by the IG militants (al-'Awwa 2006, 102; IG member 2002). Caught by surprise, several officers were unarmed, and several of whom were shot unarmed by the attackers (al-'Awwa 2006, 102; IG member 2002). After hearing that account in 1983, Umar Abdul Rahman, Emir of the IG back then, ordered the perpetrators of the attack to fast 60 days in their prison cells to repent their sins (a theological ruling for killing innocents by "mistake") (Abdul Baqi 1994; al-'Awwa 2006, 104).
22 He means Nagih Ibrahim, the principle ideologue of the IG.
23 That argument can be easily refuted. Ibrahim himself has participated in the Assyut operation which, as discussed in note 20, was "excessively" violent even by the standards of the IG and its radical leadership represented by Sheikh Abdul Rahman at that time. In addition, Ibrahim has authored the book *Inevitability of Confrontation* (1990) in which he argued that the "soldiers of good" and those of "evil" will inevitably and violently clash, without any clear definition of what represents "good" or "evil," thus leaving these broad categories for his followers' to fill. In 2005, however, Ibrahim has authored a new edition of the book in which he criticized the older version and argued in favor of uncertainty and dynamism of views, *fatwas* and ideas as well as against cultural clash (Ibrahim *et al.* 2005).
24 The relationship between the IG and the Algerian FIS is no secret. Several IG leaders had ties with FIS figures in the late 1980s and early 1990s. Muhammad al-Islambulli and his mother have visited Algiers and participated in one of the FIS rallies in 1990, in which they were greeted as heroes by FIS supporters. Talaat Fu'ad Qasim (alias Abu Talal al-Qasimi), former IG spokesperson, has issued several statements supporting the FIS in the 1990s. In his sermons recorded on audio tapes, Qasim prayed for the release of Madani and Belhaij (Talaat Fu'ad, Friday Sermon, Cassette, 1994). In 1997, the IG historical leaders have issued a statement congratulating Abbasi Madani, the FIS leader, for his release from prison (see Zuhdi *et al.* 2003, 136).
25 It is worth mentioning that in the old literature of the IG, most of these arguments have been refuted as a form of heresy and/or conspiracy (see for example Ibrahim *et al.* 1984; Ibrahim 1990).
26 The new development here is that the condemnation was directed against *some* leftists. Usually, the IG would attack the whole ideological camp.
27 One example is Dr. Farag Foda, a leading secular intellectual who was assassinated by IG activists in June 1992.

28 The general features of the new ideology are based on the first four books that were mentioned before.

29 These are the leaders who ran the IG outside the prisons throughout the 1980s and led the confrontation with the regime in the early 1990s.

30 For the reasons behind the 1990s insurgency and the demands of the IG see Chapter 3.

31 I found one exception of that "defensive reaction" argument, the account of Tal'at Fu'ad Qasim, one of the historical leaders who disappeared in 1995 and allegedly murdered by one of the Egyptian security agencies. In his book *Death of Egypt's Pharaoh*, he claims that the meetings held in September 1981 aimed for establishing an Islamist state in Egypt. However, Qasim did not attend any of those meetings since he was detained on September 3rd (Hammuda 1985a, 81; al-Awwa 2006, 95). In addition, after reading some of his works, interviews and hearing his sermons, it can be concluded that Qasim constantly tends to exaggerate, overstate and use propaganda. At one point in 1993, he publicly told a journalist that there is a "secret" IG unit in the Egyptian army planning a coup soon (Qasim 1996, 44).

32 Former Emir of Assyut University, Dr. Shu'ib spent 14 years as a detainee without a charge.

33 Hafiz constantly opposed violence since the 1980s, including opposing the assassination of Sadat and attempting to stop the Assyut operation in 1981 (al-'Awwa 2006, 95–99). In addition, some sources attribute the lack of violence in al-Menya, al-Fayyoum and Beni Sueif in the period between 1992 and 1994 to Hafiz's control over his follower in those areas (State Security Major 2002; Al-'Awwa 2006, 95). Following his re-detention in 1994, the situation deteriorated and violence ensued in those areas.

34 The argument in this section is based on empirical observations and inductive analysis. At the core of it, there is an obviously problematic moral element which is not addressed here. However, the argument should not be understood as recommending or supporting state repression or any violations of human rights.

35 Which means in this case, the IG's understanding of Islam.

36 For example, former detainees who were held in the Scorpion Prison mention that they were held in solitary cells from 1993 till 1997. In addition to bimonthly beatings and torture, they were not allowed to get out of these cells for four years. When they have interacted with the outside world in 1997, the last news they had heard about the world was in 1993 (Former IG Detainee, Interview by author, October 2002, Cairo, Egypt).

37 I have to mention here that the strategy of "health-oriented" repression inside prisons was not limited to Islamist radicals. It was applied to many political prisoners from different ideological camps. Saad Eddine Ibrahim and Ayman Nour, another liberal politicians and presidential candidate in 2005, are among the high-profile victims of that strategy (interview with Ibrahim 2007).

38 Where the overwhelming majority of IG members were present.

39 That practice was not only observable in the IG case. In 1993, al-Jihad Organization recruited two officers from the air-defense army unit. The latter planned to shoot down Mubarak's airplane over Suez city in 1994, but the plot was foiled. The planners were all executed at the orders of a military committee, except for the ones who gave orders. Those were two well-known imprisoned leaders from al-Jihad Organization (Former Islamist Leader, interview by author, July 2002, Cairo, Egypt).

40 The exact time period depends on which prison is in questions.

41 For example, Samir al-Arky, one of the IG members who was detained in al-Fayoum prison explains that since January 2000 when the ban on visits was revoked, there were usually two fences between the detainee and his visitors. Given the large numbers of detainees and visitors in the same location at the same time, it was very difficult to hear or to interact with each other. By late October 2001, the detainees

were allowed to sit with their families with no fences in between. Al-Arky mentions that when this happened, many detainees went down on their knees and prostrated to perform *sujud*, an Islamic ritual for thanking God (see al-'Arky, Samir. "*Rihlat Al-Fayyum ... Zikrayat wa Shujun* (The Fayyum Trip ... Memories and Grievances)." Interview by Islamic Group. [Online]). Available: http://egyig.com/Public/articles/mobadra/6/38809650.shtml (accessed 1 January 2007).

42 It is noteworthy here to mention that before 9/11 there was the regime was less supportive of the ICV and the IG transformations. The "coordination with the leadership" policy did not start except after 9/11. The IG leaders were allowed to tour the prisons, the state media gave extensive coverage of the transformations and the regime went as far as funding and disseminating the IG new books (in 2002, a major from the SSI gave the author of this chapter the four books. Since there were a few more copies in stock, the major asked the author to purchase what was left!). Due to space limitations, I will not be able to discuss the causes of the policy change.

43 See interview with Nagih Ibrahim, "*Ibrahim Yakshif al-Sitar 'an Ahdath Akhbar al-Mubadara* (Ibrahim Unveils the Newest Developments of the Initiative)" [Online] Interview by Usama Abdul Azim. Available: http://egyig.com/Public/articles/interview/6/83640472.html (accessed 20 July 2007).

44 Although the history and the old literature of the IG are not available on it.

45 Ahmad, "*Al-Qawa'id Tunaqish*," 16.

46 The stances varied between early support (1997–2004), late support (2007) and rejection.

47 The only exception is 'Abbud al-Zumur. However, he switched to the IG (al-Jihad rival) in the early 1990s and that undermined his standing within al-Jihad members. In addition, his initiative for ceasing violence required immediate political gains, something that Mubarak's regime refuses (Ghurab 2007, 11).

48 Perception plays a crucial role in creating charismatic leadership. Al-Sharif for example was not a military commander during the Soviet–Afghan conflict. His role was mostly limited to medical aid and Jihadist ideological production and propaganda (al-Siba'i 2007. 6).

49 Like Salih Jahin (see Jahin 2007, 5).

50 Such as some of al-Azhar scholars who tried between 1988 and 1994 to convince al-Jihad leaders that violence against the state and society is not sanctioned by Islam.

51 Like Nabil Na'im for example, who was described by other Jihad figures, such as Hani al-Siba'i, as an "SSI servant" (Al-Siba'i 2007, 1).

52 Al-Safty's group attempted to assassinate two former interior ministers and a pro-regime writer in 1987.

53 See for example Ashour (2007); Ashour and Unlucayakli (2006); Hafez (2004), Ibraihm (1980).

54 This is in addition to secular opposition figures and groups like the liberals and the communists.

55 For more details see the Human Rights Watch reports on Egypt (1992–2007) as well as the UN Committee Against Torture reports.

56 The IG was given much more extensive governmental media coverage, however (see Ahmad 2002a, 2002b, 2002c).

57 He was also the Imam of a mosque in Milan, Italy who was allegedly kidnapped by the CIA and handed over to the Egyptian State Security Investigations in 2003 (Zinah 2007, 1). He is suing the US for that and the case is being looked in Italy (Zinah 2007, 1).

58 He was a member of the Foreigners Brigade (Kwon as *Kattibat al-Ghurab*').

59 As mentioned above, seculars, with no exceptions, were usually the targets of Salafi-Jihadists' harsh criticism, fiery rhetoric and sometimes their bullets. The two famous cases of secular victims of Jihadist violence are Naguib Mahfuz and Farag Fuda. The first is a Noble Prize Laureate who was stabbed by IG militants in 1994.

The second was an outspoken secular intellectual who was gunned down by IG militants.

60 An organization that represents many Egyptian Shi'ites and defends Shi'ites' rights in general.

61 The center mainly defends the rights of Egyptian Copts and its headed by a Coptic human right and democracy activist Mr. Mamduh Nakhla.

62 Give that regime denies political recognition not only to Islamist movements like the Muslim Brothers, the Islamic Group and al-Wasat, but also to secular groups with some popularity in the street.

63 Interactions between the AIS and factions from the GIA and the GSPC had also led to the de radicalization of some faction within the latter as shown in Chapter 6.

64 I used the adjective theological to distinguish him from other ideologues such as Abu Mus'ab al-Suri (Mustafa al-Sit Maryam) whose works are more strategy-oriented (as opposed to theology-oriented) and Ayman al-Zawahri whose works are more history-oriented.

65 Muntasir Al-Zayat, "*Muhami Al-Usuliyyin: Mawqifi Sa'b Fi Bulaq al-Dakrur* (The Lawyer of the Fundamentalists: My Situation is Difficult in Bulaq al-Dakrur)." *al-Sharq al-Awsat*, 9 November 2005, 5.

66 Interview with Karam Zuhdi, Liqa' Khas. *Al-Jazeera Satellite Channel*, Cairo. 23 August 2006.

67 As opposed to the organizational leaders of a group.

68 As emphasized by interviews with leaders from the two groups.

6 De-radicalization in Algeria: successes and failures

1 For definitions of these terms see Chapter 1.

2 Although from the very beginning the AIS wanted to disarm in exchange for returning to the electoral process (Merzaq 1995a, 4; 2005, 6), which did not happen in any case.

3 Also know as secular eradicators as opposed to secular dialogists like Louisa Hannoun (Worker's Party) and Hocine Ait Ahmad (Socialist Forces Front).

4 Even by AIS commanders (see for example Mezraq 1995a, 16).

5 Most notably the faction of Dr. Saïd Sadi in the Rally for Culture and Democracy (RCD), as well as the left-leaning, state-sponsored General Union of Algerian Workers (UGTA).

6 Jamal is also written as Djamel.

7 As previously mentioned, this term usually refers to Algerian generals in the security, intelligence and army bureaucracies who believed that the solution to the Algerian crisis lay in eradicating the armed Islamist opposition. To a large degree they were the mirror image of the GIA, upholding its slogan of "no truce, no dialogue and no reconciliation."

8 Even in 1997, Isma'il Lamari, the deputy head of military intelligence, took a great risk by visiting the headquarters of the AIS in the Beni Khattab mountain near Jijel to initiate a reconciliation process (Tawil 1998, 330; Mezraq 2004).

9 Some of these acts will be elaborated upon in the following sections.

10 Those organizations include al-Rahman Brigade (led by Mustafa Kertali), Islamic League for the Call and the Jihad (LIDD – led by Ali Ben Hajar), Islamic Front for Armed Jihad (FIDA – led by Abdul Wahab Lamara), Movement for an Islamic State (MEI – led by al-Sa'id Makhloufi) and the Armed Islamic Movement (MIA – formerly led by Abdul Qadr Chabouti). This is in addition to a major FIS faction mainly from *al-Jaz'ara* trend (led by Muhammad Sa'id and Abdul Razzaq Rajjam). Most of these united organizations/factions operated in Central Algeria, but the Eastern and Western parts were also represented in the "unity" meeting. The AIS however strongly opposed that unity (Mezraq 1996, 6; Tawil 1998, 199).

11   Excluding Mahfuz Nahnah's movement (Movement for Islamic Society – HAMAS in 1991 and now Movement of the Society of Peace – HAMS or MSP), which represent the mainstream Muslim Brothers in Algeria. MSP sided with the junta and launched severe criticism against the St. Edigio Platform and participants in it.

12   An ultra-secular, left-leaning party whose support comes mainly from some of the ethnic Berbers.

13   Belhaj views on democracy were mentioned before in Chapter 3. In 1990, he considered it a form of *Kufr* (infidelity) and a *Bid'a* (sinful innovation). He has a book in which he details his views on democracy and attempt to support them with theological and ideological argumentation. The book is titled *al-Hujja al-Shar 'iya al-Qawiyya fi Damgh al-Dimuqratiyya* (The Strong Theological Proof for Refuting Democracy).

14   He was the President of Algeria between 1962 and 1965. He was also the FLN's leader and co-founder, and was perceived as an independence hero for his struggle against French colonialism.

15   One of the co-founders of the FLN and a leading figure in the anti-colonial struggle against the French. In 1995, he headed the left-leaning, Berber-supported party of the FFS. In the elections of 1991, the FFS came third after the FIS and the FLN.

16   Referring to the fact that a Catholic Community had led the initiative and brokered the accords.

17   There were several factors behind that position upheld by Mezraq. First, several analysts pointed out that the GIA was the militarily stronger organization and AIS was unable to protect the families of its own soldiers from the GIA's reprisals (Ait Larabi *et al.* 1999, 103; Aroua 2001). This claim is probably accurate but only until mid-1995. After that the AIS started gaining more momentum. Another possibility was the fact that the regime was blaming "Islamists" for all kind of violent acts against civilians. The AIS wanted to distinguish itself from the GIA's behavior and send a message to the Algerian people, that despite being oppressed, they are willing to cease violence. Finally, there was a big question of who is in control of the GIA after the death of Gouasmi, its most influential emir. Many figures in Algeria and outside have argued that the GIA was infiltrated by the military intelligence and was being used as a counter-insurgency tool. Those figures include high-ranking intelligence officers like Colonel Mohamed Samraoui, former counter-terrorism officers like lieutenant Habib Souidia, massacre witnesses like Nasurallah Yous, and diplomats like Muhammad Larabi Zitout (see Samraoui 2002; 2003, Souidia 2001; 2002; Yous 2007; Zitout 1999; also see Wafa and Isaac 373–459).

18   Madani's letter did not include anything new when compared to the St. Edigio's accord. However, it was directed this time to the ruling junta and not the Algerian people or to opposition representatives, like the case of St. Edigio.

19   The regime wanted Medani to head the delegation and to exclude some of the FIS leaders. The FIS refused and wanted the freedom to choose its own delegation (Kabir 1995 qtd. in al-Tawil 1998, 322).

20   The FIS wanted all members of its negotiating delegation released from prison and that the negotiations take place away from prison. The regime refused.

21   There was a primary agreement on the release of all prisoners. However, the differences were over when and how (the mechanism of release).

22   The FIS leaders wanted to keep the name *Front Islamique du Salut* and the regime refused.

23   Between 1992 and 1998, there were 642 massacres in Algeria (a massacre is defined here as the murder of more than five civilians). The overwhelming majority of them took place in 1997 and 1998, mainly in electoral districts that supported the FIS in the 1990 and 1991 elections.

24   Kertali was the FIS municipal deputy of the town of Larbaa after the 1990 munici-

pal elections. He was also head of the FIS branch in Larbaa (Muqqadim, 2000b, 8). He later led al-Rahman Brigade, which briefly joined the GIA in 1994 and 1995, and then went to war against it between 1995 and 2000, after the murder of Said and Rajjam. Kertali joined the AIS in 1997. In 2007, his car was blown up by QICM's operatives – he survived but lost one leg (Ghimrasa 2007 b, 6).

25 The dominant two trends before the coup were Salafism and *al-Jaz'ra* (Algerianization). Even within these two trends there were multiple factions with allegiances to different leaders. For example within Salafism it was mainly Belhaj (hardliner, radical) versus Sahnoni (more pragmatic), and within *al-Jaz'ara* there were multiple leading figures like Abd al-Qadr Hachani, Muhammad Said and Abdul Razzq Rajjam.

26 A decision that was taken by Medani and Belhaj and led to the split of several FIS leaders including Sahnoni (Sahnoni 2000, 14; Marani 1999, 6). The decision was in reaction to the electoral laws that were designed by the regime to increase the FLN's chances of winning.

27 Established by Mustafa Bouya'li and recycled by Abdul Qadir Chabouti, a leading member during the time of Bouya'li, the Armed Islamic Movement (MIA) vowed to overthrow the military regime through guerrilla warfare strategies (Martinez 1998, 198). Chabouti was an officer in the Algerian army and he was given the title *"Liwa'"* or "general" by his militant followers for his military skills (Martinez 1998, 68). For more details see Chapter 3 on the history of Algeria's armed movements.

28 As will be discussed in the following sections, Mezraq was not in control of other armed organizations, especially the GIA. Once the peace deal was reached with Mezraq and the AIS, the de-radicalization process attracted other organizations as well as factions from the GIA.

29 I will not address the factional struggle within the military establishment, since the unit of analysis is the armed Islamist movements. However, for more details on that struggle see Samroui (2003), Habib Souaidia (2001), Bedjaoui *et al.* (1999), Yous (2007).

30 There is an additional known interaction between Kamal Goumazi, a FIS leader and a co-founder, and the GIA commanders that will be discussed later in the section on the de-radicalization failure of the GIA (Sheikhy 2007, 8).

31 Assuming that it was not infiltrated by the regime and used as counter-insurgency tool to eliminate armed Islamists and terrorize their possible supporters.

32 Isam'il is also written as Smain or Smail in some literature.

33 Mezarq pointed in one interview to the fact that Isma'il Lamari came to their headquarters in the mountains. Surrounded by armed AIS militants, Lamari was risking his life. Mezraq mentioned that the AIS appreciated the gesture (Mezraq 2004).

34 Provisional leader of the FIS in 1991 and widely perceived as the engineer of the electoral victory of December 1991.

35 He was one of the FIS *Shura* Council members who opposed the 1991 strike. He switched sides at a later stage and became an advisor to Prime Minister Ahmad Ghozali (1991–1992).

36 An elected MP in 1991 and head of the parliamentary delegation of the FIS abroad. He was one of the supporters of unity with the GIA in 1994 and became a harsh critic of the GIA in 1995 after the murder of al-Jaz'ara leaders (Said, Rajjam and others).

37 Former spokesperson of the FIS Coordination Council Abroad, an entity that opposed the Executive Committee of the FIS headed by Rabih Kabir.

38 His brother Mustafa Kabir was among the AIS' co-founders and became the commander of the east in 1995.

39 The term "political leaders" and "military/paramilitary leaders" can be misleading. To clarify, most of the "military commanders" of the FIS were civilian political

activists (such as Mezraq and Mustafa Kabir) and/or elected MPs (such as Ben Aicha, Ben Hajar and Mustafa Kertali) before the coup. These figures were not soldiers or military officers and they had no prior experience as guerillas before the coup.

40   The position of Belhaj and Madani was different in the GIA's case. They were admitted in the *Shura* Council of the GIA in 1994, without their consultation or consent, following the "unity" (GIA Communiqué 1995, no. 36, 1; al-Tawil 1998, 210). They were subsequently removed from that council, again without their consultation or consent, in 1995 (GIA Communiqué 1995, no. 36, 1).

41   Excluding Mahfuz Nahnah's movement (HAMAS in 1991 and now HAMS or MSP) and Abdullah Djaballah's movement (*Al-Nahda* in 1991 and now *Al-Islah*), who are more loyal to the Muslim Brothers' traditional ideology. Jihadi groups, like the remnants of Bouya'li's Islamic Armed Movement (MIA), refused to participate in elections on a religio-ideological basis and therefore can also be excluded as groups. Individuals from this current did join the FIS however.

42   Both Belhaj and Sahnoni requested a *fatwa* (religious ruling) from Sheikh Nasr al-Din al-Albani, a Syrian-Albanian Sheikh who is a leading reference in the international Salafi movement, regarding the religious "legality" of participating in parliamentary elections (Atayliyah 2000, 14).

43   Some analysts argue that Sahnoni represents that Takfiri trend in the FIS (Shahin 1997, 133; Abd al-Razzaq 2000, 11). However, these analysts have not supported their claim with empirical arguments. After reading some of Sahnoni's interviews and statements, and monitoring his political actions, it seems that the behavior and ideology more closely matches Salafism and not Takfirism. Also, Takfirists in general rarely form alliances with other Islamist factions, as they believe that other Islamists are "apostates."

44   The name *Al-Jaza'ra* was given by Mahfouz Nahnah, the leader of MSP (representing a faction of the Algerian Muslim Brothers) to distinguish them from other Islamist movements with international connections (Shahin 1997, 120; Burgat and Dowell 1997, 317). As mentioned in Chapter 1, the ideology of the *Al-Jaz'ara* current is inspired by the thought of Malek Bennabi, a French-educated Algerian intellectual who was the director of Higher Education during the Boumedienne era. Bennabi's writings focus on the reasons behind the decline of predominantly Muslim countries and the ways to progress through the interactions between ideas, cultures and individuals. The ideology of *Al-Jaz'ara* is characterized by its nationalist-Islamist agenda and its rejection of any forms of non-Algerian Islamist interpretations of Islam or influences in Algeria. These rejections include the influences of both the Muslim Brothers, who inspired parties like HAMS, *Al-Nahda* and *Al-Islah*; those of the Saudi-sponsored international Salafi current, which influenced Algerian Salafis; and those of the more extreme, international Jihadi and Takfiri groups and figures.

45   This was created by Abdullah Djaballah, and was mainly based in eastern Algeria (and is therefore sometimes known as the "eastern group").

46   There was an initial assumption that all armed Islamist organizations in 1992 were fighting for the FIS and its leaders. That assumption was incorrect as mentioned in Chapter 3, especially after the GIA's official establishment in September 1992. Also, in 1991, when tensions were rising between the FIS and the Algerian regime, one of the FIS leaders suggested to Abbasi Madani that the FIS should form an armed wing as a precaution. Madani refused the suggestion (Ben Aicha 2000, 8).

47   He co-established an autonomous armed organization (Movement for the Islamic State – MEI) in 1992; this organization joined the GIA in May 1994.

48   Said and Rajjam probably joined for pragmatic reasons rather than ideological affinity. Those reasons included the actual strength of the GIA, its control of "liberated zones" in the Algerian Center and the large number of Afghan veterans and Alge-

rian army personnel who joined the GIA and therefore contributed with their experience to its military might.

49 The AIS activists usually mean by the "original lines of the FIS" the acceptance of electoral democracy, to distinguish themselves from the GIA and Salafi-Jihadi groups who reject all forms of democracy. They also mean loyalty to the leadership of the FIS (Madani and Belhaj).

50 The LIDD avenged the murder of Said and Rajjam by assassinating Jamal Zitouni, the Emir of the GIA, in July 1996 (Ben Hajar 2000, 8; Hattab 1998, 6; al-Tawil 1998, 246).

51 It is perceived as one of the armed organizations currently affiliated with al-Jaz'ara. Its founder, Abdul Wahab Lamara was executed by the GIA under Zitouni leadership in 1996. The FIDA was involved in several terrorist attacks in the capital, including the multiple assassinations targeting secular intellectuals.

52 One of the most active GIA's brigades in the capital as it controlled several districts of Algiers at night (Kertali 2000, 8; Mezraq 2005a, 8). The Calitos Brigade was notorious for its excessively violent tactics and terror operations. Many of its members were ex-convicts in criminal cases.

53 Known as the Umm al-Thalathin massacre; it occurred in July 1997.

54 That problem did not only confront armed Islamists leaders but also the FIS leaders from the very beginning. Due to the populist rhetoric of the FIS leaders, outbidding by followers was a common phenomenon. For example, there was a widespread chant used by FIS supporters in 1991 before the elections, which was heard again in 1997 after the ceasefire declaration: "*ya Ali, ya Abbas al-Jabha rahu Hamas*" (O Ali [Belhaj], O Abbas [Medani], the Front had become like Hamas." Hamas (Currently Hams or MSP) is the Algerian Muslim Brothers party, which has been in an alliance with the military regime since 1992. It is perceived by FIS supporters as being too compromising and as betraying Islamist ideals (Muqqadim 1999, 6; Shahin 1997, 160). That chant was a condemnation of the FIS leadership's "lenient" positions by FIS followers.

55 Those included the freedom for him and other FIS leaders to consult with the military commanders of the AIS and other groups. In addition, Madani insisted that any agreement with the regime should have neutral witnesses (Ben Hajar 2000, 8).

56 He meant by that the fact that AIS had struck a deal with the regime and was already dismantling its armed units. The LIDD was a part of those units at this point in time, and Ben Hajar was following Mezraq's orders.

57 He was assassinated on 22 November 1999, allegedly by a GIA member named Fouad Boulemia. His death mainly served military generals who did not want a political role for the FIS. Hachani was coordinating with several political leader from the left (Louisa Hannoue – WP) and the right (Abd al-Hamid Mehri – FLN), demanding more political freedoms in the country as well as the rehabilitation of the FIS. His alleged "assassin," Fouad Boulemia, was convicted in a controversial one day trial, sentenced to death, and then released in 2006 (Rédaction de Liberte 2006, 3). Boulemia mentioned during the trial that he was tortured by the military and threatened by General Toufik (the alias of Mohamed Mediene – Head of *Département du renseignement et de la sécurité* – DRS) to write a confession saying that he had killed Hachani by mere "coincidence."

58 Most of the numbers mentioned in this section are mere estimates due to the lack of records, especially between 1992 and 1997. Within these years, both the security services and armed militias often burned the bodies of some of their victims (Souidia 2001). The phenomenon of "disappeared persons" resulted from these practices. Taking the "disappearances" into account, other sources claim that the number of fatalities from 1992 to 2001 exceeded 200,000 people (see: Ait Ahmad, Hussein. "Al-Zikra Al-Arba'un Li Istiqlal Al-Jaza'ir (The Fortieth Anniversary for Algerian Independence)." Bila Hudud. *Al-Jazeera Satellite Channel*. Al-Doha. 3 July 2002, 18:35 GMT).

59 A massacre is defined as a violent event in which more than five civilians were murdered (see: Abdul 'ati, Muhammad. "Muhasilat Al-Sira' (The Result of the Conflict)." 27 May 2002. Available www.aljazeera.net/in-depth/aljeria-election/2002/5/5–25–2.htm (accessed on 25 November 2002); Urwa, Abbas. "Al-Mazabih Fi Al-Jaza'ir: Huwar Ma' Al-Profissir Abbas Urwa (The Massacres in Algeria: An Interview with Professor Abbas Urwa)" Bila Hudud. *Al-Jazeera Satellite Channel*. Al-Doha. 19 February 2001, 18.

60 In addition to the humanitarian tragedy, Algeria's economy was devastated with the loss of billions of dollars in revenue (an estimated 30 billion dollars between 1992–1998), a dramatic increase in security expenditures by the regime, ballooning of the external debt ($30.7 billion in 1997) and rampant unemployment.

61 According to Faruk Costantini, the head of the regime's Consultative Commission for Human Rights in Algeria, this number does not include the supporters of armed Islamists inside cities and towns (Costantini 2006, 19).

62 The war with the GIA started with skirmishes in 1995 and intensified in 1996 and 1997 (see Hattab 1998, 8).

63 Bentalha is a small town south of Algiers that voted for the FIS in the 1991 elections. Many inhabitants were initially in favour of the FIS/AIS Islamists and some had joined them (Yous 2007, 4).

64 It was unclear what he meant by "too late." However, during the massacre the army was blocking all entrances and exits to Bentalha and reportedly shot dead a policeman who attempted to interfere. Security forces were stationed on the edge of Bentalha and were aware of what was going on without interference. The neighbourhood of Haï El-Djilali, which was specifically targeted by the attack, was repeatedly illuminated by huge projectors recently installed in a nearby field by the police (as if to light the attackers' way). Also, a military helicopter hovered over the scene throughout much of the six hours that the massacre lasted (Yous 2007, 33–47; Roberts 2001, 3). Given these conditions, it was almost impossible for an AIS detachment to reach Bentalha.

65 For statistics see Ait Larabi *et al.* (1999) and Aroua (2001).

66 In his book *La Sale Guerre* and in several interviews, Lieutenant Habib Souidia mentions that he drove some Algerian Special Forces officers and soldiers to the houses of Algerian civilians who had voted for the FIS. The group that he drove massacred the former voters. Souidia mentions that he is ready to stand trial for these and similar actions (Souidia 2001). If these accounts are correct, it shows that some units in the army were directly involved in the massacres, and not just lacking the will to interfere or providing indirect support for the GIA like in the case of Bentalha (Souidia 2001; Yous 2007, 3; Roberts 2001, 3). For comparative cases of targeting civilians as a counter-insurgency tool, see Wafaa and Isaac 1999, 391–397.

67 Like an infiltration of the GIA's units or even leadership structure as Colonel Mohamed Samraoui and others argue (Samraoui 2002; 2003). Given the simplistic mobilization and the lack of recruitment screening, as well as the basis for "promotion" inside the GIA, the infiltration scenario is not highly unlikely (see for example al-Suri [No Date], 34–42; Mezraq 2004; Mustafa Kabir 2002, 8; Wafa and Isaac 1999, 398–417).

68 Those were "No Dialogue, No Truce and No Reconciliation."

69 One of the leaders of the Muslim Brothers in Egypt. His three volume book is one of the most detailed accounts of the history of the MB in Egypt.

70 The latter book is a classic of four volumes that deals mainly with theology, jurisprudence, spirituality and Islamic philosophy. It is one of the classics that the Muslim Brothers teach and emphasize in their curricula (Abdul Khaliq 2004, episode 6).

71 His brother Mustafa Kabir was the AIS emir of the east starting in 1995.

72 Kabir could not attend because the German authorities prevented him from going (he sought refuge in Germany). Abd al-Karim Walad 'Idda was representing him in the meeting.

73 Not an end per se. The latter was an ideological preference for the GIA.

74 See Chapter 3 for more details.

75 After apologizing, Bouteflika said that the AIS militants honored their word (with regards to abandoning violence), whereas the state did not honor its commitment towards them (Bouteflika 2005, 1).

76 This was the second attempt on Kertali's life. The first was organized by a pro-regime militia in Larbaa town. It ended with a gun fight in which one of the assailants was injured and Kertali survived unharmed.

77 Al-Qa'ida later "apologized" for the attack, mentioning that one of its members decided to act on his own, that is, without the leadership's consent (Ghimrasa 2007b, 6).

78 For example, former AIS members were not allowed to run in the Algerian parliamentary elections of May 2007 (Mezraq 2007, 4).

79 This group included Khalid Nazar, the incumbent Defense Minister at the time of the coup; al-Arabi Belkhair, the incumbent Interior (Security) Minister at the time of the coup; Muhammad Lamari, the incumbent Commander of the Land Forces at the time of the coup and Chief of Staff from 1993 to 2004; Lamari's deputy General Sharif Fouday; Muhammad Médiène (alias Tawfiq) head of the military intelligence (DRS) (1988–present); General Isma'il Lamari his deputy and General Muhammad Towati (Razaqi 2000a, 8; Hafez 2000, 590; Samraoui 2001; Ben Bella 2002; al-Saydawy 2002, 17; Muqqadim 2005, 6; Unnamed Algerian General 2005, 5).

80 For example, Benjedid was forced to resign when he hesitated to cancel the elections against the wishes of the generals. Zeroual resigned in September 1998 and discontinued his presidential term when he refused to acknowledge the AIS ceasefire, again against the wishes of the generals (Muqadim 2005a, 6).

81 It should be noted that before his removal, Lamari was criticizing Bouteflika's policies that controlled the army, resulting in a decrease in the army's influence. He went so far as to threaten a coup to "correct" the democratic process in Algeria if there was fraud in the presidential elections of 2004 or if the presidential candidates withdrew (Muqqadim 2005, 6).

82 See Chapter 3 for more details.

83 The second zone comprises the eastern part of Algiers province, its suburbs and the neighboring towns and villages (Ghimrasa 2005, 6).

84 10,000 is probably a conservative estimate. Some estimates claim that the GIA in 1994 had more than 20,000 fighters (Ben Uthamn 2007, 129).

85 As noted in Chapter 1, religious/theological education is an important quality for leading an Islamist movement, as it provides the leader with crucial religious legitimacy for his actions/policies.

86 See Chapter 1 for more elaboration. Also among the reasons that Zitouni's supporters list for executing Mahfuz Tajeen, fifth emir of the GIA, was that he asked Zitouni to take Arabic lessons under Muhammad Said (al-Tawil 1998, 222). This was perceived as an insult by the supporters of Zitouni.

87 Said was a student of Malik Bennabi, a French-educated Algerian intellectual who was the director of Higher Education during Boumedienne's era. Bennabi is considered to be the godfather of *al-Jaz'ara* Islamist current (Algerianization), which presents a national-Islamist ideology (See Laremont 2000, 186).

88 GIA affiliated newsletter that was published in London between 1993 and 1997.

89 Groups like Egyptian Jihad, Libyan Islamic Fighting Group as well as several other international Jihadist figures like al-Qa'ida's Abu Mus'ab al-Suri and others, announced that they had withdrawn their support for the GIA in early 1996, after

the news of Said and Rajjam's killings was confirmed (al-Zawahri 1996, 17; al-Tawil 1998, 230–240; al-Suri [No Date], 50–56).

90   Who were a numerical minority and were purged under Zitouni and Zouabri. Also, the faction that was relatively pragmatic with regards to its position on violence was al-Jaz'ara.

91   He was widely regarded as the second man in the Algerian Muslim Brothers movement after Mahfuz Nahnah (see for example al-Tawil 1998, 116).

92   The other being Abdul Haqq Layada.

93   Commanders who attended the meeting included Zitouni, Zouabri and Said.

94   He stayed in his house fearing assassination if the GIA interpreted his position as being a "betrayal" (Sheikhy 2007, 8; al-Tawil 1998, 209).

95   Medani and Belhaj were never consulted before being declared GIA members of the consultative council. They were appointed and removed without their consent.

96   It was the Direction de la Surveillance du Territoire (DST).

97   He received a degree in Shari'a law from a Jordanian university.

98   Hattab argues that he had never resigned from leading the GSPC and that the only authentic GSPC statements have to be signed by him and stamped by his seal. However, practically he does not represent except a small GSPC faction.

99   At that time, the GSPC was operating under the title of "GIA – Second Zone."

100 Hattab also claims that the delegate was not sent to the leadership of the GSPC and that he was holding talks with grassroots and mid-ranking members (Hattab 1998, 6).

101 Mainly if the de-radicalized militias will get their political rights back or not, and how will the state treat them after abandoning arms.

102 This group operated in western Algeria and was known under the GIA as the "Horrors Brigade – Fourth Zone." It broke away from the GIA when Zouabri took over. The latter sent one of the GIA's strongest militias in the west to quash the dissent. The pro-Zouabri militia was victorious after a bloody battle in the forest of al-Taquriya on 26 September 1996 (see for example GIA-Fourth Zone, Communiqué dated 21 October 1996, 2; see also al-Tawil 1998, 255).

7 A world without violent Jihad?

1   See the following section on directions for future research.

2   See Chapters 3 and 4 for more details. Also, in the case of the IG, this explains the vying for the approval of Dr. Umar Abd al-Rahman regarding the de-radicalization process (see al-Tawil 2007, 265–268), given his theological credentials (he holds a doctorate degree from al-Azhar University). This is despite the fact that he is imprisoned in the United States and completely detached from organizational matters.

3   From Saudi Arabia Dr. Safar al-Hawali, Salman al-Audeh and 'A'id al-Qarny (al-Audeh 2007), from Yemen the late Muqbil al-Wadi'y and Hamoud al-Hitar (Johnsen 2007) and from Jordan, more recently and surprisingly, Abu Muhammad al-Maqdisi who was the theological teacher of the late Abu Mus'ab al-Zaraqawi, the former commander of al-Qa'ida in Iraq (Abu Ruman 2008, 6). It should be noted here that most of these religious leaders (excluding al-Wadi'y, who is a mainstream scientific-Salafi leader) have supported various types of Salafi-Jihadism during the 1980s and 1990s.

4   These could range from a degree from a prestigious university like al-Azhar of Egypt (such as the degree held by Umar abd al-Rahman and other IG leaders) or Umm al-Qura in Mecca (such as the degree held by Safar al-Hawali) to informal self-teaching and, based on that, showing a command of theological knowledge and issuing fatwas (like al-Maqdisi of Jordan and al-Sharif of al-Jihad Organization have done).

5   Participating in armed action against a perceived "secular" and repressive regime or against a foreign force would usually count as a history of struggle in the eyes of followers.

6 Like being the emir, the former emir or a member in the leadership council (usually called the consultative council or the elite council in armed Islamist movements).

7 Ranging from better treatment in detention centers to release from prisons and some financial assistance/compensations (see Ashmawy 2005, 136). Also see Chapter 4, section on selective inducements under Sadat.

8 The few members who agreed to declare "loyalties" or to "repent" were punished by the MB and the IG. The punishment ranged from social alienation to physical abuse (see al-Ashmawy 2005, 136; IG member 2002).

9 See Chapter 2 for more discussion.

10 The latter was mainly due to leadership beliefs and disregard for violence in general.

11 *Al-Tali'a al-Muqatila* (The Fighting Vanguards – FV), one of the armed organizations affiliated with the Muslim Brothers in Syria, is one of the few examples. The Asad regime carpet bombed the City of Hama, which was the stronghold of the organization, in February 1982. That led to the infamous Hama massacre in which somewhere between 10,000 and 38,000 people were killed in less than a week (See Amnesty International report and other estimates quoted in Friedman 1998, 78–105; see also Fisk 1990, 181–185). The structure of the organization was destroyed, but many of its commanders fled (including Mustafa al-Sit Maryam – alias Abu Mus'ab al-Suri – one of al-Qa'ida's ideologues). According to al-Suri, who took part in the combat, the FV had made the tactical mistake of holding on to a city and confronting the Syrian army in a conventional fashion, without however having a comparable fighting capacity. After the "Syrian experience," al-Suri wrote a book calling on armed Islamists to use guerilla tactics rather than conventional confrontations. It is interesting to note that Che Guevara's book on guerilla warfare was recommended by al-Suri, translated to Arabic, and posted on several al-Qa'ida affiliated websites (al-Suri 1991).

12 The two recent cases are those of Ali Ben Hajar, the emir of the LIDD, who refused a request from the regime to call on armed organizations to put down their arms as a result of the regime reneging on their promises (Ben Hajar 2005, 1). President Bouteflika had realized the importance of acknowledging the state's failure to fulfill its promises, and as a result, he "apologized" publicly to the former militants.

13 Following the regime's failure to fulfill a power-sharing formula that granted the Untied Tajikistani Opposition, led by the IRP, 30 percent of the ministerial positions, several IRP commanders started rearming and taking positions in the mountains surrounding the capital of Dushanbe in 1999 and 2000.

14 These estimates are controversial however. The IG leadership claims that the members of the armed wings were in the thousands.

15 The main exceptions are al-Zawhiri's faction and two other small factions in Egyptian prison, as discussed previously in Chapters 3 and 5.

16 Please see the section on future research agendas for the "domino effect" hypothesis: de-radicalization of one group could lead other individuals, factions or violent groups operating in the same context under similar conditions to de-radicalize via interaction.

17 See Chapter 6 for details.

18 Except for al-Jihad, all groups investigated in this book attempted to de-radicalize before the attacks of 9/11 (that is, by the mid to late 1990s). However, several Middle Eastern regimes, most notably the Egyptian one, were more responsive and supportive of de-radicalization efforts following the attacks. This was probably done to limit the chances of al-Qa'ida activities taking place on their territories and/or of an alliance between domestic groups and al-Qa'ida occurring. Additionally, these regimes wanted to limit a possible US intervention in their domestic and security policies.

19 This was done under the variable of external interaction, like the interaction between one of the French intelligence agencies (DST) and the former emir of the GIA Mahfuz Tajeen. That interaction failed, leading eventually to the execution of Tajeen in January 1996. Also, in many cases, a foreign presence acts as a hurdle to de-radicalization because the violent struggle is able to take on the mantle of an

anti-colonial struggle, which is harder to de-legitimize on both a national and/or a religious basis.

20 Currently written as Emomalii Rahmon, in a national attempt to "de-Russify" names of persons and places.

21 See the section below on policy recommendations.

Bibliography

Al-'Arky, Samir. "Rihlat Al-Fayyum ... Zikrayat wa Shujun" [The Fayyum Trip ... Memories and Grievances]. Interview by the Islamic Group. [Online]. http://egyig.com/Public/articles/mobadra/6/38809650.shtml (accessed 1 January 2007).

Al-'Awwa, Salwa. *Al-Jama'a al-Islamiyya al-Musallaha fi Misr* [The Armed Islamic Group in Egypt]. Cairo: Al-Shuruq, 2006.

Abu Ruman, Muhmmad. "al-Maqdis Kharij al-Qudban" [al-Maqdsi Outside The Bars]. *Al-Hayat*, 13 March 2008, 6.

Abd al-Halim, Mahmud. *Al-Ikhwan al-Muslimun: Ahdath Sana'at al-Tarikh. Ru'ya min al-Dakhil* [The Muslim Brothers: Events that Created History. An Insider's View]. Vol. 1. Alexandria: Dar al-Da'wa, 1970.

Abd al-Majid, Ahmad. *al-Ikhwan wa Abd al-Nasir: Al-Qissa al-Kamila li-Tanzim 1965* [The Brothers and Nasser: The Complete Story of the 1965 Organization]. Cairo: al-Zahra lil I 'lam al-'Arabi, 1991.

Abd al-Ra'uf, Abd al-Mun'im. *Arghamtu Faruq 'ala al-Tanazul 'an al-'Arsh* [I Forced Faruq to Abdicate the Throne]. Cairo: al-Zahra lil I'lam wa al-Nashr, 1989.

Abdennour, Ali Yahia. "On Human Rights in Algeria." In Youcef Bedjaoui *et al.* (eds.) *An Inquiry into the Algerian Massacres.* Plan-les-Ouates, Genève: Hoggar, 1999, 5–13.

Abdul Ghani, Safwat. An Interview with Safwat Abdul Ghani. Interview by Salwa al-'Awwa in *Al-Jama'a al-Islamiyya al-Musallaha fi Misr* [The Armed Islamic Group of Egypt]. Cairo: Al-Shuruq, 2006.

Abdul Fattah, Ali. *Al-Hala al-Diniyah fi Misr* [The Religious Situation in Egypt]. Cairo: al-Ahram Center for Strategic Studies, 1996.

Abdul Khaliq, Farid. *Al-Ikhwan al-Muslimun fi Mizan al-Haqq* [The Muslim Brothers in the Righteous Balance]. Cairo: Dar al-Sahwa, 1987.

——. "*al-Ikhwan al-Muslimun Kama Yarahum Farid Abdul Khaliq*" [The Muslim Brothers are Perceived by Farid Abdul Khaliq]. Interview by Ahmad Mansur in Shahid 'ala al-'Asr. Al-Jazeera Satellite Channel. 7 December 2003 to 7 March 2004.

Abdul 'ati, Muhammad. "Muhasilat Al-Sira" [The Result of the Conflict]. 27 May 2002. www.aljazeera.net/in-depth/aljeria-election/2002/5/5–25–2.htm (accessed 25 November 2002).

Abdul Rahman, Hamdi, Nagih Ibrahim and Ali al-Sharif. *Taslit al-Adwa' 'ala ma Waqa'a fi al-Jihad min Akhta'* [Shedding Lights on What Went Wrong during the Jihad]. Cairo: Al-Turath al-Islami, 2002.

Abdul Rahman, Omar. *Kalimat Haqq* [A Righteous Word]. Cairo, 1984.

Abdul Rasul, Magdi. "al-Jihad wa al-Jama'a Yatafiqan 'ala Awlawiyat al-'amal al-Siyasi" [The Jihad and the Group Agree on the Priorities of Political Action]. al-*'Arabi al-Nassiri*, 16 March 2006, 1.

Abu Rumman, Muhammad. *Muraja'at Harakat al-Jihad al-Masriyya fi Mir'at Muraja'at Jihadiyyn fi al-'rdun* [The Revisions of the Egyptian al-Jihad Movement in the Mirror of the Revisions of Jihadists in Jordan]. *Al-Hayat*, 17 June 2007.

Abu Zakaria, Yehia. *Al-Haraka Al-Islamiya Al-Musalaha Fi Al-Jaza'ir* [The Islamic Armed Movement in Algeria]. Beirut: AlArif, 1993.

Ahmad, Makram. "Ahmad Yuhawir al-Qiyadat al-Tarikhiyya lil Jama'a al-Islamiyya fi Sijn al-'Aqrab" [Ahmad Interviews the Historical Leadership of the Islamic Group in the Scorpion Prison]. *Al-Mussawar*, 21 June 2002a, 4–22.

——. "Al-Qawa'id Tunaqish Qiyadatiha fi Liman Wadi al-Natrun" [The Grassroots Debates with Its Leadership in Wadi al-Natur Prison]. *Al-Mussawar*, 28 June 2002b, 4–20.

——. "Ahmad Yuhawir Qiyadat al-Jama'a al-Islamiyya Kharij al-Sujun" [Ahmad Interviews the Leadership of the Islamic Group outside Prisons]. *Al-Mussawar*, 5 July 2002c, 4–18.

——. *Huwar ma' Qadat al-Tataruf* [Dialogue with the Leaders of Extremism]. Cairo: Dar Al-Shuruq, 2003.

Ait Ahmad, Hussein. "Al-Zikra Al-Arba'un Li Istiqlal Al-Jaza'ir" [The Fortieth Anniversary of Algerian Independence]. *Bila Hudud*. Al-Jazeera Satellite Channel. Al-Doha. 3 July 2002, 18:35 GMT.

Ait Larabi, Mohammed *et al.* "An Anatomy of the Massacres." In Youcef Bedjaoui *et al.* (eds.) *An Inquiry into the Algerian Massacres*. Plan-les-Ouates, Genève: Hoggar, 1999, 13–267.

Allam. Fu'ad. *Al-Ikhwan wa Ana* [The Brothers and I]. Cairo: al-Maktab al-Masri al-Hadith, 1996.

Amanpour, Christiane. *In the Footsteps of Bin Laden*. CNN Documentary. 23 August 2006.

Anderson, Lisa. "Fulfilling Prophecies: State Policy and Islamist Radicalism." In John Esposito (ed.) *Political Islam: Revolution, Radicalism or Reform*. Boulder: Lynne Rienner, 1997.

——. "Policy-Making and Theory-Building: American Political Science and the Islamic Middle East." In Hisham Sharabi (ed.) *Theory, Politics and the Arab World*. New York: Routledge, 1990.

Anon. "*L'Assassin de Hachani Libéré*." *Rédaction de Liberte*. 11 September 2006, 3.

Anon. "Le GIA est Mort" [The GIA is Dead]. *Le Quotidien d'Oran*. 4 Janvier 2005, 1.

Anon. "Muraja'at al-Jihad" [The Jihad Revisions]. *Al-Masy al-Youm*. 14 April 2001, 1.

Anon. *Muslim Brothers Newspaper*, 26 Muharram 1353 (10 May 1934), 1.

Anon. "Al-Rakha' al-Zahir" [The Apparent Affluency]. *Al-Sharq al-Awsat*, 2 October 2000, 1.

Anon. "Tatwurat al-Jaz'ir" [Developments in Algeria]. *Al-Hayat*, 12 January 2000, 1.

Ansari, Hamied. "The Islamic Militants in Egyptian Politics." *International Journal of Middle East Studies* vol. 16, no. 1 (March 1984): 123–144.

Aroua, Abbas. "Al-Mazabih Fi Al-Jaza'ir: Huwar Ma' Al-Profissir Abbas Urwa" [The Massacres in Algeria: An Interview with Professor Abbas Aroua]. *Bila Hudud*. Al-Jazeera Satellite Channel. Al-Doha. 19 February 2001, 18:35 GMT.

Ashmawy, Ali. *Al-Tarikh al-Sirri li Jama'at al-Ikhwan al-Muslimyin* [The Secret History of the Muslim Brothers]. Cairo: Ibn Khaldun, 2005.

Al-Ashmawi, Hasan. *Al-Ikhwan wa al-Thawra* [The Brothers and the Revolution]. Cairo: al-Maktab al-Masri al-Hadith, 1977.

——. *Hasad al-Ayyam: Muzakarat Harib* [Harvests of the Days: Memoirs of a Fugitive]. Cairo: Dar al-Tawzee' wa al-Nashr, 1991.

Ashour, Omar and Emre Unluckayakli. "Islamists, Soldiers, and Conditional Democrats: Comparing the Behaviors of Islamists and the Military in Algeria and Turkey." *Journal of Conflict Studies* vol. 26, no. 2 (Summer 2006): 99–135.

Ashour, Omar. "Lions Tamed? An Inquiry into the Causes of De-Radicalization of the Egyptian Islamic Group." *Middle East Journal* vol. 61 no. 4 (Autumn 2007): 596–627.

Atayliyah, Muhammad. "Huwar ma' Al-General Muhammad Atayliyah: Istaqalt Mina Al-Jaysh Bisabab Ta'yin Khalid Nazar Waziran Lil Difa" [An Interview with General Muhammad Atayliyah: I Resigned from the Army Due to Appointment of Khalid Nazar as a Defense Minister]. Interview by Abd Al-'ali Razaqi. *Al-Hayat*, 25 March 2000, 8.

Ayachi, Ahmed. *Al-Haraka al-Islamiyya fi al-Jaza'ir: al-Juzur, al-Rumuz, al-Masar* [The Islamist Movement in Algeria: Roots, Symbols and Path]. Casablanca: Ouyun al-Maqalat., 1993.

Ayub, Usama. "Qiyadi al-Jihad Rahn al-Iqama al-Jabryyia" [A Leader of al-Jihad Under House Arrest]. Interview by Muhammad al-Shaf'i. *al-Sharq al-Awsat*, 28 April 2007, 7.

Ayubi, Nazih. *Political Islam: Religion and Politics in the Arab World.* London, New York: Routledge, 1991.

Al-Bahnasawy, Salim. *Al-Hukm fi Qadiyat Takfir al-Muslimyin* [The Judgment in the Case of Muslim Excommunication]. Cairo: Dar al-Tawzi', 1977.

Al-Banna, Hasan. *Mujmu'at Ras'il al-Imam al-Shahid Hasan al-Banna* [The Complete Collection of Letters of the Martyr Imam Hasan al-Banna]. Beirut: Dar al-Qalam, 1990.

———. *Muzakkarat al-Da'wah wa al-Da'iya* [The Memoirs of the Call and the Preacher]. Cairo: Dar al-Tawzi' wa al-Nashr al-Isamiyya, 1986.

———. *Khutwatuna al-Thaniya* [Our Second Step], *al-Nadhir*, no. 1, 1938.

Al-Baquri, Ahmad. *Baqaya Dhizkrayat* [Remains of Memories]. Cairo: Markaz al-Ahram, 1988.

Bedjaoui, Youcef *et al.* (eds.) *An Inquiry into the Algerian Massacres.* Plan-les-Ouates, Genève: Hoggar, 1999.

Beinin, Joel and Joe Stork (eds.). *Political Islam: Essays from the Middle East Report.* Berkeley: University of California Press, 1997.

Bellin, Eva. "The Robustness of Authoritarianism in the Middle East." *Comparative Politics* vol. 36, no. 2 (January 2004): 139–158.

Belhaj, Ali. *Fasl al-Kalam Fi Muwajahat Dhulm al-Hukkam* [The Decisive Statement on Confronting Oppressive Rulers]. Algiers: Islamic Salvation Front Publications, 1992.

Ben Aicha, Ahmad. "Ben Aicha: Haqq al-'Amal al-Siyasi Madmun fi Itifaq al-Hudna" [Ben Aicha: The Right of Political Action is Guaranteed in the Truce Agreement]. Interview by Muhammad al-Muqqadim. *Al-Hayat*, 3 February 2000, 8.

———. "*Al-Hayat Tuqabil Emir al-Gharb Ahmad Ben Aicha* [al-Hayat Interviews the Emir of the West Ahmad Ben Aicha]. Interview by Muhammad al-Muqqadim. *Al-Hayat*, 8 June 1996, 8.

Ben Bella, Ahmad. "An Interview with the Ahmad Ben Bella." 19 November 2002. www.aljazeera.net/programs/century_witness/articles/2002/11/11–19–1.htm (accessed 25 November 2002).

Ben Hajar, Ali. "Ali Ben Hajar Yarwi Lil Al-Hayat Tajribatoh Dakhil Al-Jama'a Al-Musalaha Wa Tafasil Inshiqaquh 'anha" [Ali Bin Hajar Tells *Al-Hayat* His Experience Inside the Armed Group and The Details of His Secession from It]. Interview by Muhammad al-Muqqadim. *AlHayat*, 5 February 2000, 8.

———. "Za'im Jama'a Musallaha Yarfud Talab al-Sulta Tawgih Nida' lil Musalahiyn" [The

Commander of an Armed Group Refuses the Demand of the Authorities to Call on Armed Militias to Cease "Violence"]. Interview by Bou Allam Ghimrasa. *Al-Sharq Al-Awsat*, 27 September 2005, 1.

——. Interview by Camille al-Tawil in *Al-Qa'ida wa Akhawatiha [al-Qa'ida and Its Sisters]*. Beirut: Dar al-Saqqi, 2007, 232–234.

Ben Uthman, Noomane. "Laqa' ma' Ben Uthman" [Meeting with Ben Uthman]. In Camille al-Tawil (ed.) *Al-Qa'ida wa Akhawatiha (al-Qa'ida and Its Sisters)*. Beirut: Dar al-Saqqi, 2007, 241.

Bermeo, Nancy. "Democracy and the Lessons of Dictatorship." *Comparative Politics* vol. 24, no. 3 (April 1992): 273–291.

Bidiwiy, Ahmad. "Difa"Abbud Al-Zumur Yantaqid Izdiwajiyat al-Ma'ayir" [The Defense of Abbud al-Zumur Criticizes the Double Standards]. *Al-Usbu'*. 12 September 2005, 1.

Binder, Leonard. *Islamic Liberalism: A Critique of Development Ideologies*. Chicago: University of Chicago Press, 1988.

Al-Bishri, Tariq. *Al-Haraka al-Siyasiya fi Masr 1945–1952* [The Political Movement in Egypt 1945–1952]. Cairo: Dar al-Shuruq, 1983.

——. *Al-Haraka al-Siyasiya fi Masr 1945–1952* [The Political Movement in Egypt 1945–1952]. Cairo: Dar al-Shuruq, 1972.

Bou Abdullah, Awad. "Nar Taht al-Ramad fi Balad al-Million Shahid" [Fire under Ashes in the Country of the Million Martyrs]. Interview by Ahmad Abdullah. Al-'Ain al-Thalitha. Al-'Arabiya Satellite Channel. 10 November 2006.

Boukhamkham, Abdelkader. "Boukhamkham Yaftah Malaf al-Sulta wa al-Inqaz" [Boukhamkham Opens the File of the Regime and the FIS]. Interview by Abd al-Aali Razzaqi. *Al-Hayat*, 31 October 1999, 10.

Boukra, Liess. *Algerie: La Terreur Sacree*. Lausanne: Favre, 2002.

Bouteflika, Abdelaziz. "Bouteflika Yatlub 'al-'Afuw' min 'al-Ta'ibiyn" [Bouteflika Asks for 'Forgiveness' from the "Repented"]. Report by Muhammad al-Muqqadim. *Al-Hayat*, 9 February 2005, 1.

Brynen, Rex, Paul Noble and Bahgat Korany. "Introduction" and "Conclusion." In Rex Brynen, Bahgat Korany and Paul Noble (eds.) *Political Liberalization and Democratization in the Arab World: Theoretical Perspectives*. Boulder: Lynne Rienner Publishers, 1995.

Brynjar, Lia. *The Society of the Muslim Brothers in Egypt: The Rise of an Islamic Mass Movement 1928–1942*. Reading, UK: Garnet, 1998.

Burgat, Francois and William Dowell. *The Islamic Movement of North Africa*. Austin: Center for Middle Eastern Studies, 1997.

Burgat, Francois. "Ballot Boxes, Military and Islamic Movements." In Martin Kramer (ed.) *The Islamism Debate*. Tel Aviv: Moshe Dayan Center, 1997.

Carey, Sabine. "Uncovering the Dynamics of Domestic Conflict: A Time-Series Analysis of Protest and Repression in Latin America and Sub-Saharan Africa." *Paper prepared for the ECPR Joint Sessions, Workshop 9: The Systematic Study of Human Rights Violations*, March 2002.

Clark, Janine, "The Conditions of Islamist Moderation: Unpacking Cross-Ideological Cooperation in Jordan." *International Journal of Middle Eastern Studies* vol. 38 no. 24 (November 2006): 539–560.

Cosantini, Faruk. "al-Jaza'ir: Tahqiq Hukumi Yuhamil al-'Amn Mus'uliyat Ikhtia' 6,146 Madani" [A Government Investigation Blames the Security for the Disappearance of 6,146 Civilians]. Interview by Bou Allam Ghimrasa. *Al-Sharq al-Awsat*, 1 April 2005, 1.

——. "Huwar ma' Ra'is al-Lajna al-Istishariyya li Himayyat Huqquq al-Insan" [Interview with The Head of the Consultative Committee for the Protection of Human Rights]. Interview by Omar Taha. *Al-Zaman*, 11 November 2006, 19.

——. "al-Amn Awqaf Nisf Million Jaza'iri bi Tuh,mat 'al-Irhab" [The Security Forces Arrested Half a Million Algerians for 'Terrorism' Charges]. Interview by Ramadan Bil'amry. *Al-Arabiya*, 24 January 2006.

Dagi, Ihsan. "The Justice and Development Party: Identity, Politics and Human Rights Discourse in the Search for Security and Legitimacy" in Hakan Yavus (ed.) *The Emergence of a New Turkey: Democracy and the AK Parti.* Salt Lake City: University of Utah Press, 2006.

Davenport, Christian (ed.). *Human Rights Violations and Contentious Politics.* Lanham: Rowman and Littlefield, 2000.

Davis, Eric. "Ideology, Social Class and Islamic Radicalism in Modern Egypt," in Said A. Arjoman (ed.), *From Nationalism to Revolutionary Islam.* Albany: State University of New York, 1984.

Dekmejian, R. Hrair. "Islamic Revival: Catalyst, Category and Consequences," in Shireen T. Hunter (ed.) *The Politics of Islamic Revivalism.* Bloomington, Indiana: Indiana University Press, 1988.

——. "The Rise of Political Islamism in Saudi Arabia." *Middle East Journal* vol. 48, no. 4 (Autumn 1994): 627–643.

——. *Islam in Revolution: Fundamentalism in the Arab World.* Syracuse: Syracuse University Press, 1995.

Dekmejian, R. Hrair and Margaret Wyszomirski. "Charismatic Leadership in Islam: The Mahdi in Sudan." *Comparative Studies in Society and History* vol. 14 no. 2 (March 1972): 193–214.

DeNardo, James. *Power in Numbers: The Political Strategy of Protest and Rebellion.* Princeton: Princeton University Press, 1985.

Dhina, Murad. "Interview with Murad Dhina." *Algerian Interface.* 19 September 2002.

Diamond, Larry. *Developing Democracy: Toward Consolidation.* Baltimore: John Hopkins University Press, 1999.

Diamond, Larry Marc F. Plattner and Daniel Brumberg (eds.) *Islam and Democracy in the Middle East.* Baltimore: Johns Hopkins University Press, 2003.

Diraz, Essam. *Al-'Ā'idūn min Afghānistān* [The Returnees from-Afghanistan]. Cairo: al-Dār al-Miṣrīyah lil-Nashr wa-al-I'lām, 1993.

Dirbala, Essam. "Al-Ahram Yuhawir Essam Dirbala" [Al-Ahram Interviews Essam Dirbala]. Interview by Ahmad Musa. *Al-Ahram*, 26 August 2006, 16.

Eickelman, Dale F. and James Piscatori. *Muslim Politics.* Princeton, NJ: Princeton University Press, 1997.

Esposito, John and John Voll. *Islam and Democracy.* New York: Oxford University Press, 1996.

——. *Political Islam: Revolution, Radicalism or Reform?* Boulder: Lynne Rienner, 1997.

Fandy, Ma'mun. *Saudi Arabia and the Politics of Dissent.* New York: St. Martin's Press, 1999.

Fisk, Robert. *Pity the Nation.* London: Touchstone, 1990.

Former IG Detainee. Interview by author. October 2002. Cairo, Egypt.

Former Islamist Leader. Interview by author. July 2002. Cairo, Egypt.

Fouda, Yusri. "Ajrass al-Khatar … al-Haqiaa Wara' 11 September – J-3" [Menacing Bells … the Truth behind September 11 – Vol. 3]. *Sirri Lil Ghaya* (Top Secret). Al-Jazeera Satellite Channel. 29 September 2005.

Friedman, Thomas. *From Beirut to Jerusalem*. London: HarperCollins, 1998.

Fry, LW and Matherly, LL. "Spiritual Leadership and Organizational Performance." Paper accepted for presentation at the August 2006 meeting of the Academy of Management, Atlanta, Georgia.

Fry, LW (2005). "Towards a Paradigm of Spiritual Leadership." *The Leadership Quarterly* vol. 16 no. 5: 619–722.

Fuller, Graham. "The Future of Political Islam." *Foreign Affairs* vol. 82, no. 2 (March/April 2002): 48–64.

Gentry, Caron. "The Relationship Between New Social Movement Theory and Terrorism Studies: The Role of Leadership, Membership, Ideology and Gender." *Terrorism and Political Violence* vol. 16, no. 2 (Summer 2004): 274–293.

Gerges, Fawaz. "The End of the Islamist Insurgency in Egypt? Costs and Prospects." *Middle East Journal* vol. 54, no. 4 (Autumn 2000): 592–612.

Al-Ghazaly, Zaynab. *Ayam min Hayati* [Days from my life]. Cairo: Dar al-I'tisam, 1989.

Ghimrasa, Bou Allam. "Al-'Amn al-Jaza'iri Ya'taqil Qa'id al-Jama'a" [The Algerian Security Detains the Commander of the Group]." *Al-Sharq al-Awsat*, 4 January 2005a, 1.

——. "Za'im Jama'a Musallaha Yarfud Talab al-Sulutat al-Jaza'iriya Tawjih Nada' ila al-Musalahin lil Iqla' 'an 'al-Irhab'" [The Commander of an Armed Group Refuses the Request of the Algerian Authorities to Call on the Armed Men to Stop "Terrorism"]. *Al-Sharq Al-Awsat*, 27 September 2005b, 1.

——. "Akbar Tanzim Musallah fi al-Jaz'ir Yu'lin Mubaya'yuh li Bin Laden" [The Largest Armed Organization in Algeria Declares its Allegiance to Bin Laden]. *Al-Sharq Al-Awsat*, 15 September 2006, 1.

——. "Qa'idat al-Maghreb Tatabanna 'Amaliyat Musllaha" [Al-Qa'ida of al-Maghreb Take Responsibility for Armed Operations]. *Al-Sharq Al-Awsat*, 3 March 2007a, 1.

——. "Qa'idat al-Maghreb Ta'tadhir" [Al-Qa'ida of al-Maghreb Apologizes]. *Al-Sharq al-Awsat*, 23 August 2007b, 6.

El-Ghobashy, Mona. "The Metamorphosis of the Egyptian Muslim Brothers." *International Journal of Middle Eastern Studies* vol. 38, no. 3 (August 2005): 373–395.

Al-Gindi, Anwar. *Al-Ikhwan al-Muslimun fi Mizan al-Haqq* [The Muslim Brothers in The Righteous Balance]. Cairo: 1946.

Guenena, Nemat. "The "Jihad": An Islamic Alternative in Egypt." *Cairo Papers* vol. 9, no. 2 (Summer 1986): 1–105.

Gurr, Ted Robert. *Why Men Rebel?* Princeton: Princeton University Press, 1970.

Habib, Kamal. *Tahawwulat al-Haraka al-Islamiyya wa al-Istratijiyya al-Amirikiyya* [The Changes of Islamist Movement and the American Strategy]. Cairo: Masr al-Mahrousa, 2006.

——. *Al-Haraka al-Islamiyy: Min al-Muwagaha ila al-Muraja'a* [The Islamic Movement: From Confrontation to Revision]. Cairo: Madbuli, 2002.

Hachani, Abdelkader. "Hachani fi Risala ila Bouteflika: al-Asbab Ghayr Muhaya'a lil Musalaha al-Watanniyya" [Hachani in a Letter to Bouteflika: The Conditions are not Ready for a National Reconciliation]. *Al-Hayat*, 22 December 1999, 6.

Hafez, Muhammad. "Armed Islamist Movements and Political Violence in Algeria." *The Middle East Journal* vol. 54, no. 4 (Autumn 2000).

——. *Why Muslims Rebel? Repression and Resistance in the Islamic World*. London: Lynne Rienner Publishers, 2003.

Hafiz, Usama. 2 February 2005. An Interview with Usama Hafiz. Interview by Salwa al-'Awwa in *Al-Jama'a al-Islamiyya al-Musallaha fi Misr* [The Armed Islamic Group of Egypt]. Cairo: Al-Shuruq, 2006.

Hafiz, Usama and Asim Abdul Majid. *Mubadarit Waqf Al-'unf: Ru'ya Waqi'iya wa Nazra Shar'iya* [Initiative for Ceasing Violence: A Realistic View and a Legitimate Perspective]. Cairo: Al-Turath al-Islami, 2002.

Haddam, Anwar. "Anwar N. Haddam: An Islamist Vision for Algeria." Interview by Daniel Pipes and Patrick Clawson. *Middle East Quarterly* vol. 3, no. 3 (September 1996).

——. "Huwar Ma' Anwar Haddam" [Interview with Anwar Haddam]. *Nuqtit Nizam.* Interview by Hassan Mu'awad. Al-'Arabiya Satellite Channel. 18 October 2006.

Al-Hakayima, Muhammad. "al-Hakayima Yarud 'ala al-Jama'a al-Islamiyya" [Al-Hakaiyma Replies Back to the Islamic Group]. Interview by Muhammad Salah. *Al-Hayat.* 9 September 2006, 6.

Hammuda, Adil. *Sayyid Qutb: Min al-Qaryah ilā al-Mishnaqah* [Sayyid Qutb: From the Village to the Gallows]. Cairo: Sina lil Nashr, 1987.

——. *Ightiyāl ra'īs bi-al-wathā'iq: asrār ightiyāl Anwar al-Sādāt* [The Assassination of President with Documents: The Secrets of the Assassination of Anwar al-Sadat]. Cairo: Sina lil Nashr, 1985a.

——. *Qanābil wa-Maṣāḥif: Qiṣṣat Ttanẓīm al-Jihād* [Bombs and Holy Books: The Story of The Jihad Organization]. Cairo: Sina lil Nashr, 1985b.

Hamrush, Ahmad. *Qissat Thawrat 23 Yulyu* [The Story of 23 July Revolution]. Beirut: al-Mu'assassa al-Arabiya, 1974.

Hamzeh, Nizar. "Lebanon's Hizbullah: From Islamic Revolution to Parliamentary Accommodation." *Third World Quarterly* vol. 14, no. 2 (June 1993): 321–337.

——. *In the Path of Hizbullah.* Syracuse: Syracuse University Press, 2004.

Hannoun, Louisa. *Al-Intikhabat al-Jaza'iriya: al-Da' wa al-Dawa'* [The Algerian Elections: The Disease and The Treatment]. *Bila Hudud.* Al-Jazeera Satellite Channel. Al-Doha. 22 May 2002, 09:35 GMT.

Harris, Christina. *Nationalism and Revolution in Egypt: The Role of the Muslim Brotherhood.* Stanford: Hoover Institute Publications, 1964.

Hashim, Salah. *'An Nash'at al-Jama'a al-Islamiyya bi Misr* [On the Birth of the Islamic Group in Egypt]. *Moragaat* vol. 1, no. 1 (January 2000).

Hattab, Hassan. "La Ya'rif Al-jama'a Man Ya'tabr Anna Al-inhiraf Fiha Qadim" [Whoever Considers the GIA's Deviation an Old One, Does not Know the GIA]. Interview by Camille Al-Tawil. *Al-Hayat,* 5 April 1998, 6.

——. "Hassan Hattab: Nuryyd al-Takhali 'an al-'amal al-Musallah ... Lakin Lana Matalib" [Hassan Hattab: We Want to Give-up Armed Activism ... But We Have Demands]. Interview by Allam Bou Ghimrasa. *Al-Sharq Al-Awsat,* 15 October 2005, 6.

——. "'akkad 'an al-'ilaqa ma' Ben Laden Kant wara' al-Khilaf ma' Tanzimuh ... Hattab lil Hayat: Talaqayna Damanat min al-Sulta al-Jaz'iriya" [He Assured that the Relationship with Ben Laden was behind the Disagreement with his Organization ... Hattab to al-Hayat: We got Guarantees from the Algerian Authorities]. *Al-Hayat,* 7 May 2007a, 8.

——. "Abu Hamza Nasha' fi 'a'ila Muhafiza..." [Abu Hamza was Raised in a Conservative Family]. *al-Hayat,* 11 May 2007b, 6.

Al-Hudaybi, Hasan. "Hiwar Ma' Hasan al-Hudaybi" [Interview with Hasan al-Hudaybi]. *al-Jumhur al-Masry,* 15 October 1951, 3.

——. *Du'ah La Qudah* [Preachers Not Judges]. Kuwait: al-Faysal al-Islami, 1985.

Human Rights Watch. "al-Jaza'ir Tatsaddar Duwal al-'Alim fi 'adad Halat "al-Ikhtifa'" al-Qassri" [Algeria Leads the Rest of the World in the Number of Forced "Disappearances"] (27 February 2003). http://hrw.org/arabic/docs/2003/02/27/algeri10645_txt.htm (accessed 9 January 2008).

Hussein, Muhammad. Interview by Camille al-Tawil in *al-Haraka al-Islamiyya al-Musallaha fi al-Jaz'ir: Min al-Inqaz ila al-Jama'a* [The Armed Islamic Movement in Algeria: From the FIS to the GIA]. Beirut: Dar al-Nahar, 1998.

Ibrahim, Nagih. *Hatmiyyat al-Muwagaha* [The Inevitability of Confrontation]. Cairo, 1990.

———. *Hatmiyyat al-Muwagaha wa Fiqh al-Nata'ij* [The Inevitability of Confrontation and the Jurisprudence of Results]. Cairo: Al-Abikan, 2005.

———. *Da'wa lil Tasaluh ma' al-Mujtama'* [A Call for Reconciliation with the Society]. Cairo: Al-Abikan, 2005.

———. *Tahiyya Wajiba ila al-Duktur Sayyid Imam* [A Necessary Salute to Dr. Sayyid Imam] (10 May 2007). http://egyig.com/Public/articles/announce/6/78784019.shtml (accessed 13 June 2007).

Ibrahim, Nagih and Ali al-Sharif. *Hurmat al-Ghuluw fi al-Din wa Takfir al-Muslimiyn* [Forbidding Extremism in Religion and Excommunicating Muslims]. Cairo: Al-Turath al-Islami, 2002.

Ibrahim, Nagih *et al. Mithaq Al-'amal al-Islami* [Islamic Action Charter]. Cairo, 1984.

Ibrahim, Nagih *et al. Tajdid al-Khitab al-Dini* [Renewing the Religious Rhetoric]. Cairo: al-Abikan, 2005a.

Ibrahim, Nagih *et al. Hidayyat al-Khala'iq bayna al-Ghayat wa al-Wasa'il* [Guidance of People between Means and Ends]. Cairo: al-Abikan, 2005b.

Ibrahim, Saad Eddine. "Anatomy of Egypt's Militant Islamic Groups." *International Journal of Middle East Studies* vol. 12, no. 4 (December 1980): 423–453.

———. *Egypt, Islam and democracy: critical essays, with a new postscript*. Cairo, Egypt; New York: American University in Cairo Press, 2002.

———. "Challenges for Islam and Democracy." *A Lecture Given at the Law Faculty, McGill University, Montreal, Quebec, Canada:* 19 February 2004.

———. "Fi Rihab Hamas" [In the Company of Hamas]. *al-Masry al-Youm*, 22 April 2006, 13.

———. Interview by author, 21 March 2007a. Montreal, Quebec, Canada.

———. "Fi Rihab Hizbullah" [In the Company of Hizbullah]. *al-Masry al-Youm*, 27 January 2007b, 13.

IG Member. Interview by author. September 2002. Cairo, Egypt.

International Crisis Group. "Understanding Islamism." Middle East/North Africa report no. 37, 2 March 2005.

Islamic Group. "Ba'd al-Taghyir Hal Sa Taqulun Bi Jawaz Dukhul Majlis Al-Sha'ab?" [After the Transformations are You Going to Say that Entering the Parliament is Legitimate?] http://egyig.com/Public/articles/mobadra/6/45352142.shtml (accessed 3 January 2007).

Islamic Group Research Unit. *Al-Ta'ifa al-Mumtani'a 'an Shari'a min Shara'i' al-Islam* [The Desisting Party from a Law of Islamic Laws]. Cairo, 1998.

———. *'ilahun ma' Allah? I'lan al-Harb 'ala Majlis al-Sha'ab* [Another God with Allah? Declaration of War on the People's Assembly]. Cairo, 1990.

Isma'il, Mamdouh. *Huwair Ma' Muhami al-Jihad* [Interview with the Lawyer of al-Jihad]. *Al-Quds al-Arabi*. 25 July 2007, 23.

Issa, Ibrahim. "Inqasam al-Ikhwan Hawl Afkar Qutb" [The Brothers were divided on Qutb's Thoughts]. *Al-Hayat*, 26 May 2004, 8a.

———. "'alima al-Murshid bi 'Amr Tanzim 1965" [The *Murshid* Knew about the 1965 Organization]. *Al-Hayat*, 27 May 2004, 8b.

———. "Al-Murshid Rad 'ala al-Kha'ifyin min 'utruhat Qutb" [The *Murshid* Responds to those Who are Afraid of Qutb's Assumptions]. *Al-Hayat*, 28 May 2004c.

Izzat, Mahmud. *Al-Amin al-'Amm lil Ikhwan al-Muslimiyn fi Hiwar Sarih Gidan* [The Secretary General of the Muslim Brothers in a Very Genuine Interview]. Interview by Abdul Mu'iz Muhammad (23 October 2007) www.ikhwanonline.com. (accessed 7 November 2007).

Jabir, Muhammad. *Al-Tariq ila Jama'at al-Muslimiyyn* [The Way to the Muslim Group]. Cairo: Dar al-Wafaa, 1990.

Jahin, Salih. "al-Muttahham el-12 fi Qadiyyat Ightiyya al-Sadat" [The Defendant Number 12 in the Case of al-Sadat Assassination]. Interview by Ahmad al-Khatib, *al-Jarida*, 2 December 2007, 12.

Jam'iyat al-Ikhwan al-Muslimin [Society of the Muslim Brothers] – Qism al-'Usar. *Nizam al-Usar* [The Families Structure]. Egypt: Jam'iyat al-Ikhwan al-Muslimin, 1953.

Jeddi, Ali. *Huwar Ma' Ali Jeddi* [Interview with Ali Jeddi]. *Al-Hayat*. 14 January 2000, 8.

Jankowski, James. *Young Egypt 1933–1952*. Stanford: Hoover Institution Press, 1975.

Jansen, Johannes J.G. *The Neglected Duty: the Creed of Sadat's Assassins and Islamic Resurgence in the Middle East*. New York: Macmillan, 1986.

Al-Jihad Organization. *Butlan Wilayat al-Darir* [The Invalidity of the Rulership of a Blind Man]. Cairo, 1984.

——. *Falsafit al-Muwajaha* [The Philosophy of Confrontation]. Cairo, 1989.

Johnsen, Gregory. "Terrorists in Rehab." *Worldview* vol. 17, no. 3 (Summer 2007).

Kabir, Mustafa. "Amir Manttiqatt al-Sharq al-Jaza'iri li Jaysh al-Inqadh: 'Awdatt al-Inqadh Mas'alat Waqt" [The Commander of the Algerian Eastern Zone in the Salvation Army: The Return of the FIS is a Matter of Time]. *Al-Zaman*, 2 February 2002, 8.

Kamal, Ahmad. *Al-Nuqat Fawq al-Huruf: al-Ikhwan al-Muslimun wa al-Nizam al-Khas* [Dots above Letters: The Muslim Brothers and The Special Regime]. Cairo: al-Zahraa, 1987.

Kalyvas, Stathis. "Commitment Problems in Emerging Democracies: The Case of Religious Parties." *Comparative Politics* vol. 32, no. 4 (July 2000): 379–398.

Kepel, Gilles. *Muslim Extremism in Egypt: The Prophet and the Pharaoh*. Berkeley: University of California Press, 1989.

——. *Jihad: The Trail of Political Islam*. Cambridge, MA: The Belknap Press of Harvard University Press, 2002.

Kertali, Mustafa. "Mustafa Kertali Lil AlHayat: Musibat Qouasmi Fi Hashitih Zaytoni Wa Zawabri [Mustafa Kertali to *Al-Hayat*: The Disaster of al-Quasmi was in His Entourage Zaytoni and Zawabri]. Interview by Muhammad al-Muqadim. *AlHayat*, 8 February 2000, 8.

Kitschelt, Herbert. "Political Regime Change: Structure and Political Process-Driven Approaches?" *American Political Science Review* vol. 86, no. 4 (December 1992): 1028–1035.

Khaled, Shawqy. *Muhakamat Fir'awn* [The Trial of the Pharaoh]. Cairo: Sina lil Nashr, 1986.

Khalil, Ashraf. "General Fi Al-Sulta: 90% Min Al-'anasir Al-Musalaha Istajabat Lil Al-'afow" [General in the Authority: 90% of the Armed Elements Positively-Responded to the Amnesty]. *Al-Sha'b*, 7 March 2000, 7.

Kharbane, Qamar al-Din. "Interview with Qamar al-Din Kharbane." Interview by Camille al-Tawil in *Al-Haraka al-Islamiyya al-Musallaha fi al-Jaz'ir: Min al-Inqaz ila al-Jama'a* [The Armed Islamic Movement in Algera: From the FIS to the GIA]. Beirut: Dar al-Nahar, 1998, 179.

Al-Khatib, Ahmed. "Qiyadat min al-Jihad fi al-Kharij Tu'ayid Muraja'at al-Tanzim

Dakhil al-Sujun" [Abroad Leaders form al-Jihad Supports the Revisions Done Inside the Prisons]. *al-Masry al-Youm*, 21 April 2007a, 1.

——. "Faqih Tanzim al-Jihad Yu'lin 'an Wathiqat Tarshid al-'amal al-Jihadiyya fi Khilal Ayyam" [The Cleric of the Jihad Organization will Declare the Document on Rationalizing Jihadi Action in a Few days]. *Al-Masry al-Youm*. 6 May 2007b, 1.

Khatab, Sayed. "Al-Hudaybi's Influence on the Development of Islamist Movements in Egypt." *Muslim World* vol. 19, no. 3 (Fall 2001): 451–470.

Kramer, Gudrün. "Islam and Pluralism." In Rex Brynen, Bahgat Korany and Paul Noble (eds.) *Political Liberalization and Democratization in the Arab World: Theoretical Perspectives.* Boulder: Lynne Rienner Publishers, 1995.

Kramer, Martin. *The Islamism Debate*. Tel Aviv: Moshe Dayan Center, 1997.

Labib, Mahmud. *Humat al-Sallum* [The Protectors of al-Sallum]. Cairo: Dar al-Ansar, 1980.

Langohr, Vickey. "Too Much Civil Society, Too Little Politics: Egypt and Liberalizing the Arab Regimes." *Comparative Politics* vol. 36, no. 2 (January 2004): 181–204.

Laremont, Ricardo. *Islam and the Politics of Resistance in Algeria (1783–1992)*. Trenton: Africa World Press, 2000.

Layada, Abdul Haqq. *Al-'yada lil Hayat: 'Assast al-Jama'a al-Musallaha Difa'an 'an al-Sha'b al-Jaza'iri wa Laysa li Qatluh* [Layada to al-Hayat: I Founded the Armed Group to Defend the Algerian People and Not to Kill Them]. Interview by Camille al-Tawil. *Al-Hayat*, 6 June 2007, 6.

Lewis, Bernard. *Political Language of Islam*. New Jersey: Princeton University Press, 1991.

——. "Islam and Liberal Democracy: A Historical Overview." *Journal of Democracy* vol. 21, no. 4 (1996): 52–63.

Madani, Abbasi. "Abbasi Madani ... al-Harb al-Ahliyya fi al-Jaza'ir – al-Juz' al-Thani" [Abbasi Madani ... The Civil War in Algeria – Part Two]. Interview by Sami Kuleib. *Ziyara Khassa* [Special Visit]. Al-Jazeera Satellite Channel. 24 September 2004.

Madi, Abul 'ila. "Egypt's Wasat Party Offers a Moderate Islamist Alternative: An Interview with A. Madi." *Daily Star* (23 December 2005) www.dailystar.com.lb (accessed 27 December 2005).

Makhloufi, Said. "*Makhaloufi Yuhadid al-Jama'a* [Makhloufi Threatens the Group]. *Al-Hayat*, 21 February 1996, 6.

Mahfuz, Muhammad. *Alladhina Zulimu* [The Persecuted]. London: Riad al-Rayyes Books, 1988.

Manoech, Richard. "The May 1984 Elections in Egypt and the Question of Egypt's Stability." In Linda Layne (ed.) *Election in The Middle East.* Boulder, CO: Westview, 1987.

Mansur, Ahmad. "al-Ikhwan al-Muslimun Kama Yarahum Farid Abdul Khaliq" [The Muslim Brothers are perceived by Farid Abdul Khaliq]. Shahid 'ala al-'Asr. Al-Jazeera Satellite Channel. 7 December 2003 to 7 March 2004.

Marani, Ahmad. "Marani lil Hayat: Belhaj lam Yuwjih Ayy Risala Ila Bouteflika" [Marani to al-Hayat: Belhaj Did Not Address any Letter to Bouteflika]. Interview by Camille al-Tawil. *Al-Hayat*, 5 October 1999, 6.

McAdam, Doug *et al. Dynamics of Contention.* Cambridge, UK; New York: Cambridge University Press, 2001.

Al-Minawy, Abdul Latif. *Shahid 'ala Waqf al-'unf* [A Witness of Ceasing Violence]. Cairo: Atlas, 2005.

Mitchell, Richard P. *The Society of the Muslim Brothers*. Cambridge: Cambridge University Press, 1969.

——. *Al-Ikhwan al-Muslimun* [The Muslim Brothers] [with Commentary of Salih Abu Ruqayq] [No Place Listed]: [No Publisher Listed], 1979.

Mehri, Abdelhamid. "Interview with Abdelhamid Mehri." Interview by Camille al-Tawil in *Al-Haraka al-Islamiyya al-Musallaha fi al-Jaz'ir: Min al-Inqaz ila al-Jama'a* [The Armed Islamic Movement in Algera: From the FIS to the GIA]. Beirut: Dar al-Nahar, 1998, 183–184.

Mezraq, Madani. "al-Nida' al-Awal: Kalimat Haqq Liman Yuhimuhu al-'Amr" [The First Communiqué: Righteous Words to Whom It May Concern]. Algeria: [No publisher], March 1995a.

——. "al-Nida' al-Thani" [The Second Communiqué]. Algeria: [No publisher], 1 April 1995b.

——. "A Meeting with Madani Mezraq: the National Emir of the Islamic Salvation Army." Interview by Maysoon Azzam. Mashahid wa Ara'. Al-'Arabiya Satellite Channel. 18 October 2004.

——. "Mezraq lil Hayat: Jihat fi al-Hukum Kant Tuharik al-Ahhdath" [Mezraq to al-Hayat: Factions in the Regime were Moving the Events]. Interview by Muhammad al-Muqaddim, *al-Hayat*, 8 March 2005a, 8.

——. "al-Rajul al-Awal fi al-Jaysh al-Islami lil Inqadh Yuqawim Tajribat al-Amal al-Musallah fi al-Jaza'ir" [The First Man in Islamic Salvation Army Evaluates the Experience of Armed Action in Algeria]. Interview by Muhammad al-Muqaddim, *al-Hayat*, 9 March 2005b, 8.

——. "al-Jaza'ir: al-Jinah al-Musallah lil Inqaz Yu'id li Tashkil Hizb Siyasi" [The Armed Wing of the FIS Prepares for Establishing a Political Party]. Interview by Bou Allam Ghimrasa, *al-Sharq al-Awsat*, 2 June 2007, 4.

——. "Madani Mezraq … Na'm Aqsayyna al-Shiyukh al-FIS li Annahum Kanu Asra al-GIA" [Madani Mezraq … Yes We Removed the FIS Sheikhs Because they were Captives of the GIA]. Interview by Wazna Husam www.chihab.net (accessed 16 February 2008).

Mubarak, Hisham. *Al-Irhabiyyun Qadimun!* [The Terrorists are Coming!]. Cairo: al-Mahrousa, 1995.

Muhammad, Mohsen. *Man Qatal Hasan al-Banna?* [Who Killed Hasan al-Banna?]. Cairo: Dar al-Shuruq, 1987.

Muqqadim, Muhammad. "Madani fi Janazit Hachani" [Madani in the Funeral of Hachani]. *Al-Hayat*, 24 November 1999, 6.

——. "Bouteflika 'General' Wahid fi al-Jaza'ir" [Bouteflika is a Lone "General" in Algeria]. *Al-Hayat*, 14 February 2005a, 6.

——. "Bouteflika Yatlub Al-'afuw 'an 'Al-Ta'ibiyn'" [Bouteflika Demands Amnesty for the "Repentants"]. *Al-Hayat*, 5 September 2005b, 6.

——. "I'taraf lil Muhaqiqin bi Qatluh Zawjatuh wa Waladayh wa 15 Tiflan wa 15 'imra'h…" [Confessed to the Investigators that he Killed his Wife, his Two Kids, 15 Children and 15 Women…]. *Al-Hayat*, 22 March 2007, 6.

Mursi, Fu'ad. *Hiwar Ma' Fu'ad Mursi* [Interview with Fu'ad Mursi]. Interviewed by Abdul Azim Ramadan in *Al-Ikhwan al-Muslimun wa al-Tanzim al-Sirri* [The Muslim Brothers and the Secret Organization]. Cairo: al-Hay'a al-'amma lil Kitab, 1993.

Nasr, Salah. *Salah Nasr Yatadhakkar: al-Mukhabarat wa al-Thawra* [Salah Nasr Remembers: The Intelligence and the Revolution]. Cairo: Mu'assasat Ruz al-Yusuf, 1984.

Nawaz, Majid. "*Muffakir Hizb al-Tahrir Yutalliq al-Usuliyya* [The Ideology of the Liberation Party Divorces Fundamentalism]. Interview by Muhammad al-Shaf'i. *al-Sharq al-Awsat*, 17 September 2005, 1, 5.

Olimov, Muzzafar, Soadat Olimova. "Region Early Warning Report: Political Islam in Tajikistan." *Forum on Early Warnings*, 31 July 2001, 10–26.

Oyahia, Ahmad. "al-Jaza'ir Tu'lin Maqqtal 17 Alf Musallah Munzu Bidayyat al-'Unf" [Algeria Declares the Death of 17 Thousand Armed Men since the Beginning of the Violence]. Interview by Bou Allam Ghimrasa. 22 March 2007, 1, 6.

Przeworski, Adam. *Capitalism and Social Democracy.* Cambridge: Cambridge University Press, 1986.

Qaradawi, Yusuf. "al-Mas'uliyya al-Shar'iyya 'an Ahdath al-Jaza'ir" [The Legitimate Responsibility for the Algerian Events]. *Al-Shari'a wa al-Hayat.* Al-Jazeera Satellite Channel. 1 February 1998.

Al-Qasim, Faysal. *Al-Harakat al-Islammiyya fi al-Maghrib* [Islamists Movements in Morocco]. Al-Ittijah al-Mu'akis. Al-Jazeera Satellite Channel. 15 December 2000.

Qa'ud, Ibrahim. *Umar al-Tilmisani Shahidan 'ala al-'asr* [Umar al-Tilmisani: A Witnesses on the Times]. Cairo: Al-Mukhtar al-Islami, 1985.

Qasim, Tala'at. *Masra' Fir'awn Misr* [The Death of the Egyptian Pharaoh]. 1993.

——. Friday Sermon. Cassette, 1994.

Qumazi, Kamal. Interview with Kamal Qamazi. *Al-Hayat*, 12 January 2000, 8.

Qutb, Muhammad. *Mazahib Fikriyya Mu'asira* [Contemporary Intellectual Ideologies]. Cairo: Dar al-Shuruq, 1983.

Qutb, Sayyid. *Limdha 'a'damuni?* [Why Did They Execute Me?]. Cairo: [No Publisher], 1965.

——. *Ma'alim Fi al-Tariq* [Milestones]. Cairo: Dar al-Shuruq, [no date].

——. *Fi Zilal al-Qur'an* [In Shadows of the Qur'an]. Cairo: Dar al-Shuruq, 1985.

Ra'if, Ahmad. *al-Bawwaba al-Sawda'* [The Black Gate]. Cairo: al-Zahra', 1986.

Ramadan, Abdul Azim. *Al-Ikhwan al-Muslimun wa al-Tanzim al-Sirri* [The Muslim Brothers and the Secret Organization]. Cairo: al-Hay'a al-'amma lil Kitab, 1993.

Rashwan, Diaa. "Hal Yakun al-Sijin Akthar Rahma min al-Watan?" [Can the Prison be More Merciful than the Homeland]" *al-Masry al-Youm*, 23 August 2007, 6.

Roberts, Hugh. "The Islamists, the Democratic Opposition and the Search for a Political Solution in Algeria." *Review of African Political Economy* vol. 22, no. 64 (June 1995): 237–245.

——. "France and the Lost Honor of Algeria's Army." *Times Literary Supplement*, 12 October 2001, 3.

Robinson, Glenn. "Can Islamists be Democrats? The Case of Jordan." *Middle East Journal* vol. 51, no. 3 (Summer 1997): 373–388.

Roy, Oliver. *The Failure of Political Islam.* Cambridge: Harvard University Press, 1994.

Rushdi, Usama. *Al-Jama'a al-Islamiyya wa Khurujiha Min Mu'askar al-'unf* [The Islamist group and Its Exit from the Camp of Violence]. Interview by Malek al-Trieky. *Qadaya al-Sa'a.* Al-Jazeera Satellite Channel. 1 October 2005.

Al-Sabbagh, Mahmud. *Al-Taswib al-Amin lima Katabahu Ba'du al-Qada al-Sabiqiyn 'an al-Tanzim al-Khaz lil Ikhwan al-Muslimiyn* [The Honest Correction for What Some of the Former Commanders have Written on the Special Organization of the Muslim Brothers]. Cairo: Al-Turath al-Islami, 1998.

Sahrawi, Nabil. "Laqa' ma' Abu Ibrahim Mustafa" [Meeting with Abu Ibrahim Mustafa]. In Camille al-Tawil's *Al-Qa'ida wa Akhawatiha* [al-Qa'ida and Its Sisters]. Beirut: Dar al-Saqqi, 2007, 242.

Salah, Mohammed. "al-Qahira Tuqir bi-Itlaq A'da' al-Jama'a al-Islamiyya 'ala Duf'at" [Cairo Admits Releasing Islamic Group Members in Groups]. *Al-Hayat*, 13 April 2006, 6.

——. "al-Sulutat al-Masriyya Tutliq Ithnan min Qadat al-Jama'a al-Islamiyya" [The Egyptian Authorities Release Two of the Leaders of the Islamic Group]. *Al-Hayat*, 3 October 2003, 1.

Salamé, Gassan (ed.) *Democracy Without Democrats? The Renewal of Politics in the Muslim World.* London: IB Tauris, 1994.

Sahnoni, al-Hashmi. "Al-Hashmi Sahnoni Yarwi Lil Hayat Tafasil Sira' Al-Ajniha Dakhil Al-Jabha" [Al-Hashmi Sahnoni Tells Al-Hayat the Details of the Factional Dispute Inside the Front]. Interview by Abd Al-'ali Razaqi. *Al-Hayat*, 13 March 2000, 14.

Samraoui, Mohamed. "Tafasil Al-Inqilab 'ala Al-Dimuqratiya Fi Al-Jaza'ir: Huwar Ma' Al-'akid Muhammad Al-Samrawy" [The Details of the Coup Against Democracy in Algeria: An Interview with Colonel Muhammad Samrawy]. 6 August 2001. www.aljazeera.net/programs/no_limits/articles/2001/8/8–6-1.htm#L1 (accessed 27 December 2002).

——. *Chronique des Années de Sang: Algérie, Comment les Services Secrets ont Manipulé les Groupes Islamistes*. Paris: Denoël, 2003.

Sartori, Giovanni. "Opposition and Control: Problems and Prospects." *Government and Opposition* vol. 1, no. 1 (Winter 1966).

Al-Saydawi, Riyad. "al-Thabit wa al-Mutahwil fi al-Nizam al-Siyasi al-Jaza'iri" [The Static and the Dynamic in the Algerian Political Regime]. *Al-Zaman*, 1 January 2002, 17.

Scheuer, Michael. "Coalition Warfare: How al-Qa'ida Uses the World Islamic Front Against Crusaders and Jews?" In Christopher Heffelfinger (ed.) *Unmasking Terror*. Washington, DC: Jamestown, 2005.

Schwedler, Jillian. *Faith in Moderation: Islamist Parties in Jordan and Yemen*. Cambridge: Cambridge University Press, 2006.

Sivan, E. *Radical Islam: Medieval Theology and Modern Politics*. New Haven, Yale University Press, 1985.

Shadi, Salah. *Safahat Min al-Tarikh* [Pages from History]. Kuwait: al-Shu'a', 1981.

Shahin, Emad. *Political Ascent: Contemporary Islamic Movements in North Africa*. Oxford: Westview Press, 1997.

Al-Shaf'i, Hussein. Interview by Ahmad Mansur in Shahid 'ala al-'Asr. Al-Jazeera Satellite Channel. 25 September 1999 to 7 December 1999.

Al-Shaf'i, Muhammad. "Munazir al-Qa'ida Yidin" [The Ideologue of al-Qa'ida Condemns]. *Al-Sharq al-Awsat*, 6 May 2007.

Al-Shahary, Abdul Fattah. "Muwajahat al-'Unf Bi al-Huwar la Bi al-Nar" [Confronting Violence with Dialogue not with Fire]. (1 June 2004) www.islamonline.net (accessed 14 January 2007).

Al-Sharif, Ali and Usama Hafiz. *Al-Nusih Wa al-Tabiyyin fi Tashih Mafahim al-Muhtasibin* [Advice and Clarification to Correct the Understandings of Moral Police]. Cairo: Al-Turath al-Islami, 2002.

Al-Sharif, Sayyid. "Al-Duktur Fadl Yad'u Jama'at al-Jihad ila Tarshid 'Amaliyatiha" [Dr. Fadl Calls on the Jihad Groups to Rationalize its Operations]. *Al-Hayat*, 6 May 2007a, 1.

——. *Wathiqat Tarshid al-Jihad fi Misr wa al-'Alam* [Document for Guiding Jihad in Egypt and the World]. *Al-Jarida*. 8 November–4 December 2007, 12–13.

——. *Hiwar Ma' Dr. Fadl* [Interview with Dr. Fadl]. Interview by Muhammad Salah. Parts 1 to 6. *al-Hayat*. 7–13 December 2007, 8.

Al-Sharif, Isma'il. *Isma'il Nigl al-Duktur Fadl Yarwi* [Isma'il son of Dr. Fadl Talks]. Interview by Rami Ibrahim. Parts 1–3. 26–28 November 2007, 7.

Al-Sheikh, Yusuf. *Ajnihat Al-Inqaz* [The Wings of the Salvation]. Beirut: AlArif, 1993.

Sheikhy, Umar. *Amir al-Akhdariyya Yakshif Asrar al-Jabal* [The Emir of Al-Akhdariyya Uncovers the Secrets of the Mountain]. Interview by Camille al-Tawil. *Al-Hayat*, 7 June 2007, 10.

Al-Siba'i, Hani. "Al-Islami al-Misri Hani al-Siba'i Yarwi Qisat Ta'sis al-Jihad" [The Egyptian Islamist Hani al-Siba'i Tells the Story of the Foundation of al-Jihad Organization]. Interview by Camille Al-Tawil. *Al-Hayat*, 1 September 2002a, 10.

——. "Al-Islami al-Misri Hani al-Siba'i Yarwi Qisat al-Khilaf Ma' al-Jama'a al-Islamiyya" [The Egyptian Islamist Hani al-Siba'i Tells the Story of the Disagreement with the Islamic Group]. Interview by Camille Al-Tawil. *Al-Hayat*, 2 September 2002b, 10.

——. "Al-Islami al-Misri Hani al-Siba'i Yakshif Qisat Intiqal Imarat al-Jihad min Imam ila al-Zawhri" [The Egyptian Islamist Hani al-Siba'i Uncovers the Transfer of Leadership of al-Jihad from Imam to al-Zawahri]. Interview by Camille Al-Tawil. *Al-Hayat*, 3 September 2002c, 10.

——. "Al-Islami al-Misri Hani al-Siba'i Yarwi al-Ikhtiraq" [The Egyptian Islamist Hani al-Siba'i Tells the Story of Infiltration]. Interview by Camille Al-Tawil. *Al-Hayat*, 4 September 2002d, 10.

Sidawy, Riyadh. "Limadha lam Tashhad al-Jabha al-Islamiyya lil Inqadh Za'iman Karizmiyyan" [Why Didn't the FIS Witness a Charismatic Leader?]. *Al-Huwar al-Mutamaddin*, 29 October 2007, 16.

——. "al-Thabit wa al-Mutahawil fi al-Nizam al-Siyasi al-Jaza'iri" [The Constants and the Variables in the Algerian Political System]. *Al-Zaman*, 1 January 2002, 17.

Siddiq, Yusuf. Interview with Colonel Yusuf Siddiq. *Al-Masry*, 26 March 1954, 5.

Siringoringo, Saut. Indonesian Counsellor in Ottawa. Meeting with author. 12 March 2007.

Al-Sisi, Abbas. *Fi Qafilat al-Ikhwan al-Muslimiyn* [In the Caravan of the Muslim Brothers]. Assyut, 1986.

Snyder, David and William Kelly. "Strategies for Investigating Violence and Social Change." In Mayer Zald and JD McCarthy (eds.), *Dynamics of Social Movements*. Cambridge: Winthrop, 1979.

Souaidia, Habib. "Al-Mazabih Fi Al-Jaza'ir: Huwar Ma' Al-Mulazim Habib Souaidia" [The Massacres in Algeria: An Interview with Lieutenant Habib Souaidia]. *Bila Hudud*. Al-Jazeera Satellite Channel. Al-Doha. 19 February 2001, 18:35 GMT.

——. *Al-Harb al-Qadhira* [The Dirty War]. Translated by Rose Makhlouf. Damascus: Ward Publications, 2002.

State Security General. Interview by author. October 2002. Cairo, Egypt.

State Security Major. Interview by author. October 2002. Cairo, Egypt.

Sultan, Essam. Interview by author. 11 August 2000. Cairo, Egypt.

Al-Suri, Abu Mus'ab. *Mukhtasar Shahadaty 'ala al-Jihad fi al-Jaza'ir* [The Summary of My Testimony on the Jihad in Algeria]. Afghanistan: [No Publisher], [No Date].

Taniyici, Saban. *The Transformation of Political Islam in Turkey*. PhD Dissertation. Pittsburgh: Pittsburgh University, 2003.

Tarrow, Sydney. "States and Opportunities: The Political Structuring of Social Movements." In Doug McAdam *et al.* (eds.), *Comparative Perspectives on Social Movements*. Cambridge: Cambridge University Press, 1996.

Al-Tawil, Camille. *Al-Haraka al-Islamiyya al-Musallaha fi al-Jaz'ir: Min al-Inqaz ila al-Jama'a* [The Armed Islamic Movement in Algera: From the FIS to the GIA]. Beirut: Dar al-Nahar, 1998.

——. "A Meeting with Madani Mizraq, the National Emir of the Islamic Salvation Army." Interview by Maysoon Azzam. Mashahid wa Ara'. Al-'Arabiya Satellite Channel. 18 October 2004.

——. *Al-Qiyadiyan Dr. Fadl wa Abdul Aziz al-Gamal Yazhara* [Commanders Dr. Fadl and Abdul Aziz al-Gamal Show Up]. *Al-Hayat*, 22 March 2007a, 1.

——. "al-Qa'ida fi 'Ard al-Kinana Tarfud Muraja'at al-Jihad" [al-Qa'ida in the Land of the Quiver Refuses the Revisions of al-Jihad]. 13 June 2007b, 1.

——. "al-Qa'ida Tu'any Khilafat Bayna 'Umar'iha" [al-Qa'ida Suffers Disagreements between its Commanders]. *Al-Hayat*, 5 June 2007c, 6.

——. *Al-Qa'ida wa Akhawatiha* [al-Qa'ida and Its Sisters]. Beirut: Dar al-Saqqi, 2007d.

——. "al-Muqtila Turid min Qaditiha fi Afghanistan wa Iran al-Musharaka fi Hiwariha ma' al-Amn al-Libiy" [The Fighting Group Wants its Commanders in Iran Afghanistan to Participate in the Dialogue with the Libyan Security]. *Al-Hayat*, 28 January 2007e, 6.

Tessler, Mark. "The Origins of Support for Islamist Movements." In John Entelis (ed.) *Islam, Democracy, and the State in North Africa.* Bloomington: Indiana University Press, 1997.

——. "Islam and Democracy in the Middle East: The Impact of Religious Orientations on Attitudes Towards Democracy in Four Arab Countries." *Comparative Politics* vol. 34 (April 2002): 337–354.

Al-Tilmisani, Umar. Interview by Ibrahim Qa'ud in *Umar al-Tilmisani Shahidan 'ala al-'asr* [Umar al-Tilmisani: A Witnesses on the Times]. Cairo: Al-Mukhtar al-Islami, 1985.

——. *Dhikrayat la Mudhakkarat* [Memories Not Memoirs]. Cairo: Dar al-Tawzi' wa al-Nashr al-Islamiyya, 1988.

Tilly, Charles. *From Mobilization to Revolution.* Reading: Addison-Wesley, 1978.

Trotsky, Leon. *The History of the Russian Revolution.* New York: Monad Press, 1961.

Umar, Ahmad. *Assyut Madinat al-Nar: Asrar wa Waqa'i' al-'Unf.* Cairo: Dar Sphinx, 1994.

Uthman, Wael. *Asrar al-Haraka Al-Tullabiyya,* 1968–1975 [The Secrets of the Student Movement, 1968–1975]. Cairo: Madkur, 1976.

Unnamed AIS commander. "Lan Nuqqadim Tanazulat Aukhra wa lil Ka'ba Rabbun Yahmiha" [We Will not Give other Concession and There is a God to Protect the Grand Mosque]. Interview by Muhammad Muaqqadim. *Al-Hayat*, 28 December 1999, 14.

Unnamed Algerian Security Official. "al-Qa'ida Tu'any Khilafat Bayna 'Umar'iha" [al-Qa'ida Suffers Disagreements between its Commanders]. Interview by Camille Al-Tawil. *Al-Hayat*, 5 June 2007, 6.

Unnamed Former GIA Member. Interview by Camille al-Tawil in *al-Haraka al-Islamiyya al-Musallaha fi al-Jaz'ir: Min al-Inqaz ila al-Jama'a* [The Armed Islamic Movement in Algeria: From the FIS to the GIA]. Beirut: Dar al-Nahar, 1998, 130.

Wafa, Izel and W. Isaac. "What is the GIA?" In Youcef Bedjaoui *et al.* (eds.) *An Inquiry into the Algerian Massacres.* Plan-les-Ouates, Genève: Hoggar, 1999, 373–459.

Waly, Abul Zahra'. "Al-Azma Al-Jaza'riya – Ru'ya Mustaqbaliya" [The Algerian Crisis – A Future Vision]. *Minbar Al-Sharq*, 28 March 1995, 102–134.

Wickham, Carrie. "The Path to Moderation: Strategy and Learning in the Formation of Egypt's Wasat Party." *Comparative Politics* vol. 36, no 2 (January 2004): 205–228.

——. *Mobilizing Islam: Religious Activism and Political Change in Egypt.* New York: Columbia Press, 2002.

Wicktorowicz, Quintan (ed.) *Islamic Activism: Social Movement Theory Approach.* Bloomington: Indiana University Press, 2004.

Willis, Michael. *The Islamist Challenge in Algeria: A Political History*. Washington Square, NY: New York University Press, 1997.

Yavus, Hakan. *The Emergence of a New Turkey: Democracy and the AK Parti*. Salt Lake City: University of Utah Press, 2006.

Yous, Nasurllah. *Qui a Tué à Bentalha?* Paris: La Découverte, 2007.

Yukl, G. *Leadership in Organizations*. New-Jersey: Prentice-Hall, 1998.

Yusuf, Mamduh. Interview with Mamduh A. Yusuf, Former Leader of IG Armed Wing. Interview by Salwa al-'Awwa in *al-Jama'a al-Islamiyya al-Musallaha fi Misr* [The Armed Islamic Group in Egypt]. Cairo: Al-Shuruq, 2006.

Al-Za'atra, Yassir. "Al-Ikhwan al-Muslimun … Hal min Khutut Humr li Furu'ihim fi al-Aqtar?" [The Muslim Brothers…. Are There Any Red Lines for their Branches in Other Countries?]. *Al-Hayat*, 24 November 2005, 10.

Zaki, Muhammad. *Al-Ikhwan al-Muslimin wa al-Mujtama' al-Misri* [The Muslim Brothers and the Egyptian Society]. Cairo: Maktabat al-Wahda, 1980.

Al-Zawahri, Ayman. *Al-Hasad al-Mur lil Ikhwan al-Muslimin* [The Bitter Harvest of the Muslim Brothers]. Beirut: Dar al-Bayariq, 1993.

——. An Interview with Ayman Al-Zawahri. Interview by Hisham Mubarak in Mubarak, Hisham. *Al-Irhabiyyun Qadimun!* [The Terrorists are Coming!]. Cairo: al-Mahrousa, 1995.

——. "al-Hijar ila Afghanistan wa al-Tahawul li Istihdaf al-Masalih al-Amrikiyya: al-Sharq al-Awsat Tanshur Kitab al-Zawhri Aw al-Wassiya al-Akhira" [The Migration to Afghanistan and the Transformation to Target American Interests: Al-Sharq al-Awsat Publishes the Book of al-Zawahri or his Last Will]. *Al-Sharq al-Awasat*, 2 December 2002, 10.

——. *Firsan Taht Rayat al-Nabiyy* [Knights Under the Flag of the Prophet]. [No Place Listed]: [No Publisher Listed], [No Date].

——. *Al-Tabri'ah* [The Vindication]. [No Place Listed]: [No Publisher Listed], [No Date].

Al-Zayyat, Muntasir. *Ayman al-Zawahri Kama 'ariftuh* [Ayman al-Zawahri as I Knew Him]. Cairo: Dar Misr al-Mahrusa, 2002.

——. *Al-Jama'at al-Islammiyya: Ru'ya min al-Dakhil* [The Islamist Groups: An Insider Perspective]. Cairo; Masr al-Mahrusa, 2005.

——. "Muhami Al-Usuliyyin: Mawqifi Sa'b Fi Bulaq al-Dakrur" [The Lawyer of the Fundamentalists: My Situation is Difficult in Bulaq al-Dakrur]. *al-Sharq al-Awsat*, 9 November 2005, 5.

——. "Huwar ma' al-Zayyat" [Interview with al-Zayyat]. Interviewed by Ahmad al-Khatib, *al-Masry al-Youm*, 17 November 2007, 5.

Zinah, Abdu, "Mu'assyis al-Jama'a al-Islammiya: Nastab'id Ta'sis Hizb Siyasi wa Nad'u al-Dawla Ila al-Tagawob ma' al-Mubadara" [The Founder of the Islamic Group: We Will Not Establish a Political Party and We Call on the State to Cooperate with the Initiative]." *Al-Sharq al-Awsat*, 22 February, 2002, 1.

——. "al-Jama'a al-Islammiya Fi Misr Tulghi Manahijiha Wa Tastabdil Kutub al-Ikhwan Biha" [The Islamic Group in Egypt Rescinds its Curriculums and Replaces them with the Brothers' Books]. *Al-Sharq al-Awsat*, 8 June 2003, 16.

——. "Qiyadat al-Jihad Dakhil al-Sujun al-Masriyya Ta'kuf 'ala I'dad Bayan Mubadarit Waqf al-'unf" [The Commanders of al-Jihad inside Egyptian Prisons are Engaging in Preparing a Communiqué for an Initiative for Ceasing Violence]. *Al-Sharq al-Awsat*, 19 April 2007a, 1.

——. "Al-'amn al-Masry Yutliq Akbar Qiyadi bi Tanzim al-Jihad Ba'd Sijnuh 26 'aman"

[The Egyptian Security Releases the Highest Ranking Commander in the Jihad Organization after 26 Years of Detention]. *Al-Hayat*, 21 April 2007b.

Zitouni, Jamal. *Hidayat Rabb al-'Alamin fi Tabyin Usul al-Salafiyin wa ma Yajib min al-'Ahd 'ala al-Mujahidin* [The Guidance of the Lord of the Worlds in Clarifying the Fundamentals of Salafists and the Requirement of Allegiance among Holy Fighters]. Algeria, 1995.

——. "al-Sawa'iq al-Hariqqa fi Bayan Hukum al-Jaz'ara al-Mariqa" [The Burning Lightening in Showing the Verdict on the Heretic Jaz'ara]. *Al-Jama'a*, 5 January 1996.

Zitout, Mohamed. "Algerian Elections." Interview by Hasan al-Rashidy. *Al-Jazeera Satellite Channel.* 15 May 1999.

Zollner, Barbara. "Prison Talk: The Muslim Brotherhood's Internal Struggle During Gamal Abdel Nasser Persecution, 1954 to 1971." *International Journal of Middle East Studies* vol. 39, no. 3 (August 2007): 411–433.

Al-Zouabri, Antar. "Sadd al-li'am 'an Hawzat al-Islam" [Repelling the Evil People from the Core of Islam]. Algeria, 1999.

Al-Zouabri, Ramadan. "Shaqiq Amir al-Jama'a Yalja' ila Britanya" [The Brother of the Emir of the Group Seeks Refuge in Britain]. Interview by Camille al-Tawil. *Al-Hayat*, 20 February 1999, 7.

Zubaida, Sami. "Islam in Contemporary Egypt: Civil Society Versus the State." *American Political Science Review* vol. 95, no. 1 (March 2001): 246.

Zuhdi, Karam. "Interview with Karam Zuhdi." Liqa' Khas. *Al-Jazeera Satellite Channel.* Cairo. 23 August 2006, 12:30 GMT.

Zuhdi, Karam *et al. Istratijiyat wa Tafjirat al-Qa'ida: al-Akhta' wa al-Akhtar* [The Strategy and the Bombings of al-Qa'ida: The Mistakes and Dangers]. Cairo: al-Turath al-Islami, 2002.

——. *Nahr al-Zikrayat* [River of Memories]. Cairo: al-Turath al-Islami, 2003.

——. *Tafjirat al-Riyadh: Al-Ahkam wa al-Athar* [The Riyadh Bombings: The Rulings and the Effects]. Cairo: al-Turath al-Islami, 2003.

Al-Zumur, 'Abbud. *Hiwarat wa Wath'iq* [Dialogues and Documents]. Giza: Markaz al-Hadara lil I'lam wa al-Nashr, 1990.

Index